New Trade Union Activism

New Trade Union Activism

Class Consciousness or Social Identity?

Sian Moore
Working Lives Research Institute,
London Metropolitan University, UK

To Eileen
Lae
Si X

First published 2011 by
PALGRAVE MACMILLAN

Palgrave Macmillan in the UK is an imprint of Macmillan Publishers Limited, registered in England, company number 785998, of Houndmills, Basingstoke, Hampshire RG21 6XS.

Palgrave Macmillan in the US is a division of St Martin's Press LLC, 175 Fifth Avenue, New York, NY 10010.

Palgrave Macmillan is the global academic imprint of the above companies and has companies and representatives throughout the world.

Palgrave® and Macmillan® are registered trademarks in the United States, the United Kingdom, Europe and other countries.

ISBN: 978–0–230–24411–5 hardback

This book is printed on paper suitable for recycling and made from fully managed and sustained forest sources. Logging, pulping and manufacturing processes are expected to conform to the environmental regulations of the country of origin.

A catalogue record for this book is available from the British Library.

A catalog record for this book is available from the Library of Congress.

10 9 8 7 6 5 4 3 2 1
20 19 18 17 16 15 14 13 12 11

Printed and bound in Great Britain by
CPI Antony Rowe, Chippenham and Eastbourne

To my Father and to the memory of my Mother

*To all the activists in this book – for their commitment
to collectivism against a tide of individualism*

Contents

List of Abbreviations   viii

Acknowledgements   ix

Introduction   1

1   Identity and Consciousness – An Unstable Relationship?   12

2   Structure and Agency – The Dynamics of Workplace Activism   30

3   The Role of Activists in Collective Mobilisation –
    Statutory Recognition Ballots   50

4   Agents of Neoliberalism? The Contested Role of the ULR   72

5   The Mobilisation of Social Identity?
    The Emergence of Equality Reps   96

6   Legacies of Self-Organisation? Migrant Worker Activists   120

7   The Ideological Dimensions of Activism – Excavating Class?   142

Conclusions   165

Notes   172

Bibliography   177

Index   187

Abbreviations

AEEU	Amalgamated Engineering and Electrical Union (now part of Unite the Union)
CAC	Central Arbitration Committee
CWU	Communication Workers Union
ER	Equality Representative
ESOL	English for Speakers of Other Languages
FBU	Fire Brigades Union
GFTU	General Federation of Trades Unions
GMB	General Municipal and Boilermakers union
LGBT	Lesbian, Gay, Bisexual and Transgender
MSF	Manufacturing, Science and Finance union (now part of Unite the Union)
NLRB	National Labor Relations Board
NUT	National Union of Teachers
PCS	Public and Commercial Services union
RMT	National Union of Rail, Maritime and Transport Workers
SEIU	Service Employees International Union
TGWU	Transport and General Workers Union (now part of Unite the Union)
TSSA	Transport Salaried Staff Association
TUC	Trades Union Congress
ULR	Union Learning Representative

Acknowledgements

My thanks go firstly to all the activists who made the book possible and who gave up their time to talk to me, but who were also so open and engaging and inspiring and encouraging. Gratitude is also due to the union officers who spared their time, in particular to Greg Thomson, Diana Veitch, Susan Cueva and Adam Rogalewski with whom I worked on UNISON's Migrant Worker Participation and Equality Reps projects.

I would like to acknowledge the support of the Leverhulme Trust for the research on statutory recognition which was dependent upon a Leverhulme Fellowship. Max Watson provided excellent research support on Chapter 3 and general technical support in moments of desperation.

Thanks to Anna Pollert, Cilla Ross and Max Watson for reading and making valuable contributions on earlier versions, but particularly to Paul Stewart for ideas and support (and canapé). Professor John Kirk gave me enormous encouragement in the writing of this book, but sadly was not able to see it published.

I am indebted to my colleagues at the Working Lives Research Institute who supported me whilst researching and writing. Collectively we owe a great deal to Mary Davis and Steve Jefferys, who in establishing the Institute, created a unique space for socially committed research, which I hope has allowed us to restore work and worker agency in a very cold climate. Jawad Botmeh, Linda Butcher and Janet Emefo released me from sufficient administrative duties to write and Pauline Windsor provided excellent transcription.

A number of friends have sustained me emotionally through the writing of this book and deserve recognition and thanks; Helen (Mrs Cut-Out) (for Geoffrey Rush), Celia and Caron (for the swordfish), Marion, Simon, Roger, Cilla, Tessa, Eric, Sonia, Liz (for discussions on identity whilst running). Also to my sisters Clare and Lynne and to Peter (for Villa tickets), Tim, Jess, Beth, Stan, Anna, Joe and Edward. Walter Llewellyn Moore was NUGMW convenor at Swansea gasworks and probably the harbinger of this.

Above all my thanks and love go to Kevin and Ella for unbelievable support and tolerance; to Kevin with infinite gratitude for the emotional and intellectual combat and to Ella (buffalo soldier) (with apologies for any neglect) for making me laugh and for her utter commitment to urban conviviality.

We are all conformists of some conformism or other...The question is this; of what historical type is the conformism, the mass humanity to which one belongs?

(Gramsci, 1971, p. 324)

Introduction

> I don't think I really have any views on society to be honest ... a lot of the time I live in a closed world ... I'm probably as normal as you could define normal, just a normal individual, everyday, hardworking, conscientious, honest individual.
>
> Nicola, Equality Rep

This is not an auspicious beginning for a study of the motivations and values of trade union activists in the 21st century and yet it is the beginning. What is it about this woman in her forties that made her become an activist and what does the term signify to her? Does the apparent absence of class consciousness or any other active social identity or consciousness reflect the paralysis of the British labour movement and its inability to play any transformative role in a period in which the economic and political power of workers is particularly weak? Nicola attributed her recent union activity to her parents (her mother had been a shop steward and her father had told her to join the union) and her personal circumstances – she was divorced with a grown-up daughter and this meant she had some spare time. She had been approached by other activists to become a shop steward 'I think it was I'd be phoning them up moaning about things' and she had subsequently become an Equality Representative. She defined herself as 'not really interested in the political side of things', she did not believe that people should be defined in terms of class, had not voted at the last election and despite being involved in the union's regional women's group did not define herself as a feminist. Like a number of the activists interviewed for this book the role of unions and personal motivations for activism were defined in terms of 'fairness' rather than any coherent political ideology. As David Lockwood concluded for the 1950s, whilst unions are class organisations there is no inevitable connection between unionisation and class consciousness (Lockwood, 1958, p. 137). Has the subsequent retreat from class meant that a wider range of social identities and interests provide a basis for collective organisation and social change?[1]

This book explores what it is that continues to motivate workers to become and remain active in trade unions at a time when the structural and ideological barriers to workplace activism have intensified. Whilst there is an extensive literature on the factors influencing the decline in collective bargaining and fall in trade union membership since 1979 (Waddington and Whitson, 1997; Machin, 2000; Freeman and Diamond, 2003; Bryson and Gomez, 2005), less has been written on the role of trade union activists within this. Yet they remain key to union recruitment, mobilisation and representation (Kelly, 1998). In an earlier and different political and economic context there was a more extensive literature on the nature of union activism. The book revisits this literature from a renewed perspective emphasising first, the impact of changes in work and the regulation of work upon union organisation and activity; second – and against the train of sociological scholarship in the past decades – the importance of work and workplace to social identity; and third, the centrality of gender, race and ethnicity to changing work relations and consequently to the production of collective identity and consciousness.

The book focuses upon workplace activists who have taken up 'new' union roles that have emerged from the specific political and economic context of the first decade of the 21st century: the establishment of statutory trade union recognition legislation, the introduction of two new trade union representative roles – the Union Learning Representative and Equality Representative – and a new wave of migration. These contexts have provided constraints and opportunities for trade unionism. Labour Government support for the emergence of these new trade union roles has been described as an attempt by the state to reshape workplace trade unionism and to constrain trade union independence and militancy (Daniels and McIlroy, 2009). At the same time there is evidence that these new roles have encouraged the emergence of new activists and that they can provide the basis for a more diverse activism. The book asks whether trade union activity and ideologies allow for the expression and mobilisation of different social identities and whether, in a changed and changing economic and political context, these eclipse class consciousness (Bradley, 1996). It raises the possibility that the 'abstract ideologies' (Kelly, 1998) that inform trade unionism have changed reflecting a discourse of 'equality' and/or 'fairness' rather than 'class'.

Above all the book aims to restore the subject to the landscape, following Gordon Marshall in resisting the reduction of social actors 'to the status of simple executants of strategies imposed on them' by their location in the relations of production (1988, p. 108) or equally as 'imprisoned within the ideological terms imposed by the hegemonic capitalist or ruling classes' (1988, p. 109). It foregrounds the experience and testimonies of union activists, how they define their activities, mediate their experiences and receive, internalise and articulate the diverse, confused and contradictory values and ideas they encounter. At the same time it attempts to firmly locate these testimonies in the social relations of work and wider political and ideological frames which shape and are shaped by these relations.

This book draws upon a range of research I have undertaken on trade union activism and this provides the wider context for each chapter. The focus is upon the oral testimonies of 30 trade union activists, that is, those with a representative role in the union and active at workplace level and possibly also in the wider union (Table 1).

Table 1   The activists

Name	Union role	Union	Job and sector	Profile
Activists in Statutory Recognition cases				
George	Shop steward	Unite	Operative, Retail	Black male
Jo	Shop steward	Unite	Lecturer, Education	White female
Ken	Activist	Unite	Production Worker, Manufacturing	White male
Mark	Shop steward	Unite	Operative, Retail	White male
Piotrek	Shop steward	Unite	Warehouse operative, Retail	Polish male
Steve	Shop steward	GMB	Electrician, Social Housing	White male
Union Learning Representatives (ULRs)				
Anand	ULR	CWU	Postal Worker, Communications	Black male
Charles	ULR and shop steward	Unite	Printer, Manufacturing	White male

Continued

Table 1 Continued

Name	Union role	Union	Job and sector	Profile
Diana	ULR and Regional Learning Officer	PCS	Job Centre Worker, Central Government	White female
John	ULR	RMT	Train Guard, Transport	White male
Lloyd	ULR	UNISON	Emergency Controller, Local Government	Black male
Oreleo	ULR and shop steward	UNISON	Crime Analyst, Local Government	Black male
Equality Representatives (ERs)				
Anna	ER and workplace contact	UNISON	Support Officer, Local Government	White female
Carrie	ER and shop steward	UNISON	Support Worker, Social Services, Local Government	White female
Dave	ER	UNISON	Civil Enforcement Officer, Local Government	White male
Elizabeth	ER and shop steward	UNISON	Social Worker, Local Government	White female
Josephine	ER	UNISON	Staff Development Officer, Local Government	White female
Kevin	ER and shop steward	UNISON	Youth Worker, Local Government	Black male
Kingsley	ER and shop steward	UNISON	Mental Health Worker, Local Government	White male
Neil	ER and Branch Equality Officer	UNISON	Records Officer, Higher Education	White male
Nicola	ER and shop steward	UNISON	Civilian Staff, Police Authority	White female
Pat	ER, ULR, Branch Equality Officer and shop steward	UNISON	Health Support Worker, National Health Service Trust (NHS)	White female

Continued

Table 1 Continued

Name	Union role	Union	Job and sector	Profile
Peter	ER, ULR, Deputy Convener and national lay rep	Unite	Production Operative, Manufacturing	Black male
Rizwan	Seconded and Branch Equality Officer	UNISON	Community Worker, Local Government	Black gay male
Simon	ER and shop steward	UNISON	Call Centre Worker, Utilities	White gay male
Migrant Worker Activists				
Cassandra	Shop steward	UNISON	Occupational Therapist, National Health Service Trust (NHS)	Filipino transgendered
Daisy	International Officer	UNISON	Community Development Worker, National Health Service Trust (NHS)	Filipino female
Jose	Branch Chair and activist	UNISON	Cleaner, Education	Latin American male
Lukasz	ER, and workplace contact	UNISON	Community Worker, Local Government	Polish gay male
Olivia	ER, shop steward and Vice-Chair, Regional Black Members' Group	UNISON	Nurse, Private Healthcare	Zimbabwean female

I make no claim that the sample is representative of UK trade union-ism, rather that oral testimonies allow for a deeper exploration of the articulation of interest, identity and consciousness. Their inclusion is defined by their activity as Union Learning Representatives, Equality Reps, migrant worker activists or activists in statutory recognition bal-lots. This means there is some variation in terms of sector, occupa-tional group and union and the latter allows for consideration of the distinctive political discourses of different unions. All but one of the activists from statutory recognition cases are from Unite, reflecting its dominant role amongst unions taking recognition cases, whilst the Union Learning Representatives are from five different unions. However, the research on Equality Reps and migrant workers involved the UK public services union, UNISON, and thus the majority of the activists are from UNISON. The sample is diverse in terms of gender, race, sexuality, disability and ethnicity with 11 women, including 1 who underwent gender reassignment in the course of writing the book; 11 black[2] activists; 6 migrant worker activists and 3 gay male activists.[3] This provides an opportunity for the exploration of social identity as a subjective dimension of union activism. The inclusion of a number of migrant worker activists allows for the consideration of the different legacies they may bring to collective organisation. Three quarters of the sample were new to UK union activism and had been attracted into activity by 'new' union roles as Union Learning Reps or Equality Reps or through recognition campaigns or specific programmes encouraging migrant worker activism. The remainder were longer-standing activists who had taken on these new roles or revived previous activism in new roles. In terms of age they were characteristic of the UK trade union movement in that only 6 were under 40 and only 2 under 30 – this generational effect is evident in their narratives and in the articulation of their activism. In terms of geography the activists were spread over a wide area, including South Wales, the North East, the North West, the South West, the South East and Midlands. The domination of UNISON means that the sample reflects the specific experience of public sector trade unionism,[4] although increasingly the union has been faced with the necessity of representing those working for private sector service contractors. As I show in Chapter 6 this has posed major challenges for union representation and organisation, in particular for the activism of migrant workers. Since the majority of UNISON members are women equality and self-organisation have been central to its identity, but also to its internal governance. This distinct context is of particular value in exploring the relationship between social identity and class consciousness.

The book responds to an earlier conviction that the study of class consciousness cannot be based upon large-scale social surveys (Marshall, 1988, p. 124), despite the prevailing trend in industrial relations studies to reduce unionisation to consumer choice and/or something that can be understood with reference to the responses of individuals at a single moment in time (Fantasia, 1995). It thus returns to narrative modes and draws upon intersectionality as a theoretical and methodological tool that can potentially capture how activists privilege one identity or switch between different social identities which then become intertwined in the construction of their self-narratives (Buitelaar, 2006). Whilst there are a number of distinct intersectional methodologies (Nash, 2008), I began my interviews with an 'anticategorial' methodological approach which meant that whilst I did operationalise *trade union identity*, I did not aim to operationalise one particular *social category* in the course of an interview. Rather, I allowed respondents to articulate their own identities, although, as Alice Ludvig (2006) has suggested in her discussion of intersectionality in relation to empirical material, it is not possible to avoid using categories altogether and I did so towards the end of the interview if the subject had not made any social identifications. This is a methodological device which uses an anticategorical approach to test theoretical frameworks. I have, however, to face the possibility that if identity is situationally contingent then the context of the interviews may have located the respondents as trade unionists first. The focus upon subjectivity may also be problematic in its tendency to understand trade unionism, identity and class consciousness as an attribute of individuals rather than collective relationships and organisation, particularly in the face of a strong historical and political literature that emphasises that class consciousness cannot be understood as the beliefs of an individual at one point in time (Lukacs, 1974). In response to this the analysis of oral testimonies, whilst exploring subjectivity, aims to locate consciousness in practical, institutional and historical processes, but also in the context of class, race and gender relations and the dynamics between and within these categories. The articulation of these potential collectivities to a concept of class consciousness is a central problematic informing the rationale of this study. In terms of intra-class relations it emphasises the way employer power shapes activists' responses and this is highlighted by the description of employer counter-mobilisation in statutory recognition ballots in Chapter 3. Rick Fantasia (1995) also advocates Michael Burawoy's social-organisational conception of consciousness and the oral testimonies upon which the book is based certainly places activism firmly in the context of workplace relations, albeit secured by wider economic, political and ideological structures. In terms of resolving the tension between individual subjectivity and collective consciousness the book looks at the role of available ideas, language and political discourses in constructing and transforming identity, values and consciousness, but also at the legacy of political defeat for not only class, but for black struggle and anti-racist and feminist movements.

For Pierre Bourdieu the social relationship between researcher and subject has an effect upon the outcomes of research, 'with all kinds of distortions...embedded in the very structure of the research relationship' (Bourdieu, 1999, p. 608). In *The Weight of the World* investigators shared a social proximity and familiarity with their respondents and engaged in conversation during the interview in a clear challenge to the interview in which 'the researcher, out of a concern for neutrality, rules out all personal involvement' (1999, p. 619). Yet as Bourdieu concedes, this could produce only 'sociolinguistic data, incapable of providing the means' for interpretation (1999, p. 612). For this reason I did not share the close relationships with respondents that Bourdieu's investigators had, yet it is important to recognise that there may have been some 'axis of equivalence' (Kirk, 2007, p. 199 quoting from Charlesworth, 2000) since I was identified as an investigator undertaking research for specific projects around equality or migrant workers for UNISON, or as a teacher on a university course on union learning.[5] My aim was to reflect Bourdieu's emphasis upon 'active and methodical listening' combining 'total availability to the person being questioned' and submission to their life history, with 'methodological construction, founded on the knowledge of the objective conditions common to an entire social category' (1999, p. 609) or, in this case, social categories.

Beverley Skeggs (1997) talks honestly about the dangers of mapping our own frames of reference as researchers onto the experiences of the subjects of the research 'without listening to or hearing what they were saying'. This is important. Yet, as Skeggs continues, researchers bring 'histories, locations and identifications' to research (1997, p. 34) – whilst the young women who were the subject of her research disassociated themselves from class she did not abandon class as a theoretical concept which could 'make sense of many disparate and contradictory experiences' (1997, p. 30). Diane Reay rightly argues that 'emotions and psychic responses to class and class inequalities contribute powerfully to the makings of class', but in doing so challenges sociologists' concern with class consciousness as the working classes 'politicised awareness of their social positioning' (2005, p. 912). In contrast, Miriam Glucksmann in the new introduction to her classic account of factory lives, written 30 years previously, suggests that sociologists have become increasingly concerned with individual empowerment rather than collective power derived from material relations of production and with rights, morality, respect and dignity at work rather than exploitation and subordination (2009, p. xxix).

Like Skeggs my research is motivated by a desire for social change. This book was written in the wake of one of the deepest global and national financial and industrial crises of recent generations. This crisis laid bare the compulsive and unrestrained greed unleashed by the deregulation of financial markets, shored up politically and almost indistinguishably by Conservative and Labour governments. It has exposed a system based upon an increasing gulf between rich and poor, with the transfer of wealth from labour to capital and in which workers are expected to pay through their jobs, pay and pension funds for the compulsion of shareholders. For Georg Lukacs (1974) the translation of class consciousness and class struggle into a wider revolutionary consciousness is influenced by the depth of economic crisis. Yet as he concluded, such conditions do not automatically produce consciousness or organisation. In the context of the financial meltdown of 2008 individual workers recognised the 'bankruptcy' of the system, but their individual fury was not harnessed or even articulated by the movement that claimed to represent them. It is in the light of this political crisis that the testimonies of activists are placed within a theoretical framework which problematises class consciousness and its absence. Yet in arguing for a reassertion of theories of class consciousness it insists that such theories must be able to capture the expression of interests generated not only by race, gender and class, but also by sexuality, disability, ethnicity and age, all, to varying degrees, central to the continual restructuring of capitalism.

Antonio Gramsci's concept of hegemony is crucial to the reading and location of activist testimony explaining how ideologies and discourses shaped by class, gender, race and ethnicity are mediated in the lives and experiences of workers – the way that people invest in and give consent to prevailing relationships underpinned by power (Skeggs, 1997, p. 139). In line with this the book is concerned with the dynamic between structure and agency and a concern that the former, whilst shaping the latter, does not imprison it, leaving no possibility of transformation through struggle and experience, as for Nicola:

> I think having contact with the union has educated me, definitely. I think things that I would have perhaps not have if I'd not been doing this, it wouldn't have even entered my head.

Outline

Chapter 1 aims to provide a theoretical framework within which to explain the relationship between social identity and consciousness. It argues that intersectionality, whilst providing a theory which can understand the interaction of social divisions over workers' life courses, in treating class as a sociological category, does not adequately locate workers' experiences in the intensification of work and restructuring of capitalist relations. Drawing upon the oral testimonies of the activists the chapter distinguishes active and passive identities and (dis)identifications. It moves on to explore consciousness as conceptualised by Gramsci in the context of hegemony and then uses Raymond Williams' (1977) notion of emergent and residual structures of feeling to illuminate the way different generations of union activists interpret or understand their social existence. Finally, the chapter considers the role of ideology and language and the dissonance between material realities and the articulation of those realities. The changed context for trade union organisation is explored in Chapter 2, which describes the structural barriers to activism in terms of changing workplace organisation and relations and the political and ideological regimes that underpin and regulate them. A transformed economic, political and legal context has seen the decline of collective bargaining coverage and the proliferation of individual workplace rights shaping the circumstances in which workplace activists operate and their roles; yet the collective nature of the employment relationship persists and the subjective and ideological dimensions of activism remain important. Chapters 3 to 6 focus upon 'the gap between the activity and the consciousness of organised workers' (Hyman, 1971, p. 38). Chapter 3 documents the crucial role of activists in providing a collective focus for workplace grievances and a basis for collective representation in workplaces with no previous union organisation and in the context of the introduction of a statutory procedure encouraging union recognition under certain conditions. It draws upon mobilisation theory to elaborate the role of six activists through case studies of five successful statutory recognition ballots. It considers how far activists are a precondition for or a product of workplace mobilisation, but refutes a characterisation of mobilisation theory in which collective organisation and action is dependent upon leaders and divorced from rather than embedded in the social relations of the workplace – in this it stresses the role of employer counter-mobilisation. Chapter 4 explores John McIlroy and Richard Croucher's claims that union involvement with New Labour's initiatives demonstrates the 'limits of trade union practice in a neo-liberal skills regime' (2009, p. 287), by implication constraining the trade union and political consciousness of Union Learning Representatives (ULRs). Drawing upon the in-depth narratives of six ULRs it presents a more contradictory and confused picture of union learning as a contested process, which can lead to activism and politicisation. Chapter 5 focuses upon Equality Representatives and the extent to which this new union role can lead to forms of collectivism based upon diverse social identities. It finds that activism may be generated by experiences of discrimination in the workplace, but that activists do not automatically construct active or politicised social identities on this basis. Their activism may be articulated in terms of a rather abstract concept of equality and/or fairness distinct from the collective mobilisation of social identity which characterised the emergence of self-organisation in UNISON in an earlier period. Chapter 6 explores the collective representation and organisation of migrant workers and how their experiences and political legacies can inform UK trade union activism. It shows how community organisations defined in terms of ethnicity can provide sources of collective strength upon which unions can draw. However, as with British-born workers, activism is based upon the ability of the union to reflect experiences rooted in the workplace. It argues for an inclusive collectivity, which transcends existing divisions of labour allowing migrant workers to transform constructed and essentialised social identities and which provides a basis for integration and collective organisation in a way that 'community' may not. Chapter 7 returns to an older literature on trade union consciousness to explore how far the values and/or language upon which union activism are based have changed. The hegemonic processes which sustain prevailing material relations and in which trade unions are embedded are important here, notably the institutional role of unions in mediating dominant ideologies to workers and, in the UK, their continued political subordination to the Labour Party (Clements, 1977, p. 316). For contemporary activists trade unionism appeared to allow for the recognition and expression of a range of interests in terms of gender, race, ethnicity, disability and sexuality. At the same time, rooted as they were in the workplace, these are implicitly class relations and not divorced from them. Class identity was not generally explicit and class consciousness is certainly latent, although not necessarily eclipsed. Its political expression through socialism was tentative and many activists were unclear about their political identity because their access to political ideas and vocabulary, whether based on class, black struggle, anti-racism or gender, was limited or lost. A political vision capturing their experiences and challenging prevailing workplace and class relations, but not subordinating race and gender to these, was elusive.

1
Identity and Consciousness – An Unstable Relationship?

> To say you're brainwashed is wrong – it's the environment that you work in and are brought up with and the beliefs.

Kingsley left school at 14 and started work as an apprentice welder in a steel works in South Wales, where as he implies, union membership was defined in part by the closed shop and in part by a strong working class community and culture. He was nearly 60 and in many ways his work history embodies not only the social change, but also the political articulation of that change, which underpins the questions asked in this book. Later in life his wife had breast cancer and when they went out for a meal to celebrate her recovery she announced that she was leaving him because, as he recalled, 'you've done everything in your life, I've done nothing, I want to go my own way'. As a consequence Kingsley had an emotional breakdown, but following his recovery was working as a community support worker in mental health for the social services department of a city council. He joined UNISON during the national one day strike over public sector pension provision and subsequently become a shop steward. His transition, from heavy manufacturing in a strong industrial working class community and overwhelmingly male working environment to the public service sector where he was now working with a predominantly female and racially mixed workforce in a large city, had raised a number of issues for him:

> From the point of view of my age, with the job that I'm doing, I was made aware that sometimes I'd come across as perhaps racist or maybe unfair, because sayings that were common to me in my age group were perhaps offensive to a younger element or 'minorities' – is that the way of saying it? So I was on a fast learning curve to sort

myself out. With my boss...we had a few things that went wrong...
We were in the office one day and she said to one of my colleagues,
'what did the brother call the other brother this morning?'; the colleague said 'a faggot', 'faggot?', she said, 'what is a faggot?' Without
thinking about it I turned and said 'it's slang, Australians use it, for
poofters'. I was nearly frogmarched out the office – 'you can't say
things like that'; I said 'but that's common'. Little things like that
sort of brought it home to me, I can't say this, the world is changing and you can't say things like that. So that was the reason why I
wanted to do this...

Kingsley put himself forward for training as a UNISON Equality Rep
as part of his own personal education and development. His narrative
conveys a sense of himself as a subject who has been disorientated and
challenged in terms of class, gender, race and sexuality. What is com-
pelling is his capacity to address the deficit he perceived in both his
values and language and the role of the union in helping him to make
sense of his identity.

This chapter problematises the relationship between material relations,
interest, identity and consciousness, restoring work as a primary location
in which they are produced. It seeks to develop a theoretical framework
which can make sense of the activism of trade unionists described in
subsequent chapters and in particular how they situate their lives within
structures composed on the basis of class, gender, race and ethnicity. It
begins by exploring the concept of social identity, reflecting upon an
epistemological shift towards a conceptualisation of class as divorced
from work and the capitalist economy which defines it and in which it
has become one sociological and cultural category amongst others upon
which identity may be based. The emphasis upon the subjective, cultural, affective and psychic dimensions of class, race and gender is rich
in terms of our understanding of social identity as lived experience, but
abandons these categories as providing any collective basis for political
change. Whilst struggles rendering the connections between class, race
and gender have been in retreat (Gilroy, 2002), these impulses are alive
in the narratives of the activists, but residual and emergent and constrained by current political vocabulary and organisation.

The destabilisation of class

For Richard Hyman, 'whether or not they endorse an ideology of class
division and class opposition, unions cannot escape a role as agencies

of class' (Hyman, 2001, p. 4). This presupposes that union activists have some form of class identity, yet this is not to be confused with class consciousness or in Perry Anderson's terms is 'an incomplete and deformed variant of class consciousness', devoid of the political consciousness necessary to challenge a class-based society (Anderson, 1977, p. 334). Hyman's sociology of trade unionism confirmed that whilst workers may recognise 'the need for collective self-activity to protect their living standards and working conditions', such activity 'does not reflect any general questioning of the relations of production in capitalist society' (1971, p. 39). The sectional nature of trade union struggle, rooted in the collective struggle against employers over living and working conditions, gives rise to trade union, but not necessarily class consciousness.

An older Marxist literature generally reduced race and gender to class (where it considered them), privileging productive relations as the site of subordination and struggle to the exclusion of other realms of human experience. If Kingsley's narrative reflects the destabilisation of class identity over a working life, then there has been a contemporaneous shift in the sociological and political literature away from studies of class consciousness to a preoccupation with social identity and multiple social identities, of which class may be one. In this formulation material relations and work have been dislodged as the foundation of social identity and basis for social change by a range of social identities and alliances constituted at a cultural and ideological level or even by language or discourse (Meiksins Wood, 1986). Postmodernism dissolved concepts of gender, race and class into 'shifting, variable social constructs which lack coherence and stability over time' and were abstracted from the social and economic relations of wider society (Walby, 1992, p. 34). Theories of intersectionality to varying degrees restore these relations, providing a methodological and theoretical approach that captures the dynamic interrelationships not only between gender, race and class, but also between sexuality, disability and age. They represent a reaction against the conceptualisation of different oppressions as unconnected or hierarchical. Intersectionality instead conveys the multiple and simultaneous oppressions that individuals experience and which cannot be abstracted or compartmentalised, finding the connections between them and the way that society is structured and experienced through multiple forms of differentiation (Brah, 1996). For Nira Yuval-Davis intersectionalty recognises that these 'social divisions are about macro axes of social power, but also involve actual, concrete people' (2006, p. 198).

Joan Acker has proposed that intersectionality, whilst capturing the ways that workers are variously situated across a number of social locations over the life course, can obscure the linkages to the capitalist economy which are necessary to an understanding of class (Acker, 2006, p. 39). In his attempt to marry class struggle and postmodernism Slavoj Žižek has argued that the 'global dimension of capitalism is suspended in today's multiculturalist progressive politics: its "anticapitalism" is reduced to the level of how today's capitalism breeds sexist/racist oppression, and so on'. Class is one of a series of political struggles (the class-gender-race series) rather than a 'structuring principle of the social totality' so that it 'encounters itself in its oppositional determination' (2000, p. 96). For Acker sociological categories such as class, race and gender cannot be divorced from relations of production within the capitalist system. The narratives presented in this book verify this at the level of the workplace, whilst suggesting how intersectionality can encapsulate the ways that workers experience and articulate structural and subjective relationships of power within social locations and practices. Theoretically intersectionality raises questions as to how far social divisions based upon race, class, gender and sexuality arise from different modes or processes of differentiation or whether it is preferable to view them as integral to one structure or mode of production. This is particularly problematic when thinking about sexuality, which is not a category around which labour markets are organised. In one response to this Nancy Fraser (1997) suggests two separate but related systems based upon redistribution and recognition, with gender and race 'bivalent collectivities' which cut across both, but class confined to the redistributive model and sexuality to the social and cultural model. Since redistributive remedies require de-differentiating social groups and recognition remedies enhance social group identity there is a tension between the systems.

An earlier literature challenged the idea of separate systems, whilst asserting that socially constructed categories of gender and race are integral to capitalism. Cedric Robinson used the term racial capitalism to capture the way that capitalism pursued a racial direction and permeated the social structures and ideology emergent from it (1982, p. 3). Anna Pollert (1996) has challenged the use of analytically separate structures, notably dual systems theory, to explain women's oppression, because of the suggestion that there are clear boundaries between class and gender. For Pollert it is not possible or analytically viable to think of class and gender as two separate structures and then to try and establish the relationship between them; all class relations are in fact gendered and all gendered social relations also have class as an integral part. For Acker 'class is still the concept that links economic inequalities to capitalist practices' and a historical-materialist analysis is still valid (2006, p. 40).

The testimonies of the older activists presented in this book reflect the restructuring of capitalist relations which marked the 1980s and 1990s shaping their experience of work. Kingsley implicitly refers to the changing nature of class, race and gender relations that underpinned this, as well as the political expression of these interests at work. Historically the continual restructuring of capitalism has involved the renegotiation of race and gender, but also a range of other categories such as sexuality, disability, ethnicity and age. This renegotiation, which is often downplayed in traditional Marxist accounts (although partially acknowledged through discussions on reserve armies of labour), is contested and produces or politicises a range of social identities which take on different configurations at different moments.[1] Social divisions have always fractured workplace and class solidarities. Historically some of the most conscious working class movements have been based upon the assertion of white skilled working class masculine identities (Taylor, 1983, Thompson, 1984, Moore, 2011).

The restructuring of gender, racial and ethnic relations is a permanent feature of the social totality of capitalism, although historically and spatially specific. For example, Jane Wills, Kavita Datta, Yara Evans, Joanna Herbert, Jon May and Cathy McIlwaine (2010) show how in London over the last decades of the 20th century and first decade of the 21st century migration has led to a division of labour based upon ethnicity,[2] but also to the re-gendering of some low paid jobs, with migrant men moving into previously feminised work. Linda McDowell's study of merchant banking shows how work is constructed in a way which combines particular versions of masculinity and sexuality with class and youth and she emphasises 'the increased centrality of the body at work' (McDowell, 1997, p. 36). A number of studies demonstrate how the intensification of capital accumulation in the interactive service sector involves the commodification of aesthetic capacities and attributes. Chris Warhurst and Dennis Nickson illustrate how in retail and hospitality employers seek to 'create congruence between employee appearance and corporate image' (2007, p. 116), with the potential for discrimination based upon appearance and, by implication, age. Sally Weller's (2007) study of the post-redundancy recruitment experiences of flight attendants in Australia exposes how the increased emphasis upon service quality and brand identity can exclude older workers, particularly women – differentiation by age is superimposed upon occupational divisions by gender. In these studies sexuality is not confined to a system of 'recognition', but becomes embodied and commodified in the labour market or system of (re)distribution.

A literature on the crisis of late capitalism and so-called post-industrial society proposed a move away from the centrality of work and identification with it. The associated decline of workers' movements was seen to be in inverse proportion to the rise of social movements based upon diverse identities challenging modes of subordination removed from the workplace (Gilroy, 2002). Yet in the UK at least, the subsequent restructuring of work has seen the expansion of the labour market, promoted by government, and its diversification in terms of gender, race, age and ethnicity. There is no clear evidence that work has been marginalised as a source of identification and collectivity. Social identities are materially rooted in changing capitalist relations of production, as manifested in the workplace, although as the narratives of the activists suggest, theorising their expression and articulation is difficult. One of the key questions that this book aims to explore is that posed by Harriet Bradley (1996): whether Marxist theories of consciousness have been eclipsed by post-modernist notions of identity or, in the context of union activists, whether these theories remain fundamental to any understanding of activism. To do so they would have to be capable of reflecting the changing relationships between class, race and gender and the articulation of the interests generated by these relationships.

Capturing identity

Bradley (1996) defines social identity as the way individuals locate themselves in society and how they perceive others as locating them, deriving from various sets of lived relationships. For Bradley there are three levels of social identity: passive, active and politicised. Passive identities reflect these lived relationships but individuals are not particularly conscious of them or do not define themselves by them. As commentators have pointed out, heterosexuals rarely articulate their sexuality, and white racial identity is often dormant and assumed (Howard, 2000). 'Active identities' involve positive self-identification which provides a basis for actions – although these identifications may be momentary and as a defence against a negative definition or action and this may particularly be the case for race and ethnicity. Politicised identities demonstrate a more constant basis for action in the form of positive or defensive collective organisation. Bradley's conception of active identities may coincide with definitions of class or gender or race consciousness, although with regard to class consciousness Gordon Marshall, David Rose, Howard Newby and Carolyn Vogler have argued that there is a distinction between identity and consciousness (1988). From a neo-Weberian perspective they see social identity as interceding between social structure, social consciousness and social action, with one such identity being with class (1988, p. 6). Gramsci suggests more of a continuum from practical activity or 'good sense' to political articulation and organisation (Rees, 1998) with no unilinear progression from one to the other, but a constant movement between – political consciousness may be fleeting and the establishment of a sustained political movement elusive. It might be further argued that gender, race and class offer trajectories across this continuum, with simultaneous and continual movement across and between them.

Whilst trade union activism assumes some form of implicit class identity, the centrality of gender, race and ethnicity to changing work relations must also impinge upon identity and consciousness. In which case how far have trade union activity and ideologies shifted to allow for the expression and mobilisation of different social identities and, in a changed and changing economic and political context, might these supersede class consciousness? The narratives of activists confirm that the subjective dimensions of union activism can be elusive. Although the interviews located the respondents within the context of their trade union activity, few actively identified themselves socially and/ or politically during the interviews,[3] although gay male activists were more likely to do so. In terms of identity Rizwan here operationalises his sexuality, but at other points in the interview he also conveyed an active race and class identity:

> Isn't it about who you are, your being? Well I think for heterosexual men – maybe not women so much – they don't necessarily have to think about that do they? They've never been asked about that, so therefore they take it for granted. It's that whole thing about you walk into a room and people presume you're straight until you happen to actually say 'hang on, I'm not, stop talking to me about football or stop giving me this banter as if to presume I'm going to just join in with you'.

Cassandra, a migrant worker activist, who during the writing of this book underwent gender reassignment, was reluctant to operationalise one identity:

> Do we really need to define? Identity for me, it can be defined in different ways, from the background of your nationality or your birth origin, from the language you speak, from the food you eat, from the friends you hang out with, from your sexuality, from your spirituality. Those would probably comprise your identity, but I think in one word, I would say that my identity is diversified.

Whilst Cassandra consciously questioned the notion of identity (and her reference to diversity reflects a contemporary discourse of equality) other respondents interpreted the question in individual rather than in social or political terms. Carrie was a union steward who had become an Equality Rep in part because of her disability; her union activity and membership of the union's women's group suggested a politicised identity, yet when asked about her identity she responded:

> I'm a bit of a plodder I think…I think other people tend to think of me as being strong, I'm a strong character, but identity wise, no I'm just me. I know people in work say 'I'll give it to you, you've got backbone', and I say 'well no I haven't'…but I do tend to be a bit more forceful over the last few years.

What is striking is not just the absence of conscious social or political identifications, but, as with a number of the working class women interviewed, a sense of denial or downplaying of their activism, despite their evident capacity and preparedness to stand up to defend fellow workers against injustice and their substantial commitment, in terms of energy and personal resources, to collective organisation.

Bradley argued that by the late 20th century class had become a passive identity, since whilst people recognised that class equalities existed, they did not think of themselves in class terms (1996, p. 25). For Savage 'class does not seem to be a deeply held personal identity, nor does "class belonging" appear to invoke strong senses of group or collective allegiance' (2000, p. 37). His interviews with middle class men and women suggested that they recognised the importance of class in social terms rather than as part of their identity, defining themselves as being 'ordinary' in a way which evokes Carrie's statement. Skeggs, in her longitudinal ethnographic study of white working class women from the North West of England talks about the (dis)identification with class. She describes how the women's class position was the 'omnipresent underpinning which informed and circumscribed their ability *to be*' (1997, p. 74), yet they refused to recognise this positioning and be fixed or measured by it and there was a reluctance to talk directly about class. Skeggs argues that this is because for women class is pathologised and demonised, but also experienced as exclusion. She emphasises the 'emotional politics of class' marked by 'insecurity, doubt, indignation and resentment' (1997, p. 162).

Skeggs' arguments have resonance for female and male, but also black and white union activists. Rod Earle and Coretta Phillips's (2009) have found that ethnicity like class can also be disavowed; in their study of young men in prisons ethnicity lacked social or political meaning despite the reality of racial and ethnic difference – understandings of ethnicity were largely cultural. Skeggs concludes that the women in her study 'did not feel a possessive relationship with their subjectivity' (1997, p. 163) and this is because theorising on subjectivity assumes the prevalence of discourses of individualism, which did not reflect the women's lives. This suggests the emphasis of an earlier Marxist literature on the need to understand consciousness as a collective rather than individual relationship. The location of identity in culture or ideology rather than in material relations or political struggle reflects, not only the defeat and decline of the labour movement, but also of social movements based upon gender and race, to which they are historically and politically connected.

Social identity and hegemony

Just as social identity has to be placed within the context of changing capitalist relations of production, so too its expression has to be seen as permeated by the hegemonic forms and impulses through which these relations are sustained. For Gramsci consciousness is firmly rooted in his conception of hegemony; in Terry Eagleton's terms this is the power of a ruling group or class as 'the common sense of a whole social order', 'subtly, pervasively diffused throughout habitual daily practices... inscribed in the very texture of our experience from nursery to funeral parlour' (Eagleton, 1991, p. 114). For Gramsci consciousness may be contradictory and ambiguous – a combination of an individual's practical experience of social reality and popular beliefs distilled from prevailing philosophies. In his frequently quoted but still salient proposition, consciousness 'even in the brain of one individual is frag-mentary, incoherent and inconsequential' and 'consciousness of being part of a particular hegemonic force (that is to say, political conscious-ness) is the first stage towards a further progressive self-consciousness in which theory and practice will finally be one' (1971, p. 333).

Williams elaborated Gramsci's concept of hegemony to emphasise it as a lived process which is continually resisted and never either total or exclusive (1977). It contains within it, not only dominant, but also residual and emergent elements. The residual is formed in previous social and cultural phases, but is also an active and effective element of current cultural processes, which can be oppositional or alternative to the dominant culture, but which can also be incorporated by it. It is brought to mind by Bourdieu's later reflection on the way the interac-tion of researcher and subject in the process of conducting work-life his-tories can 'deliver' (using Bourdieu's metaphor of researcher as midwife) or at least legitimate a fragile or buried political critique – as Bourdieu puts it, 'giving vent, at times with an extraordinary *expressive intensity*, to experiences and thoughts long kept unsaid or repressed' (Bourdieu, 1999, p. 615). Some of the most significant moments in the research process underlying this book occurred after the digital voice recorder had been turned off. A number of the respondents acknowledged that reflecting upon their life stories had evoked strong feelings and emotions – in the words of Daisy, who had discussed her politicisation through the struggle of the Filipino people against the military repres-sion of the Marcos regime, 'I had to pause to draw up the appropriate emotion'. This is suggestive of Williams' structure of feeling – a social experience still in process or 'not yet recognised as social but taken to be private, idiosyncratic, and even isolating', the affective elements of con-sciousness and relationships; 'not feeling against thought, but thought as felt and feeling as thought' (Williams, 1977, p. 132). It may also be detected in Kingsley's statement at the beginning of his interview, 'I'm struggling for words here to express myself' or Jo's response in discuss-ing her motivations as an activist: 'I'm not much for self introspection, sorry [*laughing*]'.

John Kirk (2007) has drawn upon Williams' concept of structure of feeling to understand the oral testimonies of workers and the way that they articulate their working identities as at once both social and per-sonal. Drawing upon an interview with a railway worker and union activist who reflected upon the impact of privatisation upon work, Kirk identifies a residual structure of feeling founded on a sense of loss, as both an individual and collective experience (2007, p. 176). For him this is 'nostalgia as critique' – not the sentimental reminiscences of an older generation, but a discursive practical consciousness reflecting the loss of a social collectivity and expressing 'a critique of perceived individualism characteristic of the neo-liberal dispensation that contributes to the transformation of the workplace' conveying a powerful feeling of alienation (2007, p. 174). Such a critique is resonant in the testimonies of the older activists presented in this book.

What is striking is the *latency* of the residual as oppositional, alternative and counter-hegemonic. Myself as interviewer precipitated the recollection of lived impulses and values (which to varying degrees had been politically articulated and acted upon) that had subsequently been silenced, restrained or confined to personal dissent in a new generation or period, leaving, in Williams' words, an unease or tension between received interpretation and practical experience (1977, p. 130), implied by Kingsley:

> I suppose at one stage the unions went too far and we went to a point where it was stupid, we were going out on strike and perhaps there was too much power – of course the employers have had their turn now, it's gone back to the other way.

Kingsley's comment about the former power of unions suggests the way that speech is constituted by 'what are perceived to be dominant narrative modes, legitimated by mainstream culture' (Kirk, 1997, p. 149), but he then qualifies this through a critic of the reversal of the balance of power between employers and unions. Throughout the interview process a number of older activists appeared to recover confidence in past interpretations of social existence and this could manifest itself, as in Kingsley's case, in a return to the room and/or a willingness to engage further after the interview and to offer political opinions. These residual values (not fixed since they were subject to being actively reformed in the present and in the telling) were precipitated by the interview process, as if they had been in solution (Williams, 1977 p. 134). When Kingsley returned to the room, he articulated a retrospectively constructed political consciousness finally embodying what had been a spectral presence throughout the actual interview, his lived experience of the 1984–1985 Miners' Strike:

> To my regret, and I know to lots of others, it's fine looking back now with hindsight, I know there's umpteen people felt that, work colleagues of mine felt the same, if only we'd had the insight to see what

was happening and supported them. Yes, we were supporting them in finances as in levies for food for the families, but I think it should have gone to a national strike right across the board... Nobody realised what was happening and I do wonder... between Swansea and Newport there were four dry docks for all the shipbuilding, numerous mines going all the way up to the Rhonda Valley. Steelworks, I've just lost count, plate works, steelworks, so there was an abundance of work and heavy manual work – all this has gone.

This is the articulation of alternative residual values beyond practical consciousness, informed by the social memory of industrial communities enmeshed in the family, the continuity and specific nature of employment and the institutional role of the trade union, where the past is struggle and is explicitly political (Fentress and Wickham, 1992) and refracted through the subsequent lived experience of deindustrialisation. As Fantasia (1995, p. 279), suggests the Miners' strike has a wider resonance – a strategic encounter with a national impact on class relations. For Lloyd, a black Union Learning Representative new to union activism, in inner London:

I knew what a union was because of going back to the miners' strike, yes, that's when I first started to learn about unions and also my father used to work for British Rail and there was always some sort of dispute going on so I got an awareness... I remember all that, I remember seeing Arthur Scargill out on the picket line trying to drum up support for the miners. I remember Thatcher how she wouldn't give in, she dug her heels in, she was unopen to change and those are some of the things I remember. I remember Derek Hatton and then talking about the 'Loony Left' and Tony Benn and those are the people that I really like, that's when I started taking more of an interest and finding out what these people had to say.... I was definitely sympathetic towards the miners. And also through reading, although it was nothing to do with over here, I read Nelson Mandela's autobiography so I know about certain struggles that took place...

Kingsley's expression of loss is informed by a residual *political* language at odds with what Williams might term the 'official consciousness' or 'received interpretation', a tension which initially constrained Kingsley's narrative. It also reflects the residue of political defeat. In Chapter 3 we see how another older activist, Ken, drew on residual political values to unionise his workplace on the basis of a collective grievance and to win a statutory recognition ballot. For John Fentress and Chris Wickham (1992) working class social identity and historical consciousness 'can lie deep' and its absence or silence can reflect its defeat, or, as Luisa Passerini's work on Italian Fascism suggests to them, its restriction, under certain political conditions, to the personal or to individual acts of resistance (1992, p. 124).

Despite the suggestion that class has been dislodged by other social identities and that class itself may have been silenced, there is also a sense that interests based upon gender and race are tolerated only so far as they can be redefined in terms of individualised discourses of equality and diversity – alternative politicised and antagonistic languages based upon race or gender have also been defeated. In his new introduction to his classic text on race in Britain, Paul Gilroy describes how 'the symbolic and linguistic system in which political blackness made sense was a phenomenon of assertive decolonisation and is now in retreat'. For Gilroy anti-racism is less politically focussed and more difficult to organise, reflecting an understanding of race deriving from 'diversified market relations' re-specifying ethnicity in the cultural terms of lifestyle and consumer preference (2002, p. xiv). More recently Gilroy has identified an unruly urban convivial mode of racial interaction sprouting spontaneously, which does not reflect the absence of racism, but suggests 'the means of racism's overcoming' – 'in this convivial culture, racial and ethnic differences have been rendered unremarkable' (2006, p. 40). This may recall Williams' notion of practical experience and be reflected in the narratives of black trade unionists where race was an active but not necessarily politicised identity.

An assertive and politically focussed feminism is recalled in one older woman's narrative and activity. Josephine, who was the same age as Kingsley, had just become an Equality Rep, reactivating in a changed context a latent commitment to the Women's Movement:

> It's something that I believe in...I've always had an interest in equalities particularly, women's rights, dating back from the early 1970s when I was part of a women's group, when they first came into being. And so it sort of – it sticks with you and yeah, I saw that [the Equality Rep role] and I thought 'ah, there's a role for me there somewhere, definitely – I can put something into that'.

Chapter 5 explores how far union Equality Reps articulate a rather abstract notion of equality and/or fairness distinct from the stronger ideologies that characterised the emergence of self-organisation amongst women and black workers in UNISON in the ten years from the late 1980s (Healy and Kirton, 2000). Josephine's use of the term 'women's rights' (and she later referred to 'the women's liberation movement') is not generalised throughout other women's narratives, despite their involvement in self-organised women's groups within the union and their concern for women's issues in the workplace. The term 'feminism' was not generally used, although when asked, Daisy responded that she was a feminist, shaped by her work with 'women at the grassroots and within the women's movement in the Philippines'. She had set up women's groups in rural villages when she worked as a community development worker there. Pat, a shop steward and Equality Rep, stated, 'I've been involved in women's issues and [they are] very close to my heart, women's working conditions and that', but when asked whether she considered herself a feminist responded:

> I don't think so really, I don't know. I do believe in some of the aspects of that, but I do believe that people still have a right to have a freedom of choice in certain things. I know there's a big debate about abortions and that, and I wouldn't say I was a feminist of either one way or the other, because I think it's an individual [thing], but I know that in some aspects … I would say in some aspects I am, and in other aspects, no. I don't hate men if that's what … I just want to be treated on the same level.

This is resonant of Skeggs' observation that young working class women's understanding of feminism was fragmented and partial as a result of its lack of clarity as a political category and confused transmission through popular culture – women did not recognise themselves as feminist, but found some feminist explanations useful (1997, p. 157).

Whilst residual values are evident in the testimonies of Josephine and Kingsley, in other, generally younger, respondents they are not. Here experiences of discrimination at work based upon race or sexuality appear to provide motivations for activism. We see the formation of some form of consciousness through lived experience at odds with received interpretation, which may reflect Williams' sense of the 'emergent'. In the case of the younger activists the fundamentally conflictual relations between capital and labour within the workplace provide the social basis for an oppositional impulse. What is important is the role of the union in translating such impulses into collective activity and a trade union consciousness. This was the case for Simon, a call centre worker and new activist with no previous trade union or political history:

> I had a problem with my employer and needed the support of the union; because of the support that I got, and how good they were, I wanted to give something back and the way to give something back is to become active yourself... I was working out in India for the company. In India, to be homosexual isn't illegal, but the act is and the previous manager that had been out in India, he himself was also gay, so there were never any problems when I went to a gay club or if I had an overnight guest. Then, towards the end, the last two months, a new manager was put in place from the UK – they swap them every couple of years. The new manager is straight, the new manager disapproved of where I went clubbing and the fact that I had overnight guests.... I got sent home because of that, but the union has taken the case and we are taking them to employment tribunal.

As Jennifer Nash (2008) has proposed, there is a distinction between the ways that 'subject's experience subjectivity' and whether they mobilise aspects of their identities at specific moments (2008, p. 11). This is born out in Simon's response to the question about identity, which chimes with Carrie's:

> The way I see it is I'm just a normal guy just getting on with life like everybody does. We all have ups, we all have downs, we all have our struggles. Some might be financial, some emotional, but just get on with it – just a normal guy.

Whilst Simon's activism was based upon discrimination at work defined by his social identity, he did not articulate it in these terms. Nash calls for intersectionality to deploy a theory of agency. Yuval-Davis similarly emphasises the importance of political values and the social agents who struggle for them in constructing identities and their potential as 'unifying factors' going beyond the individual towards the collective (2006, p. 199). In Simon's case the union appears to have both reflected and shaped his experience and values; his subsequent activity as an Equality Rep had led to a critique of the company's policy of offshoring work to India:

> I hadn't realised the politics of it prior, I just thought 'oh it's an opportunity', but having come back now, got the support I did from

the union and realised I'd like to give something back…as a rep now I wouldn't go because obviously we disagree with sending work offshore.

In the absence of residual political values and language his activism, in contrast to Josephine, was expressed in terms of equality and/or fairness and this is explored further in the focus upon Equality Reps in Chapter 5. In Chapter 4 we see how Union Learning Representatives, in discussing their trade unionism, move between contested and contradictory discourses, at times adopting the language of the government skills agenda. The narrative mode lends itself to an exploration of the tension between the lived experience of workplace relations, the generation of interest and collective organisation based upon these, and the availability of ideas and language which construct and which may constrain them.

Rearticulating experience, ideas and language

The tension between interest, ideas and language as reflected in the narratives of activists is a preoccupation of this book. Williams has argued that language is not a medium, but 'a constitutive element of material social practice' (1977, p. 165). Gareth Stedman-Jones' (1983) revisiting of the history of Chartism highlighted the role of politics and language in shaping consciousness, arguing that experience cannot be abstracted from the language which structures its articulation. He went further to claim that the discursive structure of political language defines interest; 'It was not consciousness (or ideology) that produced politics, but politics that produced consciousness' (1983, p. 20), pre-empting a torrent of postmodern literature which subsequently freed language from its social and historical location.

In his exploration of Williams' conception of base and superstructure, Eagleton has criticised him for 'materialising' cultural processes and 'rendering them equivalent with other forms of material production' (1989, p. 171) with the implication that social change is as likely to occur through the superstructural – emergent structures of feeling – as the transformation of productive relations that are its basis. As Ellen Meiksins Wood concedes, the non-correspondence of material conditions and political forces is entirely compatible with Marxism. Yet the 'ultimate disassociation of ideology and consciousness from any social and historical base' and the 'dissolution of social reality into language' reflects a retreat from class and class struggle as the basis of socialism

(1986, p. 5) – both subject and structure are evacuated since 'social reality is constituted by autonomous discourse and all social identities are discursively negotiable' (1986, p. 78). For Meiksins Wood the possibility that there is no political programme, language or ideology that articulates the interests of workers does not deny the reality of the exploitative nature of the relationship between capital and labour. It rather raises the issue of how material interests are translated into political terms and the fact that there is no easy and mechanical translation; 'the absence of explicit "class discourses" does not betoken the absence of class realities and their effects in shaping the life-conditions and consciousness of the people who come within their "field of force"' (1986, p. 97). Similarly, the vocabulary of class analysis has been insufficient to address political struggles based upon race and gender (Gilroy, 2002, p. 5; Moore, 2011). Whilst historically trade union consciousness has been seen to constrain class consciousness, more recently for Bradley, 'euphemistic terms such as poverty, exclusion, equality for all, social justice' abound, but 'few unions present themselves openly as vehicles of working class interests' (2008, p. 345).

Conclusions

In seeking a framework in which to understand social identity and class consciousness and their relationship I challenge two related epistemological developments. First, the shift away from the centrality of work as a basis for identity so that class becomes one of a range of equivalent social identities, as likely to be constituted by culture, ideology or language as material relations. Here I argue that intersectionality is useful to an understanding of lived experience and in exploring it methodologically, but that social divisions are fundamental to the restructuring of capitalist relations and have to be seen as integral to this system. Second, I question the emphasis upon social identity and particularly class as an individualised, affective and psychological experience, which can become divorced from class as our collective and political history, legacy and future. In this book I attempt to place the narratives of activists within a context which restores the link not only between work and identity, but also between the affective and political dimensions of class.

If identity is rooted in changing material relations of production, reproduction and consumption then it will also reflect the shifting social divisions that are integral to these material relations and which are played out in the workplace. Consciousness is not a pure expression of either gender or race or class interests, since gender, race and class are not experienced separately, but are entangled. Anna Pollert in her study of women factory workers in 1980s Bristol drew upon Gramsci's notions of consciousness to demonstrate how working class women both accepted and rejected their inferior position at work and were 'at once satisfied and dissatisfied', living an unresolved conflict (1981, p. 87). This ambivalence was rooted in their simultaneous location in the structures of social production and human reproduction – the workplace and the family. The women had an ambivalent class consciousness, since at certain moments class was overshadowed by consciousness of their oppression as women – a gender or feminist consciousness.

Like Pollert and Skeggs I draw upon Gramsci's notion of hegemony to conceptualise consciousness, but also upon Williams to identify both residual and emergent consciousness in the narratives of activists. Chapters 3, 4, 5 and 6 demonstrate how union activism is constrained by trade union consciousness and shaped by the values and ideologies of trade unions. Consciousness is transitory and contradictory and whilst it cannot be an individual phenomenon Chapter 7 probes the values of the activists to explore how far they articulate a wider class, race or gender consciousness as a basis for an alternative social structure. Older activists may have access to residual values and language which are counter-hegemonic, yet in retreat, devalued and tentative. There is a lack of confidence in critique whether this is based upon class, gender or black struggle or anti-racist politics. Younger activists may articulate more emergent meanings and values, which are generational and refracted through the dominant language in different ways to the residual. These reflect a palpable unease with relationships at work, but a language of class antagonism and rights may be constrained or displaced by new languages of justice and equality and in the case of union learning of individual employability and opportunity. The silencing of class does not reflect the material reality of workers' experience, but a prevailing political language imbued by a legacy of political defeat not only for class politics, but for wider social movements and struggles.

2
Structure and Agency – The Dynamics of Workplace Activism

> I mean some people are a steward, but they're not necessarily an activist. An activist is someone who's quite au fait with issues, understands the dynamics, understands how to mobilise people as an activist. But a steward, maybe they've got a sickness hearing and you're there just to make sure that the managers have gone through the correct procedures. So to be a steward and an activist are not one and the same, but I think the starting point usually is a steward. And you develop into an activist depending on your level of passion and commitment.
>
> Oreleo, ULR

As Laurie Clements argued in the 1970s, 'it is necessary to insert any analysis of trade union consciousness within specific structural locations and historical periods; changing socio-economic and political conditions will affect the balance upon which a "progressive" or "reformist" consciousness will dominate' (Clements, 1977, p. 328). This chapter explores the changed context for trade union organisation since the 1970s. It describes the structural barriers to activism, particularly those arising from changes in work organisation and the intensification of work over the past 30 years, but also the shift in the political and ideological climate undermining government and employer support for collective bargaining and collective organisation. The chapter explores how far these structural constraints and an increasing tension between collective organisation and individual representation influence the subjective and ideological dimensions of union activism.

The context

In line with the decline in UK union membership throughout the 1980s and early 1990s[1] there has been a reduction in the number of workplace trade union representatives and an increase in workplaces without union representation (Kersley et al., 2006). There were also fewer activists in workplaces where there was trade union representation. The nationally representative WERS 2004 survey (Kersley et al., 2006) showed that members had access to a lay representative at their workplace in 45 per cent of recognised workplaces in 2004, compared with 55 per cent in 1998. There is a substantial difference between the public and private sectors with five per cent of private sector workplaces having a union rep on-site compared to 34 per cent of public sector workplaces (BERR, 2007). WERS 2004 also showed that the average age of senior workplace trade union representatives was 46; that women, although an increasing proportion of the total, were under-represented (43 per cent compared to 36 per cent in 1998) and that only a tiny proportion were from black or minority ethnic backgrounds (4 per cent). However, whilst almost three quarters (72 per cent) of union reps in the private manufacturing sector were white, male, full-time and 40 or over – the equivalent figures for the public sector and private services were just over one third (35 per cent and 36 per cent respectively). Unsurprisingly, there is a dynamic relationship between workplace union organisation and activism and the presence of representatives at the workplace is integral to union effectiveness (Bryson, 2001; Kilkauer, 2004; Charlwood and Terry, 2007), yet the literature also suggests it is not just the presence of representatives, but the nature of their activism.

The changing organisation of work

The impact of increased international competition, the restructuring of the national economy, the restoration of employer power and reassertion of managerial prerogative in reshaping workplace employment relations and interest representation have been well documented (Terry, 1995; Cully et al., 1999; Heery et al., 2004). Yet the challenge of these developments for workplace union activism has been less well explored. Drawing upon national surveys Francis Green has elaborated the impact of work intensification, driven by technological change and work reorganisation, on the quality of work at macro level. He concludes that 'evidence of a widespread intensification of work effort and its detrimental impact on well-being is unambiguous' (2006, p. 174). Stuart White (2004) has argued that the increased importance of market activity and the intensification of work 'crowds out the time and energy needed to develop, maintain and exercise the capacities of competent, democratic citizenship' and that this undermines voluntarism and active democratic participation in society. Martin Upchurch, Andy Danford and Mike Richardson (2002) recognise the pressure on the time of stewards due to the intensification of work as well as the greater range of substantive and other issues needing to be dealt with. In their survey of the members of three unions (MSF, the GMB and the AEEU) between 1998 and 2000, 80 per cent of representatives reported that increased pressure of work had made their role as a union rep more difficult.

This chapter draws upon earlier research undertaken with Sonia McKay (McKay and Moore, 2009) for the UK Government's 2006 Review of Facilities and Facility Time for trade union representatives in the workplace[2] and based upon focus groups of trade union representatives from the public and private sector. It found that organisational change involving restructuring, cuts in staffing, privatisation and contracting out were all seen to have undermined the effectiveness of representatives and the time they could spend upon representation and their own training. There were specific issues arising from the reform of the public service sector and the introduction of performance management and targets. The tension between union activity and work may be particularly strong in the public sector where there is a commitment to providing a service – the notion of a public service ethos (Terry, 2000, p. 3). Elizabeth, a workplace rep, Equality Rep and social worker in children's services talked about the way changes in her work had affected her activism:

> It's difficult really because there's a conflict, I carry a large caseload and it's conflicting priorities really and I'm finding that obviously I have to prioritise children. There's lots of changes in the way that we're monitored, the role that we have, just lots of different expectations which are just snuck in through the back door. Government makes big decisions for instance about how we're going to monitor social work and they're doing lots of back covering exercises. Just things like databases, our role is to protect children but to protect children we have to actually see them, and if we're spending 60 to 80 per cent of our time ticking boxes and ending up with repetitive strain injury, that's ridiculous ...

McKay and Moore (2009) found that a number of workplace representatives had difficulties in securing paid time-off for union duties in spite of formal agreements. The main barrier was the issue of staff cover and the pressures that time-off placed upon work teams and work colleagues – reps reported limiting themselves in taking the time they were entitled to for union duties because of this, as suggested by Pat a long-standing activist who was a support worker in a mental health trust:

> People have got to balance so many things in their lives and also it's the time off element... And sometimes if you're the rep and you're being pulled away from the work area, you've got to think of your colleagues who you work for and sometimes it's not easy. I think over the years that I've been in it, I think it's becoming harder to be a rep because of the ultimate pressures of the Trust... the pressure of the amount of work you're expected to do... the support worker's role now is more intense, more paperwork, there's more expectation of you attending things than it's ever been.

The pressures faced by activists in terms of time also meant that they did not take up the opportunity for union education and training, crucial for their development and effectiveness.

The privatisation of public services has presented specific challenges for union representation and organisation and this is particularly the case for UNISON. Surveys undertaken by Jeremy Waddington and Allan Kerr (2009) show that the proportion of members reporting a steward in their workplace fell from 60 per cent in 1998 to 51 per cent in 2008. The total number of stewards had not, however, substantially changed over this period and this implies an increase in the number of employers and workplaces and fragmentation as a result of privatisation. Waddington and Kerr suggest that whilst union recognition is wide-ranging in the public sector and employer opposition is not generally an issue, privatisation, contracting out and decentralisation have had a substantial impact upon collective organisation. Whereas UNISON branches have historically been based upon a single employer (a health trust, local authority, police authority or higher education institution) their survey revealed that just under half (45 per cent) had relationships with more than ten employers and almost 17 per cent with 51 or more employers, placing 'an enormous burden on activists within the branch' (2009, p. 31). Employers were reluctant to grant time off for these activists to represent members who had been outsourced to other employers under contracting out arrangements and where there may be no trade union recognition or organisation. Existing representatives increasingly had to cover larger groups of workers, spread over diverse locations and with varied working patterns and arrangements. Ian Kessler and Paul Heron (2001) found that the size and structure of steward constituencies had a significant effect on the character and level of steward-member contact and thus may influence their effectiveness.

McKay and Moore (2009) showed that activists spent a substantial amount of their own time, outside work, undertaking union activities and this was seen to discourage new representatives from coming forward. WERS 2004 revealed that senior union representatives at recognised workplaces spent an average 12.5 hours a week on their union duties, and most was taken during working time. However, their seniority means they were more likely to have facility time and the Government's review acknowledged that representatives spend substantial amounts of their own time (BERR, 2007). Waddington and Kerr's more recent survey (2009) of UNISON activists found that shop stewards on average received 6.2 hours per week facility time and spent an additional 3.4 hours of their own time – the figures for branch secretaries were 19.9 hours and 10.2 hours respectively (2009, p. 39). Such commitment was reflected by the activists interviewed for this book; Simon worked in a call centre and was a workplace representative and Equality Rep:

> With the job that I do I work four days a week Monday to Thursday 9am till 7pm – by the time I get home I'm a cabbage and I tend to do a lot of the union stuff, one or two weekends a month.

Whilst it might be assumed that such pressures have a particular impact upon women, Gill Kirton's study of women's trade union activism (2006) showed that although their participation was shaped by the relationship between work, family and the union, the gendered division of domestic labour was not as influential as the structure of women's employment and trade union culture. Gill Kirton and Geraldine Healy (1999) have suggested that women's activism has to be seen over the life cycle – senior female trade unionists may be older and without dependent children and partners. In line with this the female activists interviewed for this book were often older women whose children had left home and who, in some cases, were without partners, although a number of the male activists were similarly free from such commitments.

Box 1

'People are so difficult to crank and motivate, that's what I've found. They could be passionate but when it comes to meeting times, I think because of just the hassles of life and having to coordinate family time, working time and all this, it's very difficult. Like for myself, it's so many things going on in my life, but I've managed to keep my head above water and it could just be trying to juggle work and things like that and some people they've reached one hurdle and they've just got this mountain that's too high to climb...I know one day [the branch organiser] left a message and it was like "come on guys!"...I just thought oh, poor woman and I did appreciate that she'd taken time to organise and put things together. So I dragged myself out of bed and because on night shifts you wake up, it's so exhausting and I'm so paranoid now as well at work that I don't even go for [a] break...I'm practically sleeping as I'm driving home. Sometimes the meeting is at 5 pm, and you just want that time to just have your dinner and just watch a bit of telly or something before you walk out again at 8 pm. So there are sometimes you go for the meeting and they don't finish until 8 pm, so you're just coming straight from there and going on night shift. So it really does need dedication and you have to be, I think, a self motivated person as well, because without that I think it can be challenging. And then, for instance, those with small kids like, one of the ladies was a black member, she's got kids, they need dropping, she needs to organise childcare. You need to cook the dinner, you need to do this...but then sometimes you're at work, so you can't get a day off and then you're frustrated again...she's in the NHS and the NHS is quite good with things like that, but with private, it's a bit dodgy'.

> (Olivia, Equality Rep, workplace representative and
> Vice-chair of the Regional Black Members' Group)

Olivia (in Box 1) sums up the barriers for women with younger children, as well as the specific difficulties for her as someone working night shifts (and often holding down two jobs). McKay and Moore (2009) found that in terms of work–life balance there was an assumption by workplace reps that union activity had an impact upon this, but it appeared to be taken for granted, or seen as a 'given'. Many shared the experience of being contacted by union members in the evenings and weekends; they were expected to be constantly available, including outside of work and they themselves felt they had to be accessible at all times. George, a key activist in a union recognition campaign, made an analogy between being a shop steward and a doctor:

When you become a shop steward you are sort of like a doctor, your surgery's got to be open all the time, your door is supposed to be open, because you could get a call or you can get HR [Human Resources], even at your work, it could be in your break, as you are leaving the building, walking along, it's like that. So it's a job which never stops.

These findings resonate with those of Allan Kerr, Linda Perks and Jeremy Waddington (2002), where respondents stated that the reason why members were not taking up representative positions was because the job was seen to involve too much responsibility and might damage career prospects. This may have always been the case; Patricia Fosh noted that 'low participation in trade union branches is a recurrent and inevitable structural phenomenon since this participation usually involves "costs" to the individual's other roles, such as familial and leisure ones' (1981, p. 1). Yet the testimonies of the activists here suggest that the intervening period may have seen a further polarisation between activity and inactivity. Even where trade union membership was relatively high, as characteristic of the public sector, activists often reported that participation by members was weak with membership meetings at best irregular or confined to an Annual General Meeting (AGM) and comprising largely of existing activists taking on an increasing number of roles,[3] as Pat described:

> [I'm] shop steward and ULR, then I've held positions in the branch, I've been a branch officer, I've been health and safety officer, education officer, and chair of the branch until we merged. And at this moment in time, I'm a branch officer, leading on equalities. That's how I ended up with a multi-skilled hat on...sometimes they come along and they're short and they haven't got stewards and you end up doing so many jobs because there's nobody else to represent the member.

Similarly, in Simon de Turberville's analysis of the implementation of UNISON's organising strategy in three NHS branches, one respondent commented that participation in branch meetings was so poor that anyone who turned up was considered to be an activist (2007, p. 252). For Ralph Darlington (1994b) contested elections for shop stewards may be associated with vibrant workplace union democracy since a lengthy uncontested tenure of office could mean stewards becoming divorced from the shop floor. Few of the activists interviewed for this book had emerged through contested elections, in most cases they had stood unopposed or been identified by existing activists and encouraged to stand. In the case of Lloyd who first became active through union learning:

> There was a void for the steward's position. I asked everybody else 'do you want to become a shop steward?' and no-one wanted to take up the mantle and I said 'right well I am putting my hat in the ring I am going to be the steward' and then they all said 'yes you've got my vote, you've got my vote, you've got my vote and that's how I became a steward'.

The pressures on activists are elaborated by Cassandra an occupational therapist and migrant worker activist, who also identified the supportive role of her manager as important:

> Initially when I moved here in London, I didn't want to be a steward, I didn't want to be active again because I know it's hard, it's voluntary work, they don't pay you, you spend so much of your time and get loads of conflicts with your manager because you're going to take the time off – you can't do your job properly. But my overall head manager, who supervised me, asked me personally because they didn't have anyone. And they knew that I had been a rep for quite some time in my previous employment and during meetings they knew that I could speak about the union and what's going on and everything and she said 'I am giving you my full support'. I really, really thought about it for a long time and when I had a meeting, a branch meeting here in my current work, I could see why they really needed someone – apparently there are only two NHS stewards representing almost 3000 NHS members … so they encouraged me, they were really begging that they needed me; so I said 'OK then' … but again, my dilemma is the time, this is the thing, it's always a battle. I'm very busy with my workload, I don't know how I am going to do the union work at the same time.

The experiences of UK activists may be shared by activists internationally: a Swedish survey concluded that 'shop stewards generally experience a situation characterised by inherent conflict and wide-ranging tasks, resulting in high demands on their skills and in role overload' (Pilemalm et al., 2001). A large survey of Australian workplace delegates found that the effects of work intensification appeared to complicate their role and to indirectly influence their subjective power in the workplace (Peetz and Pocock, 2009). As Cassandra indicates the support of management in this context can be important, yet evidence suggests that in the UK at a national level and particularly in the private sector this has dissipated.

The withdrawal of managerial support

Kerr et al.'s study of UNISON representatives (2002) asserts that 'union influence in the workplace depends on paid facility time and concrete management support in the shape of good facilities'. Andy Charlwood and Michael Terry (2007) similarly recognise that union presence depends upon employer support and goodwill. McKay and Moore (2009) found that continuing workforce reductions together with the widespread use of performance targets in the public sector meant that immediate managers and supervisors were often reluctant to agree to time off where this would have an impact on overall productivity. A number of representatives identified distinctions between immediate supervisors who were seen as hostile to their union activity and senior management who were perceived as more supportive. Local managers were seen as unaware of the content of union agreements or of contractual or legal rights – management and union interpretations of what was 'reasonable' in terms of time off did not generally coincide. Carrie was a support worker in social services and a workplace representative, branch officer and Equality Rep:

> Time off has never really been an issue with me in work up until now, and suddenly they're wanting all my [time] sheets, when I've applied for time off for anything and they're sort of questioning it 'oh you can't have time off for this'. So I've got to go back to the branch and they've got to chase it up through personnel... I'm not sure but apparently somebody has made a comment, not in our team, about people getting time off for things. And it's not just me... everybody is being monitored, 'why do you want this time off? Have you got to have this time off?' and they're sort of pushing to find out what they can get away with, keeping people in work, and saying 'well no you can't have the time'. I dare say it will calm down again, give it a few months, but they're on a bit of a purge at the moment.

Nicola, a civilian officer for a police force and a workplace representative and Equality Rep, suggests how time-off can depend upon the attitude of individual managers:

> I've recently changed stations where I work, I used to work in one police station … but now I've transferred to another station and I've never ever had a problem with my boss in [the previous station], he always authorised the time off, no problem at all. But I've had terrible problems with my new inspector, he won't sign the forms, he won't authorise if I'm working, he'll only authorise them if I'm on a day off. We've got a very good facilities agreement actually within the force, they don't get any problems getting time off – I never used to, but it's just a nightmare.

There is evidence of wider pressure on time-off for union duties; Waddington and Kerr's survey showed that employers recognising UNISON had cut facility time (2009, p. 34). McKay and Moore (2009) found that while employers might grant time off for duties that were directly relevant to workplace representation, they were less willing to do so for activities that were perceived as being outside the employer's core interests, including rights to time off for trade union training. A number of focus group participants reported that pressures from colleagues, as well as those generated by their work, made them reluctant to pursue training. Although participants generally got time off to formally represent their members and for meetings with managers, many said that they did not get time to talk to members about union or workplace issues.

Paul Willman and Alex Bryson (2006) have used WERS data from 1980 to 2004 to show that although there is little evidence of large-scale withdrawal of employer recognition or facilities; managerial support for trade unions in terms of check-off, management recommendation of membership or a closed shop; and having an on-site union representative, had all declined since 1984. Management endorsement of union membership in workplaces with more than 25 employees reduced dramatically from 34 per cent to 21 per cent between 1990 and 1998, with the decline most marked in the private sector. In addition the probability of lay representation in unionised workplaces fell by 17 per cent between 1984 and 2004. John Goodman and Terence Whittington writing in 1973, stated that management 'enhance the scope, power and authority of shop stewards'; 30 years later Bryson (2006) concluded from his survey that employees' perception of employer support for unionisation raises union effectiveness and 'unions therefore need the active support of management, something that is often lacking' (2006, p. 37). Other studies have confirmed this dynamic between activism and management support, which can undermine the independence of union representatives (Kessler and Heron, 2001; Oxenbridge and Brown, 2002) and this complexity was articulated by Simon, a steward in a call centre in the privatised utilities sector:

> The business aren't happy we've got so many reps. I think the reason I get away with it within my department is with the union we've got a very good relationship with our business manager. So whereas other departments, they're clamping down, our business manager realises and knows the benefits of working in partnership with us as the union. I'm the only rep from our department, my business manager knows that I carry a lot of influence if you like with the agents on the floor and we've gone through major change over the last 12 months and we've worked very closely in partnership to make this a very smooth change and the business manager has seen and reaps the benefits from that. So I think my facility time isn't really in question because he personally knows the benefits of working with us.

The shift in the political climate since the 1970s and strengthening of managerial prerogative appear to have had some impact upon union workplace activity. McKay and Moore (2009) reported that a number of the long-standing activists engaged in their focus group research identified a reduction in the legitimacy of the union in the workplace and placed this in the context of wider political changes. They felt strongly that their work as union representatives was not valued and that this reflected the wider weakness of trade unions in the law and society.

The proliferation of individual rights

For Allan Flanders writing in 1970 the activity to which unions 'devote most of their resources and appear to rate most highly is collective bargaining', providing rules which protect not only their members' material standards of living, but equally their security, status and self-respect; in short their dignity as human beings' (1970, p. 41). WERS 2004 reports that the percentage of workplaces covered by collective bargaining over pay fell from 30 per cent to 22 per cent between 1998 and 2004; this decline was largely accounted for by the private sector where it went from 17 per cent to 11 per cent (Kersley et al., 2006, p. 182).

The decline in collective bargaining has coincided with historically low levels of collective action and an increase in individual cases taken by workers against employers (Cully et al., 1999: Drinkwater and Ingram, 2005). William Brown and Sarah Oxenbridge (2005) have identified a shift in the role of unions since the 1970s to one where they have become upholders of a growing number of statutory individual employment rights in the workplace. Whilst the Conservative Government's legal programme to undermine trade union legitimacy both within and outside the workplace heralded the decline in collective bargaining, the Labour Government did little to reverse this. For Pollert 'individual statutory rights are now the key form of employment regulation for the majority of workers', and were 'the main emphasis of New Labour's employment relations strategy' (2007, p. 111). According to WERS 2004, 79 per cent of senior union reps spent time on terms and conditions; 73 per cent on individual disputes; 69 per cent on selection, development and staffing issues and 68 per cent on welfare issues (Kersley et al., 2006). For the union reps participating in McKay and Moore's (2009) focus groups union work was dominated by individual representation and casework. Many did not feel adequately equipped to deal with their members' stress and wider emotional and mental health problems, which they perceived had increased as a result of organisational change and which may demand counselling skills. Jo described the high expectations of members after the union had won a ballot for union recognition through the statutory procedure:

> What people don't understand is winning wasn't what worried me, it was keeping the momentum going afterwards. Basically it's mainly me, you know and it's a huge organisation. The other reps, no-one's got any background in employment or unions, so I have to do all the grievances... so much time it takes and when there's only a few of us and most of it still falls on me and then we've got to do disciplinaries on top, which are very stressful. Not just the time but the emotional dependence of the person on you is very wearing. It's quite hard. But they have – I've just negotiated time off – they've given me proper time off.

Following a campaign based upon the collective mobilisation of the workforce in the face of employer hostility and the conclusion of a recognition agreement which allowed for collective bargaining over pay, hours and holidays, Jo was preoccupied with individual grievances and disciplinaries in the workplace. Changes in the organisation of work would appear to have increased the tension between individual and collective activity.

Structure versus agency – the subjective and ideological dimensions of activism

The prevailing climate may therefore serve to reinforce the role of activists in defending individual rights in the workplace at the expense of a more collective and organisational role. Gary Daniels and John McIlroy provide a detailed overview of industrial politics since 1997 situating trade unions firmly in the context of 'the current stage of capitalism and the dominant ideology which shapes economic, political and employment policies in Britain today' – neoliberalism (2009, p. 2). They argue New Labour sought to remould unions in its own image rehabilitating trade unions so long as they restructured their ideology, politics and activity to act as lubricants of the labour market and as agents of supply-side neoliberalism, doing the work of New Labour and the market inside the enterprise (2009, p. 80). They suggest that this represents a real constraint on the activity of workplace representatives and by implication their consciousness.

For Eric Batstone, Ian Boraston and Stephen Frankel the conditions of class consciousness involve a more complex interplay of structural factors, workers' attitudes and process of negotiation at the level of the workplace (1977, p. 267) than Daniels and McIlroy imply at the macro level. Their detailed observational study of shop steward activity in the 1970s argued that the dynamics of behaviour in domestic organisations was key to understanding workplace industrial relations and that the 'leadership' provided by shop stewards was one factor conventionally ignored. In the opening quote to the chapter Oreleo's distinction between a representative and an activist conveys the subjective elements of activism – he went on to describe how he had been motivated to stand as a steward:

> I became active because the steward in the workplace in my perception was weak. In my perception he allowed management to bully you. In my perception he didn't actively stand up for members and represent members and really told them off as opposed to giving them support. So after three years he resigned and then another person said 'oh I'll do it'. And I realised that's more of the same. So I

thought if I get the sack, and if you defend me I'm going to be gutted because I know you're no good. Whereas I know I can defend myself and I could probably defend others. So on that criteria, I asked to be put forward and my workshop voted me in.

Similarly, Diana, a Regional Learning Organiser who had become active through union learning, suggested the importance of reminding both ULRs and managers of statutory rights to time-off:

It can be difficult, but again, some of that's down to how individuals present it as well and how unions present it and you have to give the role equal weighting to your official role. Certainly at the moment there's a lot of pressure and I have heard individuals – ULRs – say 'oh we've got a lot on, this, that and the other'. I say 'well hang on a minute, you're entitled to the time for union learning and you should be treating that as if you work part-time. How would you be if you had two official roles? You'd have to share your time between those two, it's no different. Don't let your union work become second place, it should have equal priority because if you don't give it equal footing, will anybody else?'

These quotes suggest the interplay of structure and agency that characterises the activist role and there have been a number of attempts to construct typologies of workplace activism. Fosh (1981) suggested that historically participation had been defined formally in terms of attendance at branch or local meetings or holding branch/local office. Her own study was more inclusive and aimed to reflect more informal workplace participation defined as knowledge of the union rulebook, reading the union journal, talking to workmates about union issues, talking to branch officers about work and conditions and canvassing in elections for the union executive. However, most other work focuses upon activists with more formal representative roles. In the 1970s Batstone et al.'s (1977) study of shop steward activity differentiated 'leaders' and 'delegates', with 'leaders' defined as a 'representative' in relation to union members, taking a proactive role and having a commitment to trade union principles. In contrast a 'delegate' was more passive and reflected members' wishes. Darlington challenges Batstone et al.'s polarisation between leaders and populists suggesting that stewards generally have characteristics of each (1994a). His definition of steward activity, distinguishes between management-facing, member-facing and union-facing activities. Management-facing activity includes dealing with management on collective issues related to pay and non-pay matters through bargaining or consultation, but can also include interacting with management on individual issues linked to grievances and discipline. Union-facing activity embraces recruitment by stewards as well as the dissemination of union information and material. Member-facing activity covers activity that requires stewards to deal directly with their constituents, primarily providing advice and information on employment rights, work and occupational issues.

For Batstone et al. (1977) shop steward leadership was associated with strong bargaining relationships with management and with outcomes in terms of bargaining, pay, overtime, work organisation and industrial action. For Daniels and McIlroy (2009) the potency of shop stewards also appears to depend upon their role in the joint regulation of the workplace and in collective bargaining. How far has the decline in collective bargaining and increase in the individual demands of members in the workplace undermined or transformed typologies of activism? Although central to trade unions' ability to protect both the standard of living and dignity of their members, collective bargaining has also been seen as integral to the fundamentally contradictory nature of trade unions – simultaneously a challenge and component part of capitalism (Clarke, 1977). For Lenin trade union consciousness rested upon sectionalism and economism (Clements, 1977). In the tradition of Marxist literature the economism of trade unions was reflected in their limited and accommodative frames of reference structured by the process of collective bargaining – a key constraint tying them into the capitalist system (Hyman, 2001). How far does the subsequent decline of collective bargaining potentially challenge these frames of reference? In Chapters 5 and 6 we note how collective bargaining could operate in a way that was exclusionary protecting the interests of skilled white male workers in periods of tight labour markets and working against the interests of black, women and migrant workers (Virdee, 2000). One hypothesis is that the recent decline of collective bargaining may allow unions to transcend such economism, although as Terry (2000) clarifies the distinctiveness of public service trade unionism is that, by definition, it has to engage with the political process and in its necessary interest in sector policy has a wider basis for engagement than that associated with collective bargaining.

For Darlington Batstone et al.'s characterisation of 'leaders' downplays the dynamic between members and activists which is as important as the relationship with management (1994a). In terms of both union and member-facing activity Fosh's later work (1993) showed that a 'participatory leadership style' emphasising communication and consultation with members at formal and informal level was integral in securing union membership participation. A number of later studies (Greene et al., 2000; Metocchi, 2002; Upchurch et al., 2002) support this view that interaction with members and inclusiveness – involving members in decision-making – influence the strength of workplace unionism and interaction with management. Peter Fairbrother has suggested that the restructuring of the state sector and shift in the locus of bargaining from national to local might provide opportunities for unions to develop more participative and active forms of workplace unionism offering the prospect of union renewal (1996, p. 111). This structural shift might support a model of activism that reintegrates representation and mobilisation and Chapter 6 explores how far this is reflected in the activity of migrant workers in privatised services with the contraction of collective bargaining encouraging unions to forge alliances with community organisations and migrant networks outside the workplace.

Alternatively union weakness, the constraints placed by the intensification of work on activism, and the focus upon individual representation and rights may further obscure the relationship between the economic and political. Waddington and Kerr have examined UNISON's membership strategy and in particular its National Organising and Recruitment Strategy (NORS) – essentially the adoption of certain elements of an organising model by the union (2009). Their survey of UNISON shop stewards and branch secretaries suggested that both undertook a wide range of duties, but concluded that providing support for existing members in terms of representation and advice inhibited their role in recruitment and organisational activity; 'a range of duties connected to individual representation and bargaining are assigned a higher priority than activities associated with the NORS by most lay representatives' and time is a key constraint (2009, p. 44).

Darlington (1994a) suggested that Batstone's emphasis upon strong bargaining relationships is predicated upon stewards and managers being on the same wavelength and that from this perspective 'by moderating their goals shop stewards can achieve more for their members than they possibly could through a more adversarial or militant perspective'. It leads to a process of 'marginal incremental adjustment', which does not obstruct managerial objectives (1994a, p. 16). This reflects Willman's (1980) earlier suggestion that management promotion of the steward role as part of the formalisation of bargaining arrangements could also be seen as encouraging more cooperative relations between them.

The debate about the independence of workplace representatives raises not only the subjective, but also the ideological dimensions of trade unionism. In the 1970s Batstone et al. showed that the way that shop stewards defined and reaffirmed trade union goals and principles was associated with their roles and effectiveness and that in this there were differences between shop-floor stewards and staff stewards (1977, p. 29). They concluded that in part the staff stewards' 'day-to-day lack of power' reflected the organisation of work and management, but, related to this, was 'their inability to create and maintain a collective approach to issues among their members' (1977, p. 254). Similarly, Fosh's 1981 study of the factors predicting the participation of Sheffield steelworkers in their local union organisation concluded that it was not possible to ignore the ideological dimension – the importance of their commitment to collectivism and to the principles of trade unionism and the labour movement. A 'collectivist' perspective, where issues are seen by representatives as relating to a shared situation of employment rather than taken up as individual grievances, has thus been seen as a key characteristic of activism (Fairbrother, 1989; Fosh, 1993; Darlington, 1994). For Huw Beynon activism is similarly directed by values and systems of belief and must take account of the ideology of both activists themselves and the organisation they are part of (1973, p. 192). In his classic study of trade union activism at the Ford Motor Company he differentiated between activists with collectivistic values and inactive members who appreciated the union in terms of the individual representation it provided. However, he argued that there is no essential contradiction between the two perspectives since 'trade unions are in fact built upon this dualism' (1973, p. 200) and there is a complementary relationship between individual ends and collective action. This is confirmed by the testimonies of activists in this book and illustrated by Diana:

> Actually I've had two [grievances]. One was prior to me becoming a rep and I did actually take that forward at the time without a trade union rep and it was successful. In some ways it was the injustice more than anything else that I wasn't happy with. There are individuals who say 'I've never needed the union, I've been able to do it myself'…now, I had an experience of doing that, but then that made me think, hang on a minute, I was OK, I managed that, but there are some people who wouldn't feel comfortable doing what I did and they need support and how do you give them the support?

You become active yourself and then you are able to support people. It makes you realise that there are folk out there who need support and some people wouldn't take these things forward on their own. They would just sit down and quietly take it, particularly if you have a background where you don't question authority in any way...and it's the same with work. Some people feel uncomfortable challenging their line manager because they believe they must know best.

As with other activists she suggests that individual grievances and the recognition that they are shared experiences of employment could generate activism, where there is a union to respond. Darlington challenges Batstone et al.'s counterposition of trade union principles and sectional interests – 'the uncertain relationship' between day-to-day grievances and longer-term protection of the interests of all workers in the organisation, suggesting, like Beynon, a more dynamic relationship. Chapters 4 and 5 explore how far the emergence of Equality Reps and ULRs reflects not only the increased focus upon individual workplace grievances, but also the role of activists in framing these collectively.

Conclusions

A changed economic, political and legal context has reshaped the context in which workplace activists operate, their roles and typologies of activism. The intensification of work has undermined workplace activity in terms of the time and resources that representatives can commit to it, whilst privatisation has fragmented collective organisation in the public sector reinforcing a more general decline in collective bargaining. This chapter has suggested that structural changes can impinge upon activists' capacity to promote collectivity, particularly the way in which they can become enmeshed in individual casework arising from seemingly individualised employment relationships, at the expense of organising activity. In their exploration of the problematic and changing relationship between individualism and collectivism Miguel Martinez Lucio and Paul Stewart are wary of research (and intellectual disengagement) that stresses the labour process as a site for the production of relations of subjectivity rather than collectivity and that suggests that increasingly 'individualised relations of conflict at work triumph over "collective" relations of conflict in work' (1997, p. 65). As Fairbrother proposes, the fact that management has attempted to reorganise collective workforces on an individualistic basis does not equate to the individualisation of social relations of production as such (1996). Martinez Lucio and Stewart similarly assert the common basis that emerges from the experience of wage labour and labour market relations despite changes in work relations and despite worker experiences which suggest otherwise – under the capitalist mode of production work is never an individual process and individualised trade union politics cannot resolve the contradictions of the collective worker (1997). In this context the collectivist perspective of the workplace representative is crucial.

For Daniels and McIlroy (2009), Fairbrother's (1996) fear that unions would be ill-equipped to deal with structural change appears to have been largely born out. Yet whilst Daniels and McIlroy (2009) certainly pinpoint the changed objective circumstances generated by neoliberalism and crucially how these circumstances have hamstrung trade unions, they downplay the subjective and ideological dimensions of activism and appear sceptical of the potential of a range of social identities to reinvigorate collective organisation. Their pessimism conveys only a limited sense of the dialectical relationship between structure and agency and a downplaying of the objective, subjective, material and ideological factors that inform workplace relations and which are informed by workplace dynamics. Within such a context activists can move between conflictual and accommodative relationships with employers and representative or participatory relationships with members reflecting the contradictory tendencies involved in trade unionism (Darlington, 1994b). Consciousness may be transformed through experience, struggle, education and political engagement, although this may be momentary.

Importantly Daniels and McIlroy extend the debate on the way the state has reshaped the context of activism to argue that Labour Government support for the emergence of two new types of union representatives – Union Learning Reps and Equality Reps – represents an attempt to channel trade unionism away from conflict and collectivism towards partnership with management and individual relationships with members (Daniels and McIlroy, 2009). In this they would appear to argue that the uncritical stance of most trade union leaderships towards the neoliberal ideologies adopted by the Labour Government has constrained the role of workplace activists themselves – Chapter 4 and 5 explore this claim in more detail. Before this we turn, in Chapter 3, to the role of activists in statutory recognition ballots, illustrating the subjective and ideological dimensions of activism, but embedded in the social relations of the workplace and necessitating consideration of employer power and behaviour. Here activists' collectivist perspective framed workplace grievances as the basis of collective organisation.

3
The Role of Activists in Collective Mobilisation – Statutory Recognition Ballots

> Somebody had to do it, I was there, I decided to do it and if you're going to achieve recognition you have to have somebody that's going to stand with their head above the parapet.

Ken was a leading activist at Groomco,[1] a company producing toiletries, where Unite won a statutory ballot to gain union recognition for over 100 production workers at one factory, in the face of stiff opposition from the US parent company which did not recognise unions in its other plants worldwide. Statutory recognition ballots represent a crucible in which the role of activists in collective organisation at workplace level can be studied. This chapter draws upon in-depth interviews with six activists who were central to five successful statutory recognition ballots, plus interviews with full-time officers and Central Arbitration Committee (CAC) documentation,[2] to explore the factors that shaped their activism. It illuminates the roles played by both the law and employer behaviour in creating or compromising the conditions for worker mobilisation and collective organisation. It considers the extent to which activism is dependent upon pre-existing ideological frames or values or whether these are forged through mobilisation.

The context

In 2000 the Labour Government introduced a new statutory trade union recognition procedure enacted in the 1999 Employment Relations Act (ERA). It enabled unions that can demonstrate majority support for collective bargaining within a specified bargaining unit to be recognised in the workplace. Once an application for recognition is accepted[3] and the bargaining unit agreed or determined, the Central Arbitration Committee (the CAC – the body responsible for handling recognition claims) is required to order a ballot if the union does not have over 50 per cent of the bargaining unit in membership. However, it also has discretion to call a ballot if there is a majority in membership, but the CAC panel deems it is 'in the interests of good industrial relations'; if it is informed by a significant number of union members that they do not wish the union to represent them for collective bargaining; if it has evidence that leads it to doubt that a significant number of union members want the union to bargain on their behalf; or if union membership has declined and the union no longer has a majority in membership. A union must secure not only a majority of those voting in a recognition ballot, but also 40 per cent of those eligible to vote. The CAC's 2008–2009 Annual Report revealed that there had been 672 applications since 2000, although 295 of these had been withdrawn at some stage during the procedure and may have resulted in a voluntary agreement; 200 cases had resulted in recognition through the procedure, 110 of them through a ballot (with 69 ballots lost). Since 2004 there had been a fall in the annual level of new recognition cases, which may suggest that unions had exhausted achievable targets and/or their increased reluctance to use the procedure (CAC Annual Reports).

Early evaluations of the statutory recognition procedure (Wood et al., 2003) broadly concluded that it was successful in the government's terms of encouraging the voluntary resolution of recognition claims, with the statutory procedure a last resort. However, they also identified some issues arising from the way the procedure could allow employers to frustrate the process legally, but also in the workplace (Moore, 2004). A subsequent amendment to the ERA in 2004 introduced the concept of 'unfair labour practices' to limit employer influence in the ballot period, but importantly employer behaviour prior to this remains unconstrained.

This chapter draws on earlier work (Moore, 2004) looking at the factors that predict success in statutory recognition ballots and arguing that for unions recognition ballots represent an uncertain terrain where membership and support is fragile. Unions have lost over a third of ballots ordered by the CAC,[4] despite the fact that on application the union either had a majority of the bargaining unit in membership or had demonstrated that a majority of the bargaining unit was likely to support recognition. In just under a third of ballots

(31 per cent) held in the first three years of the statutory procedure, the proportion of workers voting in favour of recognition in the ballot was below the membership level as verified before the ballot. An analysis of ballots held between 2006 and 2009 suggests that this trend continued. This means that membership levels or density (through changes in the bargaining unit) fell during the procedure and/or that union members abstained or voted against recognition in the ballot. Having a higher proportion of the bargaining unit in union membership on application was not related to ballot success, suggesting that during the statutory recognition process a number of contending factors come into play introducing uncertainty and this encourages employers to intervene in the procedure to ensure there is a ballot. Analysis of 64 ballots held between June 2000 and May 2003 found that the orientation of the employer towards the union, but more explicitly, whether employers were willing to turn opposition into counter-mobilisation, was important in the outcome of ballots. At the same time activists played a crucial role in sustaining support for recognition and countering employer mobilisation against the union campaign (Moore, 2004). The absence of union activists in the workplace made it virtually impossible for the union to win a recognition ballot. The chilling effect of firing activists was absolutely clear – there was a highly significant relationship between voting figures in ballots and the dismissal of activists. For a union to succeed it had to have a visible presence in the workplace and activists were key to ensuring such a presence because they were prepared to be identified as union leaders and able to instil confidence in other workers to declare their union membership. Activists countered the threats of workplace closure made by employers and prepared the workforce for the likelihood of such threats.

These case studies of statutory recognition ballots supported arguments in the US literature on union organising (for example, Rundle, 1998) that activists must be seen to challenge the employer, engage in arguments for recognition with other workers and stand up to intimidation – to 'take risks on behalf of their desire for a union' (1998, 229). Where employers raised the costs of unionisation in UK statutory recognition ballots a number of the activists were prepared to stand up to the threat of collective job loss and to run the risk of personal job loss. This chapter extends this earlier research on recognition ballots held under the statutory procedure, but focuses upon the role of activists in later successful recognition ballots, in particular their motivation, values and consciousness.

Mobilisation theory explores the factors predicting collective organisation in the workplace. John Kelly, drawing upon the work of Charles Tilly (1978) and Doug McAdam (1988), has conceptualised it as a dynamic and comprehensive explanation of workers' collective agency underpinned by social processes and structural factors, including the legal framework and national and international labour markets and product market competition. At the macro level, mobilisation reflects the opportunity structure including legislative support for unionisation (Kelly, 2005) and this would include the introduction of a statutory recognition procedure. Crucially mobilisation theory allows for agency; the role of employer counter-mobilisation, but also union organising strategies and the activity and character of activists. For Kelly, 'perceived injustice is the origin of workers' collective definitions of interests, and from those definitions in turn flow collective organisation and action' (1998, p. 64). Yet the process of collectivisation is 'heavily dependent on the actions of small numbers of leaders or activists' (1998, p. 44). This emphasis has led Fairbrother (2005) to characterise Kelly's conceptualisation of mobilisation as vanguardist and counterposed to an analysis grounded in the social relationships of work and employment, considerations of class structure and consciousness and the participative struggles that define such processes. For Fairbrother the logical outcome of mobilisation theory is a concept of individuation where collective organisation and action hangs upon leaders, divorced from rather than embedded in the workplace. Yet this conceptualisation bears little resemblance to the dialectical relationship between individual activists and collective workplace struggle actually offered by Kelly. As Darlington rightly argues (2009), a crucial feature of mobilisation theory is the way that it locates agency in the context of structural conditions. For Darlington union leadership can be seen to be as important as any structural or institutional complexity in shaping the nature of collective action. In considering this I now turn to the process of collective mobilisation in five statutory recognition campaigns in which the union was successful in winning a ballot; a test of support for collective organisation which introduces uncertainty into the recognition process and which consequently illuminates the role of activists in mobilisation.

Shared grievances

For Bert Klandermans 'felt injustice is at the roots of any protest' (1997, p. 205). His social psychology approach, conceptualising the relationship between individual and collective beliefs and actions, emphasises the role of grievance rather than rational choice or resource mobilisation, theories stressing collective action as a means to achieve a goal. As Kelly acknowledges people are not mobilised solely on the basis of 'instrumental calculations of individual self-interest (1998, p. 34). In the context of the workplace in the first instance mobilisation is based upon a sense of injustice amongst workers based upon the conviction that employer decisions are illegitimate. This is born out by the case studies of recognition which form the basis of this chapter. At Groomco unionisation was a result of changes to shift patterns and working hours and the perception by workers that they had not been consulted on this change. Although this involved those on the night shift losing money and those on the day shift gaining some extra pay, it was the impact upon work–life balance which caused anger:

> Everybody was going to swap and to rotate days and nights with the option of 'flexibility' – in their words – of changing shifts more or less at three or four weeks' notice, something like that. And imagine, that went down like a lead balloon. ... the money wasn't an issue with people, it was the fact that 'I worked ten years on days', 'I've got my personal life', 'I've got my children at home', etc etc. 'The whole of my life revolves around me coming to work on day shift... all of a sudden [I have to] turn the lifestyle upside down and accommodate night shift working'.

Departmentco was a large department store where Unite approached the company for recognition for over 100 cleaners. Like Groomco changes to shift patterns and the implications for work–life balance, along with dissatisfaction with pay and holidays and allegations of bullying, promoted unionisation. These were placed within a wider context of the absence of representation – as one of the key activists, George, put it:

> They wanted someone who can listen to them and solve their problems, because most of them weren't treated fairly – so therefore they wanted something to get done about it. So a lot of people suddenly, they didn't like it and all of them wanted to join the union, so suddenly it was getting ten forms, 20 forms, 30 a week – it's quite a lot.

At Sportsco, a sports retailer, Unite submitted a recognition claim for nearly 500 operatives working in its distribution centre. The company had relocated a largely migrant and agency workforce to a new site in a different part of the country, promising permanent contracts, higher pay and an improved bonus scheme. The improved bonus did not materialise and Piotrek, the leading activist in the campaign, described 'a lack of respect' and a climate of fear in which workers were too scared to raise issues about health and safety or to report accidents. The company regularly sacked people by mobile phone or text message on the slightest pretext; 'if you reported anything, if you had a problem, you were basically "thank you very much, we don't require your service any more".' Another worker there contacted a Polish Organiser who had been helping to recruit migrant workers for Unite where she had previously worked and where there had been union recognition. The organiser then started to meet with some of the workforce and here an organising approach[5] was used to identify specific workplace issues which were consciously framed collectively and to encourage 'small actions' which gave workers the confidence to act collectively and start to raise issues with management in a way they had been too frightened to do before. The Regional Union Organiser considered the fact that the local union organiser was Polish to be crucial in gaining the trust of eastern European workers with legacies of living in a communist state and under a culture of surveillance where involvement in any independent political activity might bring reprisals.

At Rentco group, a provider of social housing formed through the merger of a number of housing associations, the unionisation of maintenance staff in two workplaces was in response to uncertainty following the transfer of staff and due to the behaviour of one or two managers. Steve, one of the activists, described grievances arising from management's insistence on workers arranging medical appointments in their own time, despite provision for time off for such appointments within the staff handbook and their difficulties in making appointments outside working hours. Steve's subsequent reflections on the difference recognition had made to the workforce focussed upon representation, voice and respect suggesting the generalised sense of grievance felt by the workforce at Rentco, but also by the workforces in the other cases:

> The management at Rentco at the time were Neanderthal, Jurassic, for want of a better word, on a good day…The recognition agreement's working a treat for the direct workforce; where we once got dictated to and trampled on – I mean it might be a bit of a bloody cliché but that's what the situation was – we're now sort of listened to and to a certain degree I would like to think we were respected.

At Educco, a national educational charity providing professional training, recognition was similarly fuelled by the perception that employees had no representation or voice; 'management had got worse and worse here over time and were very dictatorial and everything was a fait accompli'. At the same time new staff were being employed on increasingly inferior terms and conditions and the teaching staff resented a performance-related pay system which included anonymous ratings by students. In response to these grievances, one of the key activists, Jo, organised a union meeting of around 40 members which elected four representatives.

For Klandermans injustice is socially constructed and not an objective phenomenon (1997, p. 19) or necessarily underpinned by material interest. Maurizio Atzeni (2009) challenges both Kelly and Klandermans' emphasis on injustice, arguing that for them it is subjective and not rooted in the contradictions created by the structural nature of the capitalist labour process. He aims to reinforce Kelly's theory of mobilisation 'as framed by a Marxist logic of society and economy'; for Atzeni mobilisation is a more spontaneous event arising from this logic. Yet, once again, a reading of Kelly would suggest that his formulation of injustice is placed firmly within the structural contradictions of capitalism. In line with Kelly, and as the case studies presented here confirm, collective organisation emerged from a sense of injustice stemming directly from the nature of the employment relation and was socially based rather than constructed. Mobilisation did, however, involve a process through which particular workers framed and articulated injustice collectively.

Promoting collective identity

For Klandermans acting collectively requires some collective identity or consciousness and in terms of labour movement activity this is deemed to be class consciousness or solidarity. In the five cases presented here collective identity clearly arose from social relations within the workplace. Yet, as Klandermans notes, collective identity is not mechanically generated. Jo described how a proportion of those joining the union at Educco were 'Tories', yet the sense of grievance that they felt produced a collective identity which transcended these values, possibly fuelled by a concept of their professional status. In the case of Sportsco it was reinforced by a shared ethnic identity and culture, but the union had to overcome a suspicion of unions, informed by a history of living under state communism and passed down through generations. Kelly describes how activists help to frame injustice and focus attribution onto the employer, encouraging group identity and cohesion (2005). At Sportsco one of the shifts employed women workers who did not receive the bonus that workers on other shifts were paid, as the union organiser describes:

> If you asked each worker to raise an individual complaint, they wouldn't because they are fearful. So we would raise a collective grievance, so they will all sign up to that. They will wear a badge about equality, 'we demand equality or everyone' or everyone goes to work with a blue t-shirt on. So there is this whole thing showing solidarity with one another, so nice gentle steps. Then what happened with that particular case was when we submitted the collective grievance, the employer said 'we don't deal with collective – if people want to raise a complaint, they have to come individually'. But because people had already made that first step and felt, 'oh my head didn't come off – I put my name to a collective [grievance] and nothing's happened, I'm still alive, I still have my job', then the braver ones were willing to have the complaint go forward as an individual [grievance].

Consequently the union submitted over 60 individual grievances, which would have had to be heard over weeks. In fact, after the first day the employer backed down and agreed to deal with the grievance collectively and eventually conceded the bonus. This event suggests a complex interaction of gender with ethnicity and class, rooted in workplace relations, but mediated through trade union identity and organisation.

Creating alternative channels for worker involvement is one pre-emptive step employers take to avoid union recognition (Ewing et al., 2003). Yet, as in other union recognition cases employee experiences of non-union representative bodies could precipitate unionisation (Moore, 2004). As Jo describes in Box 2, at Educco a staff forum was established by management under the Information and Consultation Regulations.[6] Whilst challenging the legitimacy of this the union representatives made sure that they were elected onto the forum, although they were not recognised in a union capacity. The forum allowed them to meet with employee representatives from other workplaces and to swap experiences of management and recruit into the union; as Jo put it 'we had this conduit which we used shamelessly'. When the representatives felt in a strong enough position they resigned en masse:

> Because we weren't going to give it the integrity, it didn't deserve it, it was a rubber stamping job and we felt the only way that there was genuinely going to be negotiation between the parties was if we were unionised.

Subsequently management sent an email to all staff personally attacking the reps for withdrawing, but this just served to alienate and anger staff further and when management called for new representatives no one was prepared to stand – the forum withered and died.

In the case of Groomco the company had a consultative committee with employee representation, but the imposition of changes in shift patterns exposed to the reps that this body gave them no real representation or voice and once again they resigned en masse. The core employee representatives, including Ken, then became central to the campaign for union recognition. Initially they collected some money and approached a solicitor for legal advice over the changes to shift patterns. However, since a small number of workers in the factory were in Unite, Ken then contacted the regional officer and undertook to increase membership to above the 50 per cent level needed to secure recognition. At Rentco the union representatives withdrew from the Staff Council because it was felt they were giving it credibility and were implicated in its decisions. At Sportsco the company established a Staff Forum after the union began organising, here union members were elected to six of eight positions and one of the other two members subsequently became a union representative. In all these cases activists used employer-led forums to expose the inadequacy of worker representation, but also to build independent organisation. Strategic withdrawal from these bodies underlined the incompatibility of management and worker interests and promoted the independent and collective identity of workers themselves. We now focus upon attempts by employers to frustrate or defeat unionisation once attempts to pre-empt independent trade union representation have failed.

The nature of employer opposition

There is variation in the extent to which employers will go to avoid recognition; whilst some are pragmatic but may wish to test majority support through the procedure, others actively organise in the workplace and invest resources to defeat recognition (Moore, 2004; Logan, 2006). One tactic is to delay the process by offering to engage in discussions over voluntary recognition either before or once the statutory claim has been submitted, thus undermining the momentum of the union campaign (Ewing et al., 2003). In the case of Educco, Rentco and Groomco the employer engaged the union in discussions, which were unproductive and which activists felt were designed to frustrate the process.

By definition recognition claims that reach the CAC are those where employers have refused to come to a voluntary arrangement with the union. Once in the CAC procedure employers can challenge the union at every possible stage with the purpose of defeating the union procedurally. In the case of Sportsco, Rentco and Educco the employer challenged the bargaining unit and in the cases of Rentco and Educco, since the unions did not have a majority in membership in the revised bargaining units, ballots were called. Where the union does have a majority of the bargaining unit in membership employers may attempt to provide information to the CAC to invoke one of the discretionary criteria upon which it can order a ballot. In the case of Groomco although the CAC confirmed that the union had just over 50 per cent of the bargaining unit in membership it concluded that letters by six members of the bargaining unit stating that they did not want the union to be recognised constituted a qualifying condition for the holding of a ballot 'in the interest of good industrial relations'. The union argued that the letters had been written as a result of a sustained campaign by the employer and at their instigation and without the opportunity for the union to put its case to the membership.

In the case of Rentco the employer was opposed to recognition and challenged the union procedurally, responding to the CAC at the last possible minute before the deadline at every stage of the procedure. However, it did not undermine union support in the workplace and once a ballot had been ordered adopted a neutral stance throughout the ballot period:

> They didn't do anything to discourage workers, it was basically the management tried to stretch the whole thing out as long as they possibly could and [the full-time officer] said, 'you know, they tried up to the very last minute basically to stick their heads in the sand'.

In contrast other employers actively interfere to try to ensure the union cannot maintain the necessary levels of support for recognition.

They may do so through persuasion and campaigning; inducements or threats; or by undermining the union's access to the workforce (Ewing et al., 2003). In particular employers exploit the period before the ballot when they can legitimately campaign against recognition and when the union may have only limited or no access to the workforce. Previous research (Moore, 2004) found that UK employers were adopting similar tactics to those used by US employers to influence the outcome of recognition ballots. These include the use of outside consultants, captive audience meetings of workers, letters to workers, supervisor one-to-ones, the dismissal or promotion of activists, redundancies, changes in pay or benefits, media campaigns and anti-union committees, plus the threat to close or relocate the workplace. The UK research found that the adoption of such tactics was related to the outcome of ballots.

A number of these tactics were evident in the recognition campaigns presented here, although not sufficient to defeat recognition and in some cases they backfired. In the cases of Groomco, Educco and Departmentco it was reported that the company secured the services of consultants with a reputation for advising employers on union avoidance. At Educco management was described by the regional officer as 'aggressive' and conducted an email campaign against recognition and gave staff a substantial pay rise during the process to discourage them from supporting the union. Prior to the ballot management sent letters to employees' homes and undertook an independent survey of staff designed to identify and respond to their concerns. However, since the survey responses gave a clear message that staff did not feel valued or heard, the results were not published until after the ballot. For Jo:

> I don't think it was so much what we did; I think it was probably the attacks on us and these constant emails to the staff from management. I felt like going round and giving them a gold star and saying 'you've recruited more members than me'. They're [the staff] quite a difficult bunch. They're not easy to intimidate, they don't like necessarily to stick their head above the parapet, they're quite happy for me to do that.

At Groomco the union informed the CAC that the employer had instituted small group meetings at which briefings against union recognition took place, with at least one manager stating that recognition would lead to the factory closing – something subsequently denied by the company. Ken had undertaken his own research on previous recognition campaigns and reported that the company utilised classic union avoidance tactics:

> They were using words like 'getting the head count down by attrition' and things like that. I think they genuinely set about trying to disrupt people's lives to the extent that they would leave rather than make them redundant or whatever. They were following a fairly set pattern and started breaking it down into small communications groups. The managers had started to walk around saying 'it's not good for the company' and they believed that if the union got recognition they would close the site etc…they were making these threats that if you got recognition the place would shut.

Previous research suggests that the credibility of such threats in the eyes of the workforce is important; Ken was asked whether he thought that the workers believed that the plant would close if the union gained recognition:

> Some, yes I mean – they really did, because they have this perception that American companies would do everything to avoid union recognition and will cut them off if they have union recognition because they see it as restrictive. So yes, they did believe that, quite a lot of them believed that.

At the same time a number of the company's tactics backfired on them, a US manager came over during the access period:

> That did the company no good, I think somebody coming across from such a high level trying to persuade people not to join the union, they were thinking 'hang on, there's something not right here, we'd better join the union'.

At Sportsco in the early stages of the campaign rumours were circulated by the agency supplying workers to the company that anyone joining the union would be sacked and the employer began disciplining members for minor offences, although this encouraged union membership as workers felt they needed protection. The company also offered various inducements to workers to pre-empt recognition, including new bonus payments, which again did not influence the workforce. Piotrek, the key activist, described a 'cat and mouse' game between himself and the employer in which they attempted to provoke him and after finally doing so they dismissed him before the recognition ballot:

> Basically they were trying to provoke me, every single week, every single month, all the time. I had a situation where they tried to grab me and when they were trying to catch me out on something I was catching them out on something all the time.

Whilst in many cases the dismissal of an activist is sufficient to defeat recognition, by this stage membership was established and members were only angered by his victimisation. During the ballot period an access agreement allowed the employer and union two meetings each to address the workforce; the management meetings were addressed by a Managing Director that workers had previously not met and who did not allow questions (unlike the union sessions), it also included a video of a Polish goalkeeper who played for a Premiership football team warning of the detrimental effects of recognition – these tactics all backfired.

In the case of Departmentco the CAC verified that membership of the bargaining unit was under 50 per cent. The union reported that recruitment had taken place in difficult conditions and outside of working hours in an environment where management disapproved of union membership, although this was disputed by the employer. Here the extent of employer opposition was such that the union made a formal complaint to the CAC that the employer had breached the statutory unfair practice provisions because it had issued a document to workers threatening redundancies or the contracting out of the cleaning service, with implied job cuts and detrimental terms and conditions of work. This was denied by the employer and although the CAC noted that the link in the document between the theoretical possibility of outsourcing and job insecurity, in the context of a recognition claim, could be interpreted as a threat it did not find that the allegation of unfair practice was founded. The activists reported that they countered the threat, 'They did introduce that, but it didn't work'. The employer had regular meetings with staff as well as producing newsletters to oppose recognition and used team leaders to convey this message. It also offered inducements in terms of vouchers for the department store and increased holidays from 25 to 27 days. Despite these tactics nearly two thirds of the bargaining unit voted to support recognition. The extent to which employers are willing to invest resources into opposing unionisation is a key factor in the success or failure of recognition ballots. In these five cases there were varying degrees of opposition, but in four of them the employer deployed aggressive tactics. In all four these tactics were unsuccessful and this shifts the focus onto union strategies and the resilience of the activists themselves.

Union organising strategies

The US literature on the determinants of union success and failure in National Labor Relations Board (NLRB) elections emphasises, not only employer strategies, but also the importance of unions adopting a comprehensive range of organising tactics (Bronfenbrenner and Juravich, 1998). In the UK the study of earlier ballots found that an organising approach was used to varying degrees in recognition ballots and this is born out by the later case studies examined here. At Sportsco a systematic organising approach was deployed, run by the regional organising team and focussed around collectivising workplace issues and inoculating the workforce against employer counter-mobilisation. The claim for recognition was not submitted until the union was convinced that members 'were strong enough to withstand the pressures that we knew would come'. Union organisers at Sportsco described how it was important to behave like a union in the workplace even though there was no recognition. This meant ensuring that activists were trained and accredited in order to accompany workers in grievances and disciplinaries during the recognition campaign, as well as to give the activists themselves some protection from victimisation. Piotrek insisted on accompanying, and effectively providing representation to, workers who were threatened with disciplinary action or called in by supervisors, as the organiser described:

> Piotrek was getting them really aggravated because he wouldn't drop it. He knew that a person is allowed to be accompanied when a worker asks for it – they can have somebody with them. So every time he was asked to go, he would go. And the manager wouldn't like it, but he would say 'no, I'm not going, they've got a right to have someone. If you want to talk to them, we'll talk to them with me or with the union representative. Otherwise you are not talking to them'.

The union became a highly visible presence in the workplace not least because activists would wear a florescent 'high visibility' jacket with the union logo and 'accredited union rep' on it.

Similarly at Rentco Steve became a representative in one of the two depots covered by the recognition claim and completed his shop steward training and began to recruit. Theories of union instrumentality suggest that it is important that workers believe the union can make a difference in the workplace (Charlwood, 2003). Steve described how he emphasised union services in order to recruit, but also how union success in individual representation began to convince workers about union effectiveness, in particular, in winning an appeal over a worker who had been disciplined over his sickness as part of the company's sickness procedure:

> I would say that there was a high chance that that was probably the first sickness appeal that was probably overturned and basically got a result for the workforce. And from that point on [there was] interest in [the] GMB, as in, 'you know, this union, has, or may have, the potential to give us a fair deal at the end of the day', which up to that point had never been heard of within Rentco, basically, it's what you would call a result for the workforce, you know.

The worker who was the subject of the disciplinary subsequently became a workplace rep. Similarly at Departmentco union effectiveness was seen to counter any fears the workers had:

> Even those who were frightened, some of them they didn't even want to join because they were frightened, they were thinking 'no, they might sack me, I might lose my job'. But then they realised, those people in the union – they'd seen a lot of difference...

Accounts of the celebrated Justice for Janitor's campaign in Los Angeles highlight the tactics, leadership and strategy of the SEIU (Service Employees International Union) in its success (Waldinger et al., 1998) and Unite's strategy clearly played a role in the success of the recognition campaign at Sports Direct. Such organising approaches, and in particular the employment of full-time organising officers, have led to suggestions of top-down 'managed activism' as a substitute for organic grassroots mobilisation (McIlroy, 2009). At the same time, in the US a similar approach has been seen to bring younger politicised organisers into the labour movement dislodging older conservative elements (Milkman, 2006). In all the cases illustrated here the union provided varying degrees of organisational support to the campaigns, but workers had contacted the union themselves and the workplaces involved were not on a list of the unions' organising targets. At Sportsco unionisation clearly emerged from organic grassroots impulses with union organisers actively targeting and training a group of activists or 'leaders', covering all shifts and nationalities in order to ensure a 'sustainable structure' that would last beyond the recognition ballot. Union support and the fact that the organiser was Polish, were seen as particularly important in the face of both workers' and activists' limited union experience.

The role and nature of activism

In the five cases presented here the development of a group of activists with a visible presence in the workplace was an important factor in union success, although in all cases there were one or two 'leaders' who played the key role. The subjective dimensions of activism were evident. Beynon's study of grass roots trade unionism at Ford found that whatever their union background the stewards often possessed 'more than a hint of bravado – a bit of go' (1973, p. 191). For the union organising officers dealing with Sportsco it was crucial to identify potential activists or 'natural leaders':

> It's really about trying to behave like a union and look like a union inside a workplace where there is no recognition, starting from trying to identify the people who others turn to, who speak for them anyway, whether that is in a community way or inside the workplace. There are natural, what we call natural shop stewards, there's always someone that someone will go to. We normally find it's a person who's got some confidence, somebody who perhaps will research on the internet what their rights are.

Piotrek was such an activist and he was quickly trained as an accredited union rep. Like the activists in the other cases he stated that he was not afraid of victimisation; 'I can't stand back when somebody is trying to exploit somebody or somebody is trying to make fear'. In the US context Milkman (2006, p. 157) has described the importance of using aggressive tactics in union organising campaigns, including legal tactics such as filing complaints with the NLRB alleging discrimination against union activists – this positions the union as the de facto representative of workers even where there is no official recognition by the employer. At Educco the representatives had been personally attacked by management when they had resigned from the staff forum, but Jo subsequently countered this by asserting her rights as a trade union representative (Box 2). When management put out information suggesting that union recognition would mean negotiations over pay which would delay pay rises, Jo responded by sending staff an email link to the organisation's accounts which revealed what senior managers were earning – the substantial pay differential encouraged recruitment. Jo confirmed the importance of union visibility and aggression when she talked about a subsequent unsuccessful voluntary recognition ballot (mirroring the statutory procedure) for administrative staff in the same organisation. Here the reps appeared more vulnerable to bullying by managers, but were reluctant to take this up and eventually organisation amongst these workers fell away. In this case the union agreed with management to keep the campaign over the ballot low-key so as

---

Box 2

'So along came a wonderful piece of European legislation called the Information and Consultation Regulations and management, because of our size – it was over 150 employees – they had to set up some sort of body, but they know nothing about the law or didn't look at it properly and we got this wonderful email from the Head of Personnel telling us what the committee would be and if you'd looked at the reg[ulation]s you know that you *negotiate* the terms of it. I replied saying "thank you very much for your proposals but you actually can't do that, you need to negotiate with us" and put a link so other staff could see what the law was. It was electric because I was getting people all over in different branches saying "Oh good for you" and "I really agree" and people were looking stuff up and sending me stuff and overnight I became the mouthpiece, you know, because, they'd checked and they knew I was right. ... I sort of just galvanised those feelings and suddenly became this figurehead.

Nationally the Chief Executive emailed every staff member, attacking us, and I went to my boss and said "Well you do understand that victimisation of trade union reps is an offence and the damages are unlimited and I will take you to a tribunal and I will make sure the press are there, and the union will make sure the press are there." So they backed off, but we actually lost reps because they were worried about the repercussions. But I thought "Well I'm protected cos I'm a rep". And I felt a bit like, not that I'm in the same league at all, felt a bit like, you know, like Nelson Mandela, they couldn't really touch me because it would be so obvious why they were touching me. They'd have to leave me alone, I'm the biggest thorn in their side but they're not going to, you know. And I was good at my job as well, luckily, so they had nothing to get me on. I always feel there's knives just waiting, so I have to watch myself'.

(Jo, activist, recognition campaign)

not to disrupt teaching – they did not put up union posters, did not leaflet staff and limited the number of meetings the union had with staff. There was a suggestion that the representatives were more passive than in the case of the lecturing staff; as Jo conceded:

> We didn't really look like a union... you can't be winding, pushing reps to do everything, they've got to take a bit of responsibility and if the reps are at that stage where they're not organising those sort of things then the members are not going to be at that stage either or behind them – are they?

At Groomco there were two key activists who met with the full-time union officer off-site and who talked to people face-to-face on both the day and night shifts. Ken played a key role in keeping the workforce updated on the campaign via email and a blog. His research on previous recognition cases prepared him for management tactics and he understood the importance of being identified with the union and in taking risks in challenging the employer:

> There was one meeting which again was reported back to me, in the early days before we got recognition, that the manager had said that the company knows who the troublemakers are and if we can get rid of them then there won't be any problems and my name was mentioned inevitably. I think it's a difficult situation because there's not many people that want to be seen to be associated with the union in that sort of situation. Understandably so, and the problem that most people would have in that situation is what's going to happen if they don't get recognition! And that did go through my mind at times. I took the view that I was going to do it. If they chose to sack me as a result of doing that then I considered I would have enough ammunition and enough arguments to claim unfair dismissal and I was prepared to do that. So you don't do it ignoring that really. I'm fairly sort of motivated and quite prepared to stand up and make arguments against or for a particular cause that I believe in.

At Departmentco Mark and George were central to the recognition campaign, they organised small group meetings and made themselves available for individual sessions with workers and put out news sheets. They described the recognition campaign as going 'by the book'. Their experience as union activists meant they could stand up to employer antagonism; for Mark, 'I've been doing this for many years, it doesn't bother me, I've been a trade union activist for all these years'. George concurred that he was not intimidated by the employer tactics. The full-time officer also pinpointed their confidence in inspiring others to stand up for themselves: 'George and Mark are leading the way in standing up to the employer, and have given them [the members] the confidence to challenge the employer individually.'

Atzeni (2009) proposes that the contradictions of the capitalist labour process can produce spontaneous, unorganised, mobilisations that cannot be attributed to the actions of an existing leadership. His research on the occupation of two car factories in Argentina show that perceptions of injustice fuelled action and become framed in the process by 'natural' leaders who emerged during mobilisation. He suggests that Kelly's model of mobilisation may be more useful for an explanation of union organising as opposed to spontaneous or even general collective action, since it locates leaders as a precondition for mobilisation rather than a product emerging from it. Whilst Kelly's formulation does not appear to distinguish between spontaneous and more organised action, it is also not at all clear that in either case it is predicated upon an existing formal leadership or 'leadership-centred' (2009, p. 6). The cases of statutory recognition presented here show that such leadership was not a prerequisite for collective organisation, but was emergent and then essential to its success. Beynon's study of Ford found that emergent shop floor organisation required 'conflict, sponsorship and a commitment to a humanistic collectivism' (1973, p. 189). For the shop stewards that he based his study upon activism was shaped by their experience of workplace conflict and their inability to stand back in the face of injustice. Most of them had no intention of becoming active when they started work at Ford, but at the same time over half had fathers that were strong supporters of trade unionism and were 'union-minded'. In the context of union mobilisation for recognition this raises the question of how far activists have to have a prior collectivist orientation to play a central role in workplace mobilisation where there is no union, or if it is possible for collectivism to emerge purely from social relations rooted in the workplace.

George and Mark were long-standing union members and had previously been representatives and Mark was a Labour Party activist. Similarly Jo had a prior history of trade union and political activism and had joined a union when she started working Saturday's at Tesco at the age of 15:

> I've got a very, very strong moral conviction of you need to be protected. There's an unequal relationship between employer and

employee. And not that I'd seen terrible things happen or anything but I just was very, very committed to that. My dad, my family were quite political anyway I suppose. My dad stood as a Labour councillor. And I'd been on demonstrations up to London so I was already a non fan of Mrs T[hatcher] and at the sixth form college I'd been involved, I'd been a member of the Labour Party, Young Socialists, and things like that. So I was already quite politicised probably.

In contrast, Ken, Piotrek and Steve had no experience of trade union activism and this suggests that collectivism may also emerge from workplace experience (Healy et al., 2004). Prior to the recognition campaign at Groomco Ken had not been a union member, but was motivated to become active by the way management had imposed changes in working practices without consultation; 'I wanted to push back a bit and there's no other way of pushing back other than having union recognition'. His father had been a union member, but neither of his parents were activists, although he described himself as coming from a 'traditional working class background'. He had, however, been a member of the Communist Party in the 1960s whilst a student and described himself as a Socialist and had been on the huge 2003 national demonstration against the invasion of Iraq. In contrast Piotrek had absolutely no experience of trade unions either in Poland or the UK and no family history of trade unionism. Steve was an electrician who had joined the AEEU as an apprentice, but was not active. He joined the GMB when a friend and workmate who was active asked him. Whilst Ken had some form of residual ideological context for his union activism, Steve did not, but, described how he was becoming more interested in politics through the union (see page 165). Whilst Ken and Steve both had some form of prior collectivist orientation, in both cases this was tentative. Like Piotrek their activism was informed and shaped by their experience of work – they responded, framed grievances and were prepared to stand up to management hostility to unionisation, and in the case of Groomco and Sportsco, counter-mobilisation. Here these characteristics would appear to be as important as a prior ideological orientation. Yet for Beynon (1973), whilst stewards might possess certain character traits, activism is a social process that goes beyond the psychological and emerges from the dialectical relationship between the activist and the workers he or she represents. In the cases presented here there is an evident dynamic between activists and other workers who wanted recognition, but were not prepared or confident enough to become activists (as illustrated by Jo in Box 2), but also between activists and the union.

Conclusions

The five case studies described here support Kelly's formulation of mobilisation theory, but not subsequent characterisations of it as vanguardist or over dependent upon injustice. Workplace grievance defined by the capitalist labour process provided the basis of collective organisation, but unions and activists were crucial in actively framing these collectively and standing up to varying degrees of employer hostility to unionisation. The political and legal context, in the form of the introduction of a statutory recognition procedure provided an opportunity structure, although the weakness of the procedure allows for employer counter-mobilisation and constrains both collective organisation and the outcome of recognition, collective bargaining. Studies of failed recognition ballots have highlighted the wider role of product and labour markets – credible threats to relocate production or to outsource services undermined union campaigns. Such threats were raised in the case of Groomco and of Departmentco – in both they were countered.

Above all the case studies underline the importance of retaining a concept of agency when situating workers within prevailing and often demoralising socio-economic conditions, reinforced by the ideological power of capital. They highlight the behaviour of employers and responses of workers and unions themselves. Whilst celebrating the possibilities that these cases represent it is, however, important to acknowledge that these mobilisations are modest in size covering small groups of workers; as Milkman concludes for such campaigns in the US, the challenge of reproducing such successes on a larger scale remains formidable (2006). They are moments of warmth in a cold climate.

Whilst three of the activists had a previous history of union activism and this was clearly important to the success of the campaigns; three did not. It could be argued that two of them had (to different degrees) a collectivist frame of reference, but in the case of Sportsco, an activist with no experience of trade unionism and a workforce with a legacy of suspicion to trade unions from former communist states stood up to a hostile and exploitative employer and delivered an overwhelming vote for collective organisation. Here collectivism was generated by the experience of employment relations located in the workplace, underpinned by a migrant (and in the organisation of one shift, gender) division of labour and informed by a shared ethnic (and gender) identity, yet transcending and transforming migrant worker identity – something we return to in Chapter 6. Pre-existing or residual or reactivated ideological frames play an important role in the emergence of activists necessary to workplace mobilisation, but they are not a precondition for activism or mobilisation and this points to the gap between activity and consciousness (Hyman, 1971).

4
Agents of Neoliberalism? The Contested Role of the ULR

The Skills for Life[1] brand, I'm not that keen on it, but it needs to have some sort of brand, I suppose. But it literally is for your life isn't it? Reactivating, bringing yourself back to life in a sense...to make sure ultimately, and one of the things I'm presenting when we do surgeries and workshops and talk about these things and why the union is present, is to make sure that we've got our jobs in five, ten, fifteen, twenty years – to make sure that we provide people with opportunities. To make sure that new members see other opportunities, other sides to the trade union – it's not all banging on the desks, it's about preparing ourselves to make sure that in the future the unions are still strong because the members have moved with the times as well, taken the opportunities. To push forward, and make sure that the companies they work for see them as valued members of staff and see that the union values them as members as well and this is another side of things.

John, ULR

This chapter explores the way in which the narratives of Union Learning Representatives (ULRs) reflect the contested ideologies and discourses surrounding trade union learning. It locates union learning in the context of the Labour Government's learning and skills agenda, essentially concerning the promotion of individual employability for national productivity and competitiveness. However, it also considers and challenges critiques of the role of union reps in workplace learning, in particular those of John McIlroy who has argued that union involvement with New Labour's initiatives demonstrate the 'limits of trade union practice in a neo-liberal skills regime' (McIlroy and Croucher, 2009, p. 287) constraining union militancy and by implication the consciousness of ULRs. Whilst in Chapter 3 we saw how workplace grievances provoked collective organisation and activism, in contrast union learning is posited as a material benefit or service to members and potential members in workplaces with existing union organisation and thus does not appear to fit within the parameters of mobilisation theory. Whilst learning has the capacity to attract new activists, Eddie Donnelly and Julia Kiely have also suggested that there might be 'a separation of learning advocacy from workplace adversarialism' (2007, p. 80) and that the 'dispositions' of new ULRs may be characterised by an instrumentalist motivation towards the role and a 'self-imposed restraint' (2007, p. 83), so that they are unlikely to engage in a sustained fashion with union mobilisation and/or employer ambivalence. At the other end of the spectrum Howard Stevenson envisages the possibility of ULRs as organic intellectuals, as conceived by Gramsci, playing a key role in 'challenging and critiquing dominant discourses of current education policy' (2010, p. 69). This chapter explores these different visions drawing upon in-depth interviews with five ULRs as well as case studies of learning and organising, including case studies written by three of the ULRs themselves reflecting upon their own practice.[2] It, does so first, by considering how far ULRs see their role in workplace learning as going beyond employer-driven agendas around productivity and government agendas promoting individual employability; second, by looking at their relationships with employers; and third, by looking at the extent to which new ULRs are divorced from branch activism in terms of collective bargaining and/or organising. Finally, I speculate on what this might mean for the trade union identities of ULRs themselves, with the unfixed and sometimes contradictory narratives of ULRs suggesting learning as a hegemonic process.

The context

The Union Learning Representative (ULR) role was first introduced in 2000 to engage and support workers – often 'non-traditional learners' – in learning at the workplace. This may be learning which 'not only meets the needs of the employer but their personal and career needs' (TUC, 1998, p. 4). Under the Employment Act 2003 ULRs were granted statutory rights to time-off in workplaces with union recognition to enable them to carry out their duties[3] and the Trades Union Congress (TUC) reported that in the ten-year period since their introduction it had trained 23,000 ULRs (TUC, 2010). Trade union learning has been funded by Government through the Union Learning Fund (ULF) established in 1998 and subsequently managed by unionlearn, part of the TUC. The Labour Government's investment in union learning was almost £100 million and the ULF had delivered learning for over 800,000 learners since 1998 (TUC, 2010). Trade unions have thus become key actors in the field of lifelong learning – especially in relation to the acquisition by workers of basic skills (Moore and Ross, 2009). They are seen as uniquely positioned because of the relationship of trust workplace union representatives are deemed to have with members.

In the UK, government investment in union learning emerged amidst evidence of high levels of illiteracy and innumeracy amongst British workers[4] which, it was argued, would leave them ill-equipped in an increasingly knowledge based society – part of a wider and contested debate that located Britain's future in a 'high skills economy' (Keep, 2002; Lloyd and Payne, 2002). Yet workplace learning has its roots in a broader concept of lifelong learning, reflected at European level in the European Employment Strategy and Lisbon Agenda (Stuart, 2007). This not only sees learning as a response to globalisation and changes in the nature of work, but also as having the potential to be a continuous educational process embracing the whole human being whilst addressing social and economic inequalities and strengthening citizenship and democratic engagement (Forrester, 2005; Fryer, 1997). This conception of lifelong learning goes beyond vocational training promoting employer productivity and, in what are seen as increasingly precarious labour markets, individual employability.

As Frank Coffield suggests, 'lifelong learning appears in the literature and in political discourse in a bewildering number of different guises' (1999, p. 487) and is contested terrain between employers, unions and the state. For Keith Forrester workplace learning may inhabit two guises – employability and democratic citizenship. Whilst recognising that employability has increasingly prevailed, he suggests that there is potential for the location of union learning within the broader framework of democratic citizenship, which may promote critical engagement with the changing nature of work and working relations, but also encourage 'the reformulation of trade unions as societal actors rather than workplace partners' (2004, p. 418). Whilst the TUC has endorsed learning as supporting employability and perceives learning as adding value to union membership by offering new opportunities to existing and potential members, it has also invested union learning with the capacity to contribute to 'wider union strategies for both organisation and partnership in the workplace' (TUC, 1998 p. 6), implying that leaning could play a role in the revitalisation of unions.

ULRs as new activists

It is clear that union learning has attracted new union activists. Earlier research with Hannah Wood (Wood and Moore, 2005) found that a proportion (around a quarter) of ULRs were new activists who were union members, but did not hold or had not held another position in the union. These new activists were more likely to be women, black or from ethnic minorities and to be younger (confirmed in more recent research by the TUC, 2006 and Hollingrake et al., 2008). The research showed that the main motivating factor for becoming a ULR was a commitment to education, albeit within the context of union activity. New activists appeared to be less motivated by political commitment and a belief in trade unionism than existing activists and some trade union officers expressed concern that new ULRs might be 'different' types of union representatives. Donnelly and Kiely (2007) have identified the 'instrumental motivations' of some new ULRs as distinct from those of existing activists. In our sample of ULRs Charles and Oreleo were existing union reps; Diana, Anand, Lloyd and John were initially drawn into union activity via learning, as illustrated by Anand, a ULR in the Royal Mail:

> I was a normal union member for a long time, then they advertised for a Union Learning Rep, because there was education involved I was keen, so I applied.

One perceived benefit of union learning for unions is its capacity to offer both existing and potential members a positive material benefit countering what might be perceived as the defensive and negative role of the union, which members may only call upon when they are in trouble. The ULR role has been characterised as attractive to new activists because it is perceived as not involving confrontation with the employer (Thompson et al., 2007). This was acknowledged by John, a ULR with a rail company:

> The idea of a rep is about leading conflict with management, which is not what a rep is about anyway…[union learning is] the non-confrontational side of trade unionism, which I'm getting better at, just like the negotiating side. It's a new era isn't it really – the vision of reps generally is you've done something wrong.

Donnelly and Kiely suggest that a preference for a non-conflictual role is gendered, appealing to women, who also may not have the confidence that they have the skills to take on a fully fledged shop steward role or who may feel that the steward role is complex and characterised by a heavy workload and 'hassle' (2007, p. 78). Yet, as Diana implies in Box 3, for older women attraction to the ULR role may be more about being at a stage in the life cycle where they have more confidence, but also time to balance work and caring commitments. As

---

Box 3

'I'd always been a union member, but no, I was never an activist prior to becoming a Union Learning Rep. In some ways it was one of those moments in your life, to be perfectly honest I was a bit fed up at work, things were a bit boring and dull and everything was getting cut back, opportunities etc. At the time I worked in close proximity to a long-standing union rep and they seemed to be always busy and it all looked quite interesting. It was just a throwaway comment one day when I just happened to say [to him], "you haven't got any jobs going have you in the union because I could really do with something new and a challenge". [He said] "Well strangely enough, we have – Union Learning Rep!" and he explained it all to me and I thought "oh yeah, this sounds right up my street, I quite fancy this".

There are folk who don't even realise they can become a rep and that's really sad. That's been my experience of talking to folk – you can see that expression on their face – "Oh! I never really thought about that before, never thought about becoming active". Then they think perhaps that they'll end up permanently on a picket line, which doesn't appeal to them. But, when you show them all the different aspects of the union and what they can get involved with, at the end of the day you find then they're quite happy to stand on a picket line because they then understand why they're doing it. It has to start with that drip feed approach and then there's a bigger picture. People have come on board and suddenly realised that they can develop themselves as individuals. That's another key reason for becoming an activist and I don't think folk necessarily realised that to begin with – they were looking perhaps to their employer to develop them.

It has changed me politically. I think there have been other factors, it's not just the union, I think maybe that's why you get a lot of middle aged women coming into this role. I think you reach a point in your life where you start looking and questioning, maybe because your kids are growing up and you're taking a view of the world and how everything fits together. I've also had some personal changes that impacted on that as well. But I don't think the change would have been as great or I could have expressed it as easily if I hadn't taken up the union role. I see things completely differently now. And again that's because of things that I've learnt through being in the union. Issues that perhaps I wouldn't have necessarily pursued, but as different papers have come across my desk, usually just for information, by picking up and reading them it's made me look at things completely differently'.

(Diana, ULR and Regional Learning Officer)

in her case it may also provide new opportunities for activism in unions where existing positions have been inhabited on a long-term basis by long-standing activists embedded in their roles by facility time. In PCS Diana described how the merger of two unions had blocked the channels for new and younger activists. For Diana and Lloyd the ULR role had provided such a space and 'an escalator' to wider activity – although their main focus was learning they quickly expanded their role in the union. As is the case for Equality Reps, existing activists may identify and encourage members who have not previously considered becoming active in the union to take on the ULR role. In the rail company where John worked, initially the ULRs were not elected but recruited on a voluntary basis without having to go through their local branch and this may have encouraged new activists. He was asked to become a ULR by his Company Council because he was already involved in a school liaison programme organised by the company; as he said 'I do believe in education massively'.

The values of ULRs

McIlroy (2008) suggests that the TUC's management of the ULF is part of the government's wider policy of contracting out the delivery of social policy to voluntary organisations and networks. In supporting the emergence of a new type of union representative focussed upon learning in the workplace he proposes that the Labour Government was attempting to reshape union representation away from conflict and militancy towards collaboration and partnership (McIlroy and Daniels, 2009). This is born out in government policy statements:

> Building future employability through skills is an essential way in which unions can support the long-term interests of their members as well as promoting the success and productivity of the economy. Supporting skills and training should be at the heart of the role of the modern trade union and we look to all unions to raise the profile of skills and training within their work. (Government Skills White Paper – Getting On In Business, Getting On At Work, DfES, 2005)

Yet how do ULRs understand their role? Whilst recognising the possibilities of union learning for active citizenship, Forrester (2004) points to the pressures upon ULRs to deliver occupationally driven and accredited learning. The TUC's Task Group on Union Learning recognised that 'the short-term requirements of companies and the lifelong needs of employees will not automatically coincide' (1998, p. 4). In the light of this do ULRs see union learning as key to promoting employer-specific training; and/or as part of a government skills agenda developing generic skills for employability; and/or do they have a wider vision of worker engagement in lifelong learning and education for personal, or even political development in the tradition of union education? As the opening quote shows John's perspective resonates with the governments' on the role of unions in promoting longer-term employability, albeit as part of a strong trade union movement. Both Anand and Oreleo reflected a key tenet of the government's skills agenda around national competitiveness:

> We have to make sure that people are up to date with modern technology as well as always trying to compete with other countries in Europe. (Anand)

> So it's about Britain upskilling themselves so they can compete in the world market and that interests me and I try to tell other members about that so they can access learning, just for their own benefit, so they're marketable and employable somewhere else. (Oreleo)

At the same time ULR support for vocational training was often accompanied by a critique of employer-driven training and the limited access that workers, particularly those defined as lower skilled, have to training and skills. Lloyd attributed his activism as a ULR to an experience of discrimination in which the only two workers in his workgroup selected for further training were white – the black workers were excluded. Charles, a ULR in a print company, fought for the extension of accredited vocational training to his workplace illustrating the divergent interests of management and unions:

> Of all the companies I've worked with this site has got some very unique training and learning methods – it is very much the old school, if there is any job related training, then it's the train yourself routine … get on with it, it was very much that, most of the training and development is done for managers.

If employers have failed to provide job-related training for lower skilled workers they have been even more suspicious of non-employer specific training which may support transferable skills and the longer-term employability of their workforces (Hollingrake et al., 2008). For John workplace learning went beyond job-related training, extending to wider employability, but the union had to convince the employer of the value of this and to match the time that workers put in to their learning with paid time-off from work – this generated tensions:

> We're advocating Skills for Life, if the educational opportunities that we can provide help you within your job, then that's good, but it's not specifically job-related. How do we now tie Skills for Life into their NVQ vocational stuff which is job applicable? What we're now in the process of embedding is how we present it to the company, 'right, listen, we don't want people to do all of this in their own time, we want something back from yourselves'.

Much union learning has been concerned with basic skills training – literacy, numeracy and language skills for migrant workers – for which unions have secured employer support on the basis that it can have a direct bearing on workers' capacities to do their jobs. ULRs alluded to the way the formal state education system has failed workers, in his case study of union learning in his workplace, John recorded the experience of one learner:

> I hated school! I was bullied right through secondary and just could not wait to leave. My dad was a railway man so I left school on the Friday and started work on the Monday. I have been here ever since, twenty five years and I need something to inspire me, I feel brain dead.

Lloyd similarly reflected upon this and also sums up the sense of real satisfaction articulated by ULRs when they feel that they have engaged, enthused and empowered workers through learning:

> I think it's a bit to do with their jobs and I think it's a bit to do with enjoying learning … I worked with a gentleman one time and he used to always flick through the [news]paper and I used to think to myself why does he always flick through the paper, and the reason why he always flicked through the paper was because he couldn't read. And it was hard to broach with him because he worked as a road sweeper and he was just somebody I saw in the works canteen and from working in the depot I used to say 'hi' and then I started talking to him. And I said 'what trade union are you in?', and he told me he was a UNISON member, I said 'they've got some fantastic courses on at the moment, like even I'm doing them', because I said, 'I don't

know about you but part of my schooling although I was an average student I didn't push myself hard enough, because I didn't think I got the encouragement and that's why I think that I've got a gap in my learning' and then he started telling me 'yes I'm the same way', he said 'there's only certain words that I can read', so I said to him 'don't take offence but what I am going to do for you, I am going to conduct a learning survey for you, if you want me to, and we'll see where your level is and I will put you on one of our courses' and I put him through two courses and he's now Level 2. He puts it down to the union and also as a road sweeper he was just a general road sweeper, now he's a supervisor so that has improved his job prospects as well at work. And he's saying to me that he wants to know what other courses do the union do.

What is striking is that the narratives of individual ULRs move between a number of discourses – learning for personal development; learning for individual employability and learning as part of improving national productivity. As we saw above Oreleo invoked both the rhetoric of the government skills agenda and its role in global competitiveness, but he also drew upon a wider concept of lifelong learning extending beyond the workplace; 'union learning is about you developing yourself as an individual so that you can be of benefit in the workplace, at home, in the community'. ULRs had a perspective on 'non vocational' education or as it is sometime termed 'learning for leisure', which they did not counterpose to vocational training. They perceived such courses as providing pathways into education or vocational learning, giving non-traditional learners confidence to go further. They challenged employer resistance to granting time-off for workers to attend such courses as short-sighted. Diana believed in a 'broader approach' to learning and suggested this could provide benefits for employers:

I've seen individuals who've done some learning outside work and prior to that they would not have stood up and volunteered to take something forward at work. Whereas after doing learning, their confidence has grown, they've learnt a few key skills, it can be something as simple as minute writing or report writing and you find that they then volunteer for things so the managers are happy because they've more volunteers who are more capable with the skills to deal with things. For me it's just part of life, if you don't learn then you just stagnate. I think once you start educating individuals, their confidence grows – they can start making choices and decisions that affect their life. They don't have to just accept stuff, that's where the education side of it and learning for me is really important.

Stevenson (2010), focussing upon the role of ULRs in the teaching unions, asks how far ULRs can challenge a current discourse dominating education policy and the professional development of teachers which attempts to align the teaching profession with state objectives undermining critical education. He calls for ULRs to uncouple learning from human resource management and to harness it to 'traditional models of trade union and political education' (2010, p. 69). In the testimonies of the ULRs drawn upon here, hegemonic discourses about individual employability are infused with more universalist educational values and ideas about the transformational role of education and the historic role of trade unions in providing education for workers, for Diana:

> Trade unionism was built on health and safety and education and to give the working class person better opportunities in life. Now, to me that's what we should be doing as a trade union, and if nobody else is picking up that tab, then it's our duty really to do that.

She was starting to organise trade union education on international issues for members as part of her role. Rizwan, a Branch Equality Officer who had encouraged union learning amongst migrant workers, similarly emphasised the role of the union in raising wider issues and providing political education; 'One of the things I think that we don't do enough of as a union is that we don't provide any learning around politics around political thought, ideals, the basis of how trade unionism came about, stuff like that'. Whilst other ULRs were not necessarily advocating political education for members as part of union learning, most of those interviewed were conscious of gaps in their own education, including trade union and political education, and were personally engaging in courses to address this.

Much of the literature on union learning and the role of ULRs is based upon large-scale surveys which can lead to researchers establishing static relationships between learning activity and outcomes, reifying the motivations, values and consciousness of ULRs. Yet focussing upon a small number of in-depth (if unrepresentative) narratives suggests a more confused picture. ULRs draw upon a prevailing language of employability, mediated by trade unions partly through ULR training, to describe their practice. Yet their narratives are messy and unfixed and dart between complementary and contradictory discourses, simultaneously refracting what might be termed dominant, residual and emergent impulses. We now turn to the relationships of ULRs to wider union activity and values.

Relationships with employers

Forrester identified the potential correspondence between the ideological nature of employability, corporate success and employer-employee partnership (2005). One formulation is of learning as largely dependent on partnership between employers and unions, representing a consensual and integrative issue for engagement where all parties stand to gain (for example Stoney, 2002; Clough, 2004; Wallis and Stuart, 2004) and this was reflected by ULRs. Oreleo had developed basic skills courses for cleaners and refuse workers in a London local authority and had been involved in negotiating a learning agreement with the employer. In suggesting that learning may be an issue which can provide a basis for partnership in a more hostile industrial relations context, he simultaneously expresses the accommodative and conflictual nature of relationships between unions and employers:

> The impact has been that it's raised the profile of the union. It's raised the profile of the branch. It's demonstrated an active partnership between the union and the authority, [where there] probably wasn't open dialogue in there before. I think the nature of the political landscape, trade unions always want to get as much as they can for their members and I think conversely, the authority want to get the maximum amount for its workforce, but then without too much capital outlay. So there's always going to be a conflict of how much we deserve to get given to do this job and how much they want to pay you. So there's always that conflict. And then there's strike actions and militant actions and all that sort of thing. So in the political landscape it was fighting every day, whereas I think once the learning situation kicked in, it's a benefit to both sides. It's a benefit to the authority and the workplace; it's a benefit to the union, and the union structures. So it's a win-win on both sides.

Yet partnership implies a genuine engagement by employers, which is not necessarily forthcoming. Catherine Cassell and Bill Lee explored the ULR initiative as a catalyst for the development of partnership between unions and employers, underpinned by statutory support. They question the notion that learning may be seen to promote partnership because of intrinsic qualities, which benefit both employers and employees (2009, p. 226). They found that there is the potential for conflict related to time off for ULRs, but also issues of to whom the learning agenda belongs, with employers sometimes suspicious that it is a union initiative extending union influence. Alison Hollinrake, Valerie Antcliff and Richard Saundry found that productive imperatives shape employer attitudes to learning and that 'ULR sustainability was contingent upon the attitudes and actions of employers' (2008, p. 407).

The experience of the ULRs interviewed here underline the importance of employer support to embedded workplace learning, but confirm Cassell and Lees' conclusions that it is also an area of contestation. John described how union learning at the rail company where he worked was based upon a learning agreement signed by the employer and three affiliated rail trade unions and established through a steering committee of eight newly trained ULRs and members of senior management. Initially he characterised this 'as a progressive, forward thinking and pragmatic steering committee', yet 'what seemed to be a company led agenda began to take over what was initially a unionised funded programme'. The union learning agenda became characterised by conflict, with barriers emerging in terms of time-off for ULRs, the cancellation of steering group meetings or meetings called at late notice, decision-making deferred to other more senior managers and the refusal to offer incentives to Skills for Life learners. This was eventually resolved following a change in company ownership and the introduction of a new management team with an interest in the learning agenda. They reengaged with the steering committee and funding was obtained through Unionlearn to bring in a project development worker to support both existing ULRs and new ULRs and to help incorporate Skills for Life into the company's five-year business plan. Full-time ULF funded project workers have played a key role in sustaining learning, something which might be seen to either compromise or support self-organisation. In this case the company subsequently committed to sign the Skills Pledge[5] and to work in partnership with the three trade unions and John argued that this reflected the negotiating skills that the senior ULRs on the steering group had developed whilst in post.

Whilst Oreleo suggested the benefits of separating learning from wider and possibly conflictual industrial relations, Charles, a Unite steward and ULR, described the difficulties of doing so. He had introduced union learning into the print factory where he worked in the Midlands, part of a larger company that had recently established a new state of the art print works in the North of England where the union had to fight to get recognition:

> Making progress as a ULR with an employer like this...it was a big ask really because there's a lot of industrial things go on on a weekly basis here, so to try and drive it [union learning] as well it's quite difficult and quite often the two things go together unfortunately...when they set up the northern greenfield site the union had a fight to protect current levels of terms and conditions.

The company attempted to introduce a workplace training scheme at the greenfield site (a College in Workplace model) through which the workforce would gain an industry recognised qualification. However, this scheme was not embraced by the workers until the union's Regional Learning Officer got involved and a ULR structure was put in place. The existing ULRs at the Midlands factory felt aggrieved that the training scheme had been piloted at the new factory and believed that 'a partnership' with their union learning team would have been more effective in delivering results. They then had to fight to ensure that the programme was extended to their workplace; eventually this was achieved through a grant from the Regional Development Agency and Charles felt that without this funding the project would not have been brought to the Midlands factory. For him, 'this illuminates industry wide employers' reluctance to provide appropriate resources and funding to meet production level training and development, which would give in return tenfold the investment'. The engagement of workers in the project was ensured by a 'floor-walking' campaign and the initial fear of volunteering for training was removed as workers talked directly to college tutors or ULRs – they did not have to go to a manager to discuss their learning requirements.

Like Charles and John, Diana expressed the view that whilst learning was potentially an issue over which there might be cooperation between unions and employers, this was not necessarily the case. She also distinguished between senior and local managers and the difficulties both ULRs and learners have in securing time-off for learning and union activity in a performance driven environment:

> It's [the civil service] such a target driven business at the moment. In theory you will have senior management signing up to all these initiatives and they can see the benefits, but then as it comes down to a local level where you have the implications of actually releasing

people and getting the time...we've had such a reduction in the staffing numbers that things are so tight it's very, very difficult for teams to let more than one person off at a time, so that causes issues. You have to convince individual managers, but once you've got past that, it's the learner themselves; they have their own targets to meet. And if they take time out to do various things, it makes it very difficult for them to meet their targets. Now if we can offer learning on site, they're more inclined to attend than even if they only have to walk five or ten minutes across the road, because one, it impacts on their time and two, there's still that element of 'oh, what am I getting myself into here?'...going out of your comfort zone. So you have to very much nurture them through it all, through that process.

These narratives undoubtedly draw upon the language of partnership and confirm the importance of positive employer-employee relationships for union learning. Yet they also suggest that embedding learning is a contested process questioning perceptions of the learning agenda as inherently consensual and as easily separated from wider industrial and workplace relations – the role of ULRs in industrial action, described below, confirms this.

Learning and collective bargaining

For Ewing (2005) union learning has moved unions towards a 'public administration function' and away from their role in regulating employment relations through collective bargaining. Kim Hoque and Nicholas Bacon (2008) have questioned the influence that ULRs have on employer training provision, drawing upon WERS 2004 to test the relationship between unions, ULRs and employer-provided training and the equality of training provision. They found there was no consistent relationship between workplaces with ULRs and training levels, although there was some evidence of greater equality in the distribution of training where ULRs were present.[6] They attributed this to the increased reluctance of employers to negotiate with unions over training. Yet this conclusion is based upon an overemphasis upon the role of ULRs in delivering employer-specific training. They acknowledge that the impact of ULRs may lie more with non-employer-provided training – training delivered by Further Education colleges, union learning centres and LearnDirect – and point to a more direct impact over non-vocational training. However, for Hoque and Bacon 'this is worrying given there is no guarantee that non-employer-provided training organised by ULRs without employer involvement will actually meet the employer's skill needs' (2008, p. 723). Yet this assumes that the sole function of union learning is to serve the employer and government's skills agenda, something which provides a basis for McIlroy's (2008) critique, but which is not fully substantiated in the testimonies of ULRs, which also refer to the personal development and the wider education of workers.

Collective bargaining over learning would encompass a wider agenda than employer-specific training. Earlier research (Wood and Moore, 2005) did suggest that union learning was not systematically incorporated into collective bargaining agendas and that in the work-place union learning could develop separately from wider employer-union structures and processes, including those supporting collective bargaining. This was initially the case in the Government department where Diana worked. Union learning had been organised nation-ally and existing activists were often not aware of its existence. This encouraged a degree of scepticism from those on the branch's executive committee, based upon fears that learning would be another task for existing activists to pick up in the context of fighting job cuts. The union learning project worker was liaising with management sepa-rately through a joint management-union steering committee within the department dealing with union learning. This meant that learn-ing fell outside of normal consultation and negotiating procedures and that union learning was not represented on the departmental trade union side, where negotiations took place. As the project worker commented:

> Originally we made a mistake because what we didn't do was to delib-erately seek out the bargaining agenda. What we did do as a matter of fact is the exact opposite...what it did was it said to those people who weren't persuaded, 'well we are different'...what we should have been doing is what we're doing now, trying to get our feet under the bargaining table.

Subsequently the union addressed the issue of integration; learning and training were brought into the departmental trade union side as a negotiating issue, dealt with by the branch negotiating officers – this also revived training as a bargaining issue. Charles also suggested the dangers of excluding learning from bargaining whilst describing how the learning agenda had changed the established collective bargaining system in his print factory, including the attitudes of the existing workplace reps:

> My belief pretty much from day one as a ULR that we must oper-
> ate outside of the industrial arena was flawed – actually involving
> and linking with my full chapel negotiating panel and committee
> enables learning information to be circulated and developed in full.
> This gives the ULR a stronger hand with the employer who realises
> that any learning proposals have the weight of the membership
> behind it. Often employers try and slip in arrangements i.e. 'you can
> come and train for nothing in your own time to get on'. Many ULR's
> have no union experience and could be exposed to being innocently
> manipulated.

These case studies illustrate how learning can develop separately from bargaining, but also demonstrate that unions can and do address this and that ULRs do have a negotiating role. In addition to formal structures ULRs were generally involved in informally negotiating with local managers over time-off for learners, even if larger learning issues were negotiated by learning committees or branch officers at a higher level.

Union learning, recruitment and organising

Early research on union learning suggested its potential for union renewal during a period of membership decline (Wallis et al., 2005; Forrester, 2004), yet later writing has been more sceptical. Donnelly and Kiely (2007) propose that the link between learning activism and union organising is tentative. McIlroy in his critique of the role of union learn-ing in union revitalisation argues that there is a distinction between 'recruitment' and 'organising' and that this has not been acknowledged in the learning literature. Organising implies systematically building the union at the level of the workplace and a degree of self-organisation, rather than simply attracting members (McIlroy, 2008; 301). A number of ULRs did emphasise learning as part of the union's offer to members, a membership service which can aid recruitment, as Charles puts it:

> Without doubt it has opened many members' eyes to a different per-
> ception on what the trade union's role is and what we can achieve.
> New starters are actively coming to union reps to sign up to join

where previously we had to find them; it gives the union a more dynamic profile.

He described how, in his print factory, it was difficult for ULRs to separate learning from mainstream union activity, because the face-to-face contact that they had with members meant that workers would raise individual grievances about wider issues with them. He refers to Monica, a female migrant worker who brought her experience of working in human resources from Poland to the ULR role before she returned to her home country:

> The new ULRs definitely seem to attract a lot of non ULR grievance problems, it's actually because some of them were so good and were the right personalities for the role and they were keen to speak to people and try and put the message over about the learning and training and especially Monica, she was really good and very personable easy to get on with, whether [because] she was trained at HR she was able to box off the [union learning] stuff that she needed to deal with, which she did, some of the others couldn't, in fact some of them got very emotive about it.

Here the integration of ULRs into wider union activity was problematic, yet learning can provide unions with a presence in the workplace and an issue over which union reps can engage on a face-to-face basis with members and potential members in a way that existing reps, weighed down by individual case work, may not have time to do. John described how he was involved in 'collective surgeries' whereby ULRs would visit workplaces on a regular basis. For Diana the face-to-face contact that ULRs had with workplace colleagues was a strength of the ULR role:

> Certainly for a lot of reps who are inundated, if you've got a personal case, you're dealing on a one to one with that individual who has an issue at the moment, but you don't go round and just generally pick up the vibes, you don't have the time, you're inundated with personal cases. Union Learning Reps, because of the nature of the way we work and the learning, you are talking to people, there's a little bit of time out if you like to start talking, and other things come up, which is just about making Union Learning Reps aware of what the other issues are so that they can talk to folk about it.

Jason Heyes has demonstrated the role of union learning, specifically English Speakers of Other Languages (ESOL) tuition, in recruiting and organising migrant workers. He argues that education and training cannot be conflated with a servicing model of trade unionism since it is 'consumed collectively' and actively rather than passively, involving 'ongoing relationships between learners and unions' (2009, p. 195). The importance of ESOL in engaging with migrant workers was emphasised by Anand, Charles and Oreleo as well as a number of the migrant worker activists featured in Chapter 6. Anand described how at the Royal Mail sorting office where he worked he offered learning to around 40 migrant workers from Angola, Brazil, Cape Verde, Columbia and Ecuador, many of whom had no experience of UK trade unions. He gave the example of a colleague, a cleaner from Brazil, who had been working for the Royal Mail for the past four years and whose first language was Portuguese – he could speak and write very basic English:

As I work on the floor on a regular basis, I am in contact with the migrant workforce. This worker approached me for advice and help after seeing my photograph as an active ULR. With the help of the ESOL tutor and encouragement from me, he successfully passed Level 1 and progressed to Level 2. He is now more happy and confident in himself. He also takes part in union meetings and also spreads the word to his friends. Migrant workers sometimes hesitate to talk to union activists in the workplace because they are frightened it might cost them their jobs, but with a bit of understanding and motivation I explained to the migrants the benefits of joining a trade union and how important it is. It is not only for job protection but it also involves learning courses for them.

In the local government branch in which Oreleo and Lloyd were active, ESOL had been provided for migrant workers and the union had held workshops in the depot to help low paid temporary and agency workers, many of them migrants, to complete application forms for permanent jobs. In the CWU learning has also been used to engage with agency workers – a group of workers who have been perceived as hard to organise – as part of organising campaigns to secure union recognition (Moore, 2009a). ESOL played a role in Unite's Justice for Cleaners campaign, which consciously went beyond learning as a recruitment tool and tied learning to organising by focussing upon learning in English around workplace issues and employment rights. There is then some evidence that unions have been consciously integrating learning into the union organising agenda going beyond recruitment to revitalise workplace, branch and regional union organisation (Moore, 2009a). Oreleo and Lloyd had become active in union learning in a branch which had been placed under supervision by the regional union, possibly because of the political activity of branch officers. They described how in this situation the ULRs and the Black Members' Group had become crucial in sustaining the branch, 'I suppose if it wasn't for those two elements, then there wouldn't be a branch – maybe that would be an accurate perception'. Whilst organising has to go beyond recruitment, the face-to-face engagement with workers and members that learning can facilitate is a crucial building block in workplace and branch organisation, particularly in an environment where existing activists may have insufficient time to do this. Yet, as we see from Charles' example, to be effective ULRs must be integrated into wider union organisation and exposed to union values.

For Donnelly and Kiely (2007) the exclusive focus of some new ULRs on learning is as much a function of the attributes of the ULRs themselves and their orientations towards union activism, as of structural factors reflecting the wider political context in which learning is situated, involving relationships with employers or their union branch's indifference or neglect. Yet this suggests a rather static and reified view of worker consciousness. The evidence of the ULRs interviewed here highlights the importance of the local union branch and its existing activists in the development and integration of ULRs. Charles alluded to the exclusiveness of some existing workplace reps, which as we see in Chapter 6, coincided with antagonism towards migrant workers. He described how in his part of the factory if someone wanted to be a ULR he would send them on a training course straight away ('to encourage quick ULR development') and they would then get formally voted in and endorsed at the next union Annual General Meeting (AGM). However, existing union reps in another section of the factory did not accept this:

> Other separately organised parts of the factory would be saying that people could only become a ULR if they were selected by the workforce and voted in at a union meeting. This method meant it was hard to get ULR's elected and trained and they got demoralised.

In the government department where Diana worked there had also been potential tension between existing activists and new ULRs. Union learning provided her with an opportunity to become active, yet becoming integrated into her union branch was a real challenge:

In some ways that's probably been the most difficult aspect to deal with for a variety of reasons; firstly, if you come in completely from outside without any background you don't necessarily understand the role, because a lot of the reps have been activists for quite some time, its like any job that you have, rightly or wrongly you speak in jargon and you assume a certain level of knowledge.

Just as existing activists initially saw ULRs as developing outside branch structures, the new ULRs had difficulties in identifying their role in the branch and finding their way around branch structures. The support of existing reps was crucial to Diana becoming active in her branch and once she had taken on a lay Regional Learning Organiser role, she recognised that a wider union perspective was necessary. However, this was a two-way process with existing reps needing to be educated about the union learning agenda; 'because some union reps don't see learning as key and there's a lot of work to be done there'. The PCS branch in the Government department took a number of small, but important, steps to ensure that union learning and ULRs did not exist separately from the branch. Initially ULRs had access to separate funding for activities (for example attending regional ULR networks) from national level. Subsequently they had to make a case to the branch for financial support, which made them more accountable. They were also encouraged to take a basic union reps course, on the basis that if they were going to become active in the union they had to know what the branch was and what the structures were. In her new role Diana addressed the dangers of ULRs developing separately from the union:

It's not one-sided; it can be that the new reps don't understand their role and how they fit into the organisation. They don't necessarily feed back enough to their branch, so again it's understanding that you must feed into your branch, you belong, you're part of the branch, you're not independent of it. Generally if I get to new reps quickly enough and explain how they fit in, we can prevent any misunderstanding and possible problems arising.

She also made the point that there are wider lessons to be learned from the experience of new ULRs:

To be honest in some ways they're only reflecting what the rest of the membership are saying and that's something we need to be aware of within the union and that needs to be fed back. I know we put out literature and if you take the time to read it you'll understand the issues and the union structure, but a lot of folk don't. I think that is one of the most important things I've learnt about how the union works with its membership and activists. If you're not careful there can be a gulf between your activists and your ordinary member.

Diana's experience suggests how the dichotomy that may exist between learning activism and branch activism can be overcome, but that branches and existing activists need to be responsive and to encourage and mentor new activists. An international debate over organising has recognised the conservative role that some long-standing and deeply embedded activists can play in representing gatekeepers to activism (Milkman, 2006) and that the 'disposition' of these activists can be as much of an issue as the 'disposition' of new activists.

The path to activism

Crucially, in terms of union organising, learning can provide pathways for new activists. Both Lloyd and Oreleo had subsequently become stewards and Lloyd was negotiating with local management over restructuring, whilst Oreleo was considering standing for branch secretary. In the opening quote to this chapter Diana talks about how learning activism has politicised her, challenging Donnelly and Kiely's emphasis upon the 'disposition' of ULRs – values and identity are subject to transformation as a result of engagement with the wider union and with union values and education. As a new ULR Diana quickly came to adopt a wider union perspective and clear union identity, whilst retaining a focus upon learning; 'we need to remember it's all part of the union, so ultimately we're trying to build up the union'. Hollingrake et al. (2008) found, in the second wave of their longitudinal survey undertaken at the end of 2005, that new activists made up 38 per cent of the total ULRs surveyed. Nearly three quarters of them said that becoming a ULR had increased their interest in the trade union movement and 43 per cent had considered standing for another union role, whilst over half (57 per cent) saw recruiting new members as part of their role. The surveys revealed a substantial level of inactivity (over a third of respondents from both waves), but this was due to redundancy, retirement or changing jobs. Hollingrake et al. concluded that increased ULR experience and activity over time results in the development and diversification of the role (2008, p. 405). Diana illustrates this in discussing a new ULR she had worked with, whilst emphasising the importance of support and mentoring:

> She's moved up through the ranks and her confidence has grown. Initially she came on board very much for the learning and was nervous of the union aspect. She didn't want confrontation or conflict and would actually physically stand back from it, but over the last 12 months she's changed and is now moving forward and is prepared to negotiate and encourage other folk to do the same.

Diana reported that in the most recent national industrial action in the civil service there had been more ULRs than other reps on the picket line and this had been 'a turning point' in getting existing activists to accept ULRs. Similarly, Anand, despite declaring his primary motivation as learning, talked about his role on the picket line in the recent national postal strike over changes to working practices. His critique of the union leadership for calling off the strike is an exposition of the role of union bureaucracies in demobilising industrial action:

> Just before Christmas the union advised us to stop the strike, but since then it has been quiet so we don't know what type of agreement will be agreed ... I think personally for myself and the people I talk with on the floor, I think so many people were not happy about it ... why they stopped it. We don't want to go on strike, but that was a crucial time for management to say 'look let's try to solve the issue', but the members I spoke to they were not happy at all; they say, especially in London, 'we've been on strike nearly 16 or 17 times from June, every week, every week one day' and when the national ballot came then it was looked at nationally everywhere in the country and then suddenly they just said 'stop'.

Although John claimed that he was currently active on learning and did not get involved in other aspects of the union, he also suggested that this was changing and his trade unionism was starting to become an extension of his political beliefs. Along with Diana, his articulation of working class identity was stronger than other activists interviewed for this book and both he and Diana were in a minority of non-migrant activists in discussing international issues; they both felt that their unions (the RMT and PCS) had a clear political role and they both actively took their trade unionism out of the workplace and into the wider community. Whilst these ULRs may not be representative, they do point to activism as a process through which identity and values can be transformed and their testimonies challenge the notion that ULRs are imprisoned by the structural and ideological conditions from which they have emerged.

Conclusions

Unlike other studies of ULRs the in-depth narratives presented here allow us to capture these activists' wider values and motivations. As we see in Chapter 7, whilst we cannot say that the six ULRs cited here are representative of ULRs as a whole, they are not distinctive from the other activists interviewed as part of this book in terms of their wider trade union or political consciousness. Whilst their focus is upon learning, this is within the context of union activity. They may seek accommodative relationships with employers, but as a number acknowledged it is not possible to separate learning from wider industrial and bargaining relations and even where it is, relationships can become conflictual.

Crucially learning offers a route to union activism and where this route is taken ULRs acquire a stronger union identity and values – the extent to which they do so is influenced by wider union organisation, by existing activists and by union education, but some are politicised by the role. There is no rigid dichotomy between learning and branch activism and Donnelly and Kiely (2007) concede that there is a continuum between the two, despite their discussion of 'the self-imposed restraint' of new ULRs and their underplaying of the role of employers and of unions themselves in inhibiting engagement. The evidence of ULR involvement in industrial action cited here further challenges this proposed dichotomy.

Moreover, the narratives of ULRs question McIlroy's somewhat blanket characterisation of union learning as a vehicle of neoliberalism, pointing to its potential in particular circumstances to broaden the union role beyond narrow economic interests, to widen constituencies and to support processes of political participation. For Coffield lifelong learning is not an unambiguous, neutral or static concept, 'but one which is currently being fought over by numerous interest groups, all struggling for their definition (1999, p. 488). For Stevenson dismissing the work of ULRs as peripheral or not within the tradition of orthodox trade unionism rules out opportunities to challenge state policy and its ideologies (2010, p. 70). The narratives of the ULRs confirm that they certainly draw upon prevailing discourses of employability, but this is informed by a critique of employer provided training, which has historically dismissed the rights and aspirations of lower skilled workers, and of an education system which has often alienated working class pupils. This recalls a wider debate about the capacity of both unions and education to challenge the wider social and economic system that they are essentially a part of. ULRs believed that they were providing workers with opportunities and in this they may have been buying into Labour's supply-side agenda. Yet, they had a wider vision of learning for personal development, which could be empowering and transformative. Ultimately these in-depth testimonies reveal the hegemonic nature of learning and the contradictory nature of trade union consciousness – a focus upon learning which takes on aspects of the government's learning and skills agenda and in particular its language does not preclude the simultaneous articulation of collectivist values and class identification, nor the possibility of politicisation, although it does focus attention upon the role of trade unions in mediating prevailing ideologies.

5
The Mobilisation of Social Identity? The Emergence of Equality Reps

> The way I see the union is an extension of my beliefs, whether political or not, because UNISON is all about equality and fairness. The politics side of it, I don't really like to focus too much on the politics, I try to keep it more real and day to day as opposed to look for the bigger game of politics and all that.... My attitude on life is, as cheesy as it sounds, I treat others how I want to be treated. And this is why I like being a union rep because I feel the union is all about equality and fairness.

Simon was a shop steward in a call centre and Equality Representative (ER), who, as outlined in Chapter 1, became active in UNISON when the union responded to his experience of discrimination at work on the basis of his sexuality. His definition of his activism is reflected in the testimonies of a number of ERs – an extension of their beliefs, which they might or might not define as political, but expressed in terms of equality and/or fairness. This chapter draws upon the narratives of the activists, including 13 ERs, to ask how far social identity and/or discrimination in the workplace provide a basis for collective organisation and/or activism addressing what Geraldine Healy, Harriet Bradley and Nupur Mukherjee have argued is 'a neglect of the link between collectivist values and gender and ethnicity' (2004, p. 452). As part of this it explores the introduction of the Equality Rep as a new type of union activist and the potential of the ER role to facilitate a more inclusive definition of activism based upon the workplace. At the same time it considers the possibility that it may be a restricted union role encouraging support for individual rights at the expense of collectivism (Daniels and McIlroy, 2009). Finally, but possibly related to this, the chapter asks how far, in the context of UNISON – a union which has led the way in terms of the self-organisation of workers – politicised and antagonistic languages based upon the collective mobilisation of race, gender, sexuality or disability have been redefined in terms of more abstract and individualised discourses of equality. This may be a response to a wider move in public policy and political language from equality towards diversity – increasingly reflected and reinforced by public sector employers. It may dissolve specific inequalities into more fluid identities based upon the individual and individual interactions, rather than defined by social relationships underpinned by power.

The context

ERs emerged before both the introduction of the Equality Bill and its final manifestation in law as the Equality Act 2010 and the formation of a single Equality and Human Rights Commission to replace the previous separate equality bodies. Yet the prospect of a new legal context and particularly the recognition of seven equality strands appear to have shaped the context for the ER role. The case for statutory rights for a new type of trade union workplace activist was made in the TUC's submission to the Labour Government's Women and Work Commission in 2005. The TUC believes that ERs are uniquely placed to promote fairness in the workplace, first by raising the equality agenda among fellow workers and in their own unions, second by encouraging employers to make equality and diversity part of mainstream collective bargaining and third by working with 'vulnerable workers' and trying to ensure that every worker receives fair treatment irrespective of gender, race, disability, religion, age, gender reassignment or sexuality (TUC, 2009). The Commission did not accept the argument that they should have statutory rights to paid time off, facilities and training, but did recommend that financial resources be made available via the Union Modernisation Fund (UMF) to train and develop networks of ERs and that unions and employers voluntarily re-negotiate recognition agreements to provide time off and facilities for them (TUC, 2009). The UMF was established in 2005 to support union adaptation to changing labour market conditions and generate transformational change within trade unions with up to £10 million allocated to the fund (Stuart et al., 2009). Mark Stuart, Miguel Martinez-Lucio and Andy Charlwood's evaluation of the first round of UMF projects concedes that the role of the state in promoting and funding union modernisation is 'not uncontroversial' and 'criticism has focused on the extent to which the UMF can be seen as an attempt by the state to reshape core trade union functions to meet government interests' (2009, p. 21).[1] The Labour Government made £1.5 million of UMF money available for pilot projects 'to help develop a union infrastructure to support the workplace activities of equality representatives – for example through training and development' (Equality Bill White Paper 'Framework for a Fairer Future'). The TUC expected that by the end of March 2010, there would be around 1,400 equality reps active in organisations in both the private and public sectors (TUC, 2010).[2]

The Establishing Equalities Reps in UNISON project was funded as part of the second round of UMF projects and began in 2008. It focused upon the establishment, training and development of Equality Representatives in UNISON as part of the union's Equality Strategy, as well as aiming to develop partnerships with employers to effectively fulfil their statutory duty to promote equality. This chapter draws upon in-depth interviews with 13 Equality Representatives, seven of whom were new activists attracted by the role. It also reflects the findings of wider research on UNISON's pilot project involving interviews with UNISON officers and a survey of ERs in 26 pilot branches across three regions covering 40 employers.

Equality Reps – a restricted union role?

Daniels and McIlroy have argued that since the functions of Union Learning Representatives and Equality Representatives do not involve collective bargaining and joint regulation 'the restricted nature of the roles they offer cannot be minimised or downplayed' (2009, p. 140). They are thus characterised as a symptom of union decline rather than regeneration. By implication those taking up the equality role are not full activists and since there is some evidence[3] that the role attracts black, disabled, LGBT (Lesbian, Gay, Bisexual and Transgender) and women workers there is the potential for a hierarchy of union representation which reinforces discrimination in the workplace.

Ironically, whilst the constrained role of the ER is seen as problematic the historically restricted nature of collective bargaining, in excluding the interests of key sections of the labour force, is not. Trevor Colling and Linda Dickens (1989) noted the exclusion of equality issues in collective bargaining and attributed this, in part, to the low levels of representation amongst women in the collective bargaining machinery. Satnam Virdee (2000) has also described the sectional basis of collective bargaining and its historical association with exclusionary practices which reinforced rather than addressed racial divisions in the labour market. Ardha Danieli (2006) has challenged the gendered nature of industrial relations and the assumption that social and personal relations, including gender relations are not its legitimate concern. She notes that more recently issues arising from wider social relationships – sexual harassment and domestic violence for example – have become legitimate issues for inclusion in collective agreements.

Yet as Chapter 2 outlined, the opportunity for ERs to take up equality through formal collective bargaining may be constrained by its contraction. There has been an increase in individual grievances as a result of the extension of managerial authority and intensification of work (Waddington and Whitston, 1996). In their research on unorganised workers, Pollert and Charlwood were not surprised by the evidence of widespread workplace problems; they argue that the decline of union power and collective bargaining has meant that 'even unionised workers became more vulnerable to unilateral managerial prerogative. In other words, the framework of collective representation and employment rights, which used to exist, has not been rebuilt' (2009, p. 355). ERs have emerged in a context in which individual grievances, often based upon discrimination, increasingly dominate the union agenda and their emergence may be a function of this.

In line with this ERs saw the workplace as their focus. Pat, a UNISON ER, described ERs as the 'eyes and ears' of the union in the workplace, 'the people on the ground floor, the people that are actually in contact with the grass roots and our members'. ERs perceived their role as identifying and promoting awareness of equality issues which could be taken up by their branches and as informing members and 'empowering' them to raise issues. In line with this the key skills that ERs were seen to require were communication and listening skills. Unlike other unions UNISON had initially made a decision that ERs would not formally represent members in grievance and disciplinary cases, although they might provide support for them. Similarly ERs might identify equal pay cases, but these would be referred upwards. The reluctance to let ERs take on individual representation was because of the requirement in the union for representatives to have the appropriate accreditation (ERs might take cases if they were already shop stewards and/ or if they had undertaken the required training), but also because of a concern not to overload or scare off new activists – this fear had also made UNISON reluctant to involve ERs in negotiating. Although not designed as such, there is a danger that these constraints result in ERs being accorded a secondary status as representatives within the union, although amongst the activists interviewed here this was mitigated by the fact that they were either existing representatives and had other union roles, or as new activists they quickly acquired other roles, or because once in the role they would not subject themselves to such restrictions.

Their narratives describe how ERs took up what were sometimes seen as seemingly small everyday grievances, standing up for workers and acting as a restraint on managerial power. Like a number of migrant workers Olivia had been attracted into the ER role; she worked as a nurse in a private healthcare facility where she was the only union representative. She had managed to recruit about ten new union members and had intervened with management when a colleague who had sustained an injury at work had had her overtime removed whilst on sick leave, thus affecting her pay:

> Yes, small things like that, but they do work for people and it can get somebody quite demoralised and frustrated and feel well what is the point really if they [management] are doing that. And they will do it and try and get away with it as well if nobody says anything, they will get away with it. It's minor but if they do that to all – because we work in a challenging environment, we've got a lot of aggressive patients and we've got a lot of things happening, we've got rib injuries, back injuries and quite dangerous things – some have been left with concussion after being attacked by a patient. And if they are to do that at each time, that's a lot of hours accumulated by the company each time and obviously, all the overtime being taken away and docking the person as sick and they are accumulating points for being off sick and actually the sickness was caused by being at work, by the work environment. It's terrible, it's really terrible.

Olivia shows the difference that union representatives can make in standing up to the abuse of managerial authority in workplaces with no union recognition. In two examples from workplaces with recognition ERs also challenged the attitudes of other workers, as Simon reported for the call centre where he worked:

> Somebody said, one of the lads was talking to him and one went 'oh you're so gay' and I looked and he went 'I'm so sorry, I didn't mean it like that'. I said 'I know how you meant it, but what I want you to do is think of why you actually used that word. You used it like being gay is a bad thing, is being gay bad?' and he was like 'no'. I said 'so

think about it'. So it's just little bits like that, but I just think that's ignorance and education, I don't think for one minute they're being homophobic or anything like that. It's just raising awareness.

Similarly, Pat described her experience of working in a Health Trust:

I still think people don't realise that if they're in a group and they're laughing, the amount of banter that could offend just one person and sometimes people don't realise you're offended. It could be anything like that, jokes. Even when sometimes just in the everyday banter of things, people will make a comment and I'm thinking 'well wait a minute, somebody's sitting there that it could be deemed as being directed at'. I think we've still got quite a long way to go and I think that's because it's become a culture. It's like the simple thing like the 'Paki shop at the bottom of the street', basically its comments like that still. We would have to challenge it.

The examples reported by ERs address just the sort of issues raised by the unorganised workers in Pollert and Charlwood's survey (health and safety, workload, work relations such as stress or bullying and discrimination) (2009). They suggest that the presence of an activist prepared to challenge inequality makes a difference, although as Rizwan suggests in Box 4, it is also difficult to distinguish or separate equality issues from general workplace issues and in the absence of shop stewards ERs may be taking up wider workplace grievances (as Olivia was doing). In terms of an older typology of union activism proposed by Batstone et al. (1977), it could be argued that ERs might fit into the mould of populist or delegate, reflecting members' wishes; as opposed to 'representative' leaders who were proactive in relation to management and had strong bargaining relationships with them. Yet Batstone et al.'s model is first, set in the private sector in the context of organisational collective bargaining, and second, may be increasingly anachronistic in an environment where individual grievances have proliferated. As Darlington (1994a) argues most representatives take on the characteristics of both typologies and Batstone et al.'s model underplays relationships with members – it may also counterpose individual and collective activity.

Whilst individual representation has become more important, William Brown, Simon Deakin, David Nash and Sarah Oxenbridge (2000) found that 'vital links exist between the enforcement of individual rights and the structure of collective representation' and that the extent to which employers are complying with their legal obligations depends significantly on the presence of active trade unions at workplace and organisation level. This is born out by Simon, who had negotiated an agreement on parking for disabled members following the relocation of the organisation:

> I tend not to do too much individual representation... I feel my strengths are more in negotiation on the bigger picture. The disabled parking is one – there are individuals in it, initially it was just one and then another and then another, so I suppose initially I took on the individual. It just happened that you ended up with five sorts of group things and now we're negotiating on a bigger picture with the company. We've suggested to them that they need to apply for planning permission outside, something that they said they wouldn't, but then when I showed them the Disability Discrimination Act document that said there is a right to request reasonable adjustment, they are now doing it.

Similarly, Neil felt that following his ER training he would be able to use the Equality Act 2010 'as a bargaining tool in negotiations with the employer or cases I take on for my members'. In another example, Nicola, an ER in a police civilian branch, had taken up the equality impact of her organisation's inclement weather policy, where she felt the requirements for attendance during heavy snowfalls worked against employees with school age children. Despite employer attempts to individualise the employment relation evidence from ERs suggest that the subjective dimensions of activism, in terms of framing issues collectively, remain important and the role does not rule out informal or formal bargaining relationships.

For the TUC, in some unions the ER role will be largely a campaigning, support or championing role, whereas others intend them to be full members of the negotiating team (TUC, 2009). In UNISON officers did not initially anticipate that ERs would have a negotiating role and their exclusion from the collective bargaining process again raises concerns that equality issues, as well as the ER role in the union, might be marginalised. However, Josephine and Elizabeth had challenged this in one local government branch. As ERs they were taking up the equality impact of a council reorganisation, which included the relocation of offices outside the city and the introduction of 'hot-desking'. Klandermans has suggested that feelings of injustice based upon perceptions of 'illegitimate inequality' can generate a collective active frame, which may lead to collective action (1997, p. 39). Josephine and

Elizabeth were convinced that this reorganisation would have a dis-proportionate impact upon women workers, since there was no pub-lic transport and unsocial hours working would raise safety issues, whilst 'hot-desking' raised specific issues for workers with disabilities. As Josephine put it, the council 'has not had a full Equalities Impact Assessment[4] done – and we are kicking and kicking and kicking about this'. Despite the UNISON ER project's explicit commitment to working in partnership with employers on equality this example questions the assumption that equality, like union learning, is necessarily an issue where there is more likely to be consensus and 'partnership' with man-agement. These ERs had also had to convince branch officers involved in negotiations on the reorganisation that there was a detrimental impact on equality, as Elizabeth said, 'I think I've been stepping on quite a few toes actually'. Both were prepared to become involved in negotiating and campaigning on the issue and there were discussions about the ERs taking up a role on the Council Employee Consultative Committee where they would be able to communicate directly with local councillors over the issue – although as Josephine explains, this was not a negotiating body:

> Well, first and foremost obviously I see it [the ER role] as for somebody for members to come to if they've got a difficulty with an equalities issue and then, I mean I know we don't do any casework, we have to then pass that along, but we would be the first port of call. And I also see us as a consultative element and a negotiating element, defi-nitely. That's the way I would like it anyway. We don't have anything to do with the negotiating because we're not the people who do the negotiating on behalf of the union and at the moment, I'm slightly critical of it. We should have a negotiating role – we kind of raised it, it's a bit difficult.

Whilst it is too early to draw conclusions on the role of ERs, their exclusion from collective bargaining and formal representation may imply a restricted role which characterises them as subordinate activ-ists. Yet, a preoccupation with collective bargaining and joint regulation can devalue the role of union representatives in challenging excesses of managerial power, often expressed through discrimination and the bullying of vulnerable workers. The renewed emphasis of the ER role on the workplace may reinvigorate trade unionism in a context in which the balance of power has swung in favour of management and away from joint regulation, generating an increase in individual grievances.

ERs were framing workplace equality issues collectively and this led them into informal and formal negotiations not only with management but with their own branch officers – the relationship between individual and collective representation is a dynamic one. The ER role appears to allow for the recognition and expression of a range of interests in terms of gender, race, age, disability and sexuality and we now explore how far activists – in particular ERs – were organising on the basis of these interests and/or mobilising their own social identities.

Social identity and collectivism

It has been suggested that the differentiation and marginalisation of sections of the workforce based upon gender and race can lead to new forms of collectivism, which may 'spring from ethnic and gender identifications as well as those of class and occupation' (Healy et al., 2004, p. 463). This chapter tests this proposition with regard to the motivations and social identities of the activists interviewed. In UNISON there is a specific question about the relationship between the ER role and the historic self-organisation of black, women, disabled and lesbian, gay, bisexual and transgender (LGBT) workers in the union and how far the two models are complementary or draw upon different discourses of representation and/or organisation.

There is some evidence that the ER role is providing new routes to activism for UNISON and other trade union members. Pat, a UNISON Branch Equality Officer, reported that the role might encourage activity amongst members who could not commit the time to being a workplace rep, particularly because of caring commitments:

> The girl in my work area, she said she wouldn't mind being an equality rep as opposed to a steward or anything, because she's got a young family, at this moment in time her husband's just been made redundant with the recession so she is the only wage earner. What she didn't want was all of a sudden to be coming in as an equality rep and all of a sudden be asked to do the stewards' role. She wanted just to come in at this moment in time as an equality rep and maybe progress later on when maybe she's got more time.

A branch secretary suggested that the ER role was a 'non-threatening introduction for new activists', reflecting the argument that new ERs should not be overwhelmed with duties at an early stage, but also the tension between this and according them a subordinate and restricted role. The TUC has reported that their ER training courses have recruited a mixture of new reps, existing reps adding a new role, and former reps wishing to remain active. In this way it argues that the equality rep initiative is helping to support and regenerate workplace representation (TUC, 2009). Its survey of 320 trained ERs found that 18 per cent were new activists (TUC, 2010). Of the 57 ERs trained by UNISON in its pilot project just over one third (39 per cent) of those responding had never held another position in the union or did not do so currently; half were shop stewards and over one third were currently branch officers (with most shop stewards also branch officers). ERs were generally not new members – they had been in UNISON for between 1 and 32 years, with a median of 10 years membership.

Similarly, a number of the ERs interviewed were also stewards and/ or branch officers and/or involved in UNISON's Self-Organised Groups (SOGs); they were already interested in or active on equality issues and felt that the ER role was 'a natural development'. For Carrie, a shop steward who had then become an ER in local government:

I tended to look more towards the equalities thing because I'm a disabled employee as well and that sort of got my interest going.

A number of new activists were motivated to become ERs by their specific experiences of discrimination and inequality in the workplace. Olivia, a migrant worker from Zimbabwe had been unfairly dismissed from her second job in a private care home allegedly for gross misconduct, but two weeks after drawing attention to a manager's racism. She was being represented by the union:

How I have managed to keep sane? I think that's what has given me a lot of passion because so much injustice is happening ... So it's quite shocking! ... I just realised that I thought my goodness, how many people are out there that actually are going through what I'm going through? And not having that [trade union] support? I've been quite fortunate that I've had that.

For Olivia and Simon their experiences of discrimination and desire to ensure that others did not have to go through something similar, but importantly the union's response and the notion of 'giving something back' to the union, were the basis for their activism. Others were motivated by grievances which were not necessarily attributed to any specific form of discrimination. Kevin was a black youth worker, UNISON steward and ER, who faced disciplinary action after he was transferred from the voluntary sector to the local authority. He felt deskilled and that the autonomy he had enjoyed in his work in the voluntary sector was undermined by the new management structure and his manager took exception to 'his attitude'. He did not identify discrimination on the grounds of race, but his activism was a result of being represented by the union and subsequently being identified as a potential activist by the branch secretary:

> The reason I joined UNISON was because of my experiences and I think one of the other reasons I joined it was to ensure that what's happened to me doesn't happen to anybody else, because people do victimise and bully and harass workers out there. I think if you've experienced it, you've got the knowledge and you can see the patterns starting to happen and you need to nip it in the bud before it actually does get too far, before grievances start and stuff like that.

Cassandra a transgendered migrant worker joined the union after an experience of bullying in the health service:

> Well it was an experience, a bad, bad experience. I don't know how to say this but I had a supervisor, she was not from this country, but I was a victim of bullying and harassment and so that really pushed me to my limit and I said I really need someone softer. But there is a certain time when I talked to one of the union reps, who wasn't UNISON, she said get someone to represent you if you want and that was the time when Agenda for Change was introduced, so I managed to come across other union reps, from other trade unions and it was UNISON – then I became a member.

As in the case of Kevin, Cassandra's activism on equality issues emerged from what was perceived as a general experience of injustice. This is also suggested by Elizabeth, a disabled worker who was prompted to become an ER and then a shop steward by a grievance at work. As with other activists she located her individual experience within a wider collective framework:

> I thought it was an issue of discrimination but probably it was much more complicated than that and on reflection I wish I had asked the union to take it up...I wrestled on my own and really that was

one of the reasons why I later decided that I would like to be a steward...I came away with a feeling of having had those bumps and bruises, but actually I didn't want anybody to go through the same sort of thing and I could use it positively – so it was a positive thing in the end.

In line with concepts of intersectionality, which capture the interplay of sexuality, disability, class, gender, race and ethnicity, workers may be unable to disentangle specific forms of discrimination since one or more forms of discrimination may be inextricably related and there may be confusion in identifying a determinant factor (Moore, 2009b). Daisy, a Filipino UNISON activist in the health service, suggested that her identity was situationally contingent and Chapter 6 explores how the identity of migrant workers could be transformed through migration, work and activism:

It depends on the context of where I am. I would define myself first in terms of my gender identity. So if I am in a context of work, I would look at myself as how am I compared as a woman or in terms of opportunity with my counterparts. And then again depending on the context, then I would also define myself as a migrant, depending on the issues. So I can pick up and use whatever becomes more relevant depending on the context or depending on the issue that I am trying to address. I think in terms of ethnicity, I would look at myself as a member of a minority ethnic group and a migrant and on the equal opportunities form I would always say 'Asian – other'.

Whilst for a number of those interviewed experiences of discrimination led to union activism, they did not generally articulate an active politicised social identity. As we saw in the previous chapter, Lloyd and Oreleo were both UNISON ULRs who described their identity as black Caribbean British and working class. The fact that workplace racism had motivated their activism, that they had initiated a local Black Members' Group and both attended their unions' Black Members' Conference suggests an active racial identity, but firmly within the context of their trade unionism (and implicitly class identity), which appeared to be a constant and conscious basis for activity. Peter, a national union activist in Unite, recalled his encounters with overt racism in a unionised factory in the car industry in the Midlands in the 1970s and 1980s, where black workers were largely confined to those jobs paying lower piece work rates. His experiences were clearly defined by race and Peter perceived that at that time union reps were complicit in this racism:

> The first day I was there I was asked by one of the lads – and he still works there – and he says 'how can a darkie like you get a job here?' ... you have to look back in the 70s, 80s, coming through the tough times for any black person, never mind the two decades prior to that ... and we was getting the backlash ... We had a manager in there, he's come in, he's seen me and he used to call me 'kaffir', 'come here kaffir, come here, kaffir' I just didn't rise to the bait because if you did you're out.... I didn't like the fact that there were stewards and convenors who used their powers to look down on others and treat them differently. ... because they [the union reps] have the power to change a lot of things and they also had the power to keep quiet and when to let things go. And they ruled with an iron fist and that wasn't a bad thing in a way, but it should have been more consistent, not just pockets of people who they got on with, but where a black worker or an Asian worker would just do something just marginally out of order and without question they were got rid of, yet I could see the same white counterpart was doing far worse or consistently more and nothing ever happened – so there's no fairness there.

Peter went on to recount how his acceptance into the union came through sport. Just after he had started work he was playing in a non-league football match and the referee happened to work for the same company and recognised him:

> The following morning after the game, the following day, when I got to work, all of a sudden I was inundated with a load of people who I had never met – 'you're the footballer?' The steward then got hold of me, said 'leave him alone, he's a new kid on the block', took me to one side and he says 'if you're the footballer, I will look after you. I'm the union rep as you well know – no one's going to interfere with you'. And he started to talk to me about the union work and all the things, and from then I just looked to him. What really got me involved in the union was him taking me under his wing. He got dismissed some three years later and by that time, I'd already served about five years, and they were looking for a new steward, and being the footballer and cricketer that I was and the character I've always

been, it became no contest. The lads said 'there's only one person for that', and that was me.

Despite identifying and recounting his experience of racism in the workplace, Peter's activism and strong trade union consciousness were not actively articulated in terms of either class or race and this was despite his attendance at the union and TUC's Black Members' conferences. This chimes with Satnam Virdee and Keith Grint's study of black self-organisation in unions (1994); they found a number of black stewards 'who subordinated the significance of their race to that of their class or union interests' and this was particularly the case when they were isolated from other black workers (1994, p. 211). In Peter's workplace and union the legacy was of racism and a struggle to integrate; over a 20-year period he was able to take a leading role in the union both in the workplace and nationally, but on the basis of his trade union interest rather than the positive mobilisation of black identity. This reflects Nash's distinction between the experience and mobilisation of subjectivity and the importance of agency in articulating a relationship (2008). The legacy of self-organisation in the union Peter had come from (pre-merger) was weaker than that in UNISON. Different unions have, to varying degrees, come to accommodate and express a range of social identities and this suggests Yuval-Davis' (2006) emphasis upon political agency in the construction of collective identities.

Political and organisational discourses

Geraldine Healy and Gill Kirtons' study of the representation of women in UK unions identified a shift over the ten years between 1987 and 1997 'from a liberal approach to more pro-active separate organising' (2000, p. 357). Radical measures involving self-organisation have been seen as the prevalent response in improving women's participation (Humphrey, 2000; Kirton and Greene, 2002). For Jill Humphrey self-organisation involves the collective mobilisation of identities 'embedded in wider histories of social movements' (Humphrey, 2000, p. 263). Similarly Virdee has documented the independent struggles of black workers in the decade prior to the mid-1970s and how 'this "process of race formation" around the identity "black"' was critical to the development of inter-racial unity in trade unions (2000). Healy et al.'s (2004) study of black and minority ethnic trade unionists demonstrated how engagement in the anti-racist and socialist struggles of the 1960s onwards, but also a commitment to minority rights and community activism around injustice, provided a route into trade unionism.

In Chapter 1 we saw how a history of involvement in the women's movement in the 1970s motivated Josephine to become an ER, framed in terms of reactivating political commitment. She expressed a social identity consciously defined by feminist political values, which was not generally the case for other women activists despite their involvement in UNISON's self-organised women's groups. One other exception was Daisy, who when asked responded that she was a feminist. She stated that her political awareness and personal experience of gender discrimination, 'all add up to a passion for helping to organise others to help change attitudes and cultural barriers towards developing more just and fair relationships in society'. Daisy and Josephine's feminism would appear to draw upon residual ideology formed through their past involvement in social movements. For other activists self-organisation within the union served to reflect, reinforce and frame active social identities, providing the motivation for membership and activity. Rizwan, a UNISON activist in local government, with a family background of trade unionism and community activism, describes in Box 4 how attendance at UNISON's LGBT conference reinforced his political convictions and helped him to make sense of his identity. Lukasz who worked on a project for lesbian and gay young people, reported a similar experience of attending LGBT conference. Unlike other new activists he defined his work, trade unionism and activity outside of work in terms of his sexuality:

> I think what I do is because of my identity. So my work is close to my identity, my trade union activity is dictated by this identity, similarly my volunteer experiences. Yes, it's the most important part of who I am and the secondary one would be my Polish identity.

At the same time Lukasz joined the union because of the unfair treatment of a Filipino colleague when he worked in a care home – relationships in the workplace provided the basis for the mobilisation of his social identity. The agency of unions in taking up discrimination in the workplace, the acknowledgement of identity on the basis of race, gender, sexuality, disability or class and the promotion of self-organisation arising from this appears to create an environment in which activism is generated.

Whilst UNISON retains its commitment to self-organisation, the development of Equality Reps (ERs) represents a new and different model of addressing inequality, informed by distinctive political and

Box 4

'It was a bit of a weird one really. I was working, I'd qualified, got my first job and just through friends, they were telling me that UNISON had a lesbian and gay conference at the time, and it was happening in, I can't remember, was it Glasgow or somewhere? And they just happened to say they were going and did I want to go? And I had no idea about anything about UNISON or conferences or anything. And I happened to just ring my branch secretary at the time and he didn't know what to do. But I ended up getting funding to go to conference...and I've never looked back since really. It was totally overwhelming...I couldn't believe it ... well I mean the thing is that I didn't know what self-organisation was about. I think it was going to Lesbian and Gay Conference at the time that really made the difference because it gave me a lot of confidence and understanding about me as a black Asian gay man being a trade unionist. And I think I just found that it was a really good avenue of being able to gain experience, develop my understanding but also in line with my politics, my own political convictions.

Prior to now, we've had very little in the way of an understanding of, is this an equalities issue or is this just an employment issue? Is this an equality issue or is this an issue around sickness absence? Is this an issue around health and safety or is this an issue about equality? So there's not been that separation out of what is intrinsically at its basis an equalities issue or what is essentially just an employment issue. So I think that once we start looking at cases with a bit more context, and start being a bit more braver about saying "yes, this is an equalities issue. Yes, we're going to fight it on the equalities agenda". I think that's when we start, the learning curve really starts kicking in. I think that's the same for most of our equality reps that we've recruited. I think their understanding of equality is fairly limited, but they would say that themselves. That they've gone into it because they're genuinely interested in doing more and learning more. I think you can't presume that every one of us goes through a process of politicisation. And I think that learning about equality and knowing what equality means and stuff like that, you inevitably are bound to go through a period, a process, of politicisation, if you haven't been through it already. In the same way that when I got involved in self-organised groups, I went through a definable process of politicisation because it was not just me as a black person, but it was also me as a gay person. And I never really understood what the politics were around both or how the two gelled together, or operated. And I still don't necessarily – I'm still learning because people's understanding of equality keeps progressing, keeps moving on'.

(Rizwan, Branch Equality Officer)

organisational discourses. Whilst ERs such as Rizwan and Josephine had emerged from participation in self-organised politics both within and outside of the union, other newer activists had not and although they might have become members of UNISON's Self-Organised Groups, their narratives did not generally articulate a strong sense of identity with one particular group or reflect the kind of self-identified politics that might be expected from such membership. Olivia had experienced racism both within and outside the workplace and had attended the regional Black Members' Group (and subsequently became its vice-chair) and Black Members' conference and was interested in women's issues. At the time of the interview, however, she was reluctant to iden-tify herself in terms of gender or race:

> A feminist? No, well, I think you've got to be quite extreme to be a feminist, I think. You've got to not like men at all...yes, I suppose I could be a feminist, yes, but obviously I just accommodate [men] as they're there, they're not going to disappear are they?
>
> I would never think of myself in terms of race. I've never identi-fied myself in that respect, and I could not say I've felt...I don't know how do I identify myself? I think I just see myself as every-body, but there again I don't know. Maybe it's a question that I've avoided and not visited. Now that you mention it, I don't drive at work, I don't drive company cars but the main reason is really I can-not be bothered being stopped by the police, being a black woman driving white patients. I'm bound to be stopped several times so I can't be bothered. So I think I just try and avoid issues that I know are going to put me in the limelight. Personally, well – I don't see myself as – well I could say yes, I could probably see myself as an ethnic minority.

This suggests an individual distancing from a gendered or racialised identity, which was not reflected in either her experience or activism. Diana, sat on the national women's committee of her union and when asked if she was a feminist similarly responded; 'I'd probably say "no I'm not", but having said that, I speak up very strongly for women's rights. So perhaps I am without even realising it...I think I've always stood up for women's rights even before I became active'. Both Diana and Olivia's testimonies suggest Skegg's (1997) finding on the confused transmission of feminist values and her conclusion that women draw upon feminist frameworks without necessarily identifying themselves as a feminist.

Thus whilst ERs drew upon individual and collective experiences of discrimination which clearly informed their activism, they did not auto-matically articulate their activism in terms of their own social interests or identities. UNISON's promotional material for the ER role appeals to a general notion of fairness ('Are you interested in fairness in the workplace?') and this was reflected by participants when they discussed their motivations. Carrie, was a support worker in social services, who was also involved in the Regional Disabled Members' Group:

> I don't like to see unfairness and I think a lot of people as well, even without meaning to be unfair, do not realise what possibilities there are with adapting hours in work or special provisions. So I do tend to jump in and say well if you go to Occ[upational] Health they can advise you on this and it's just general day to day things, I just don't like seeing unfairness.

Anna was a new ER working in local government:

> I've always taken an active interest in equalities issues, from the point of view of equality of opportunity. And I've always taken notice of things and I've got very strong views on personal circumstances where I believe that it can be a thing in society that everybody should be married with 2.4 children, and the world isn't like that. Where people's relationships and marriages don't necessarily work out and not everybody meets the right person, not everybody is heterosexual, and not everybody wants to or is able to have children. And I think that should be respected.

Nicola an ER in UNISON's police civilian branch expressed similar views: 'I think everybody should be treated fairly, no matter what race, sexuality etc'. As we have seen a rather abstract notion of fairness could also extend to workplace issues themselves with confusion as to whether they were a result of specific discrimination or a function of the wider employment relation. This point is made by Rizwan in Box 4 and his emphasis on the process of politicisation resonates with Virdee and Grint's conclusion that participation is a skill acquired through experience and that individuals are not inherently participationist, but become so (1994, p. 215).

The focus amongst ERs on a wide notion of equality and/or fairness appears to be distinctive from the stronger ideologies that characterised the emergence of self-organisation in UNISON, but which now seem elusive in the wider political landscape. In general whilst there were active SOGs at regional level, activity at branch level was weaker. Humphrey (2000) suggests that self-organisation is a way to mobilise groups that are historically excluded from the union and to reflect wider social identities in union strategy and activity. At the same time she also acknowledges critiques of self-organisation; their bureaucratisation within the union apparatus and the essentialism and exclusion which may be inherent to identity politics. Anne Munro suggests that despite self-organisation UNISON has not been able to address the workplace issues faced by black female ancillary workers (2001). Waddington and Kerr's' examination of UNISON's National Organising and Recruitment Strategy (NORS) similarly concludes that SOGs have 'tended to focus their activities on regional and national-led activities rather than those at workplace or branch level where NORS activities are concentrated' (2009, p. 43). Bureaucratisation may have detached self-organisation from its political roots, whilst the Public Sector Equality Duty has prompted employer consultative bodies or staff forums for black, women, disabled and LGBT workers which can compete with, undermine or confuse union self-organisation and in some cases conflate individuals' work and union roles – some ERs attended these groups and raised issues through them, but in the absence of formal union representation they generally had limited power.

The potential of ERs to represent a wider range of inequalities may signify an approach which is more inclusive than self-organisation, whilst reflecting the prevailing legislative agenda. As a UNISON National Officer suggested:

> One of the benefits I think about the [equality] rep role is that it means that anybody can be an activist around equalities without having to identify as one of the self organised, as part of one of the groups who might be experiencing discrimination. So you could have somebody who's a white middle aged guy who cares about these things and wants to get involved and wants to do stuff and has got lots of good skills to bring to it and they can do that. Or you might have someone who is disabled or gay, but doesn't want to be out, but would like to do something. So you can be involved in it without having to be discriminated against or without having to be out.

Three of the 11 ERs interviewed were white heterosexual men who had developed an interest in equality issues; as we saw in Chapter 1 Kingsley had a background in male-dominated heavy industry and was now trying to come to terms with working in a more mixed workplace in terms of gender and race – in his case becoming an ER was about personal education and development. Neil had been involved in delivering training on equalities as part of a previous job in the civil service and had become an ER to develop this interest. He was aiming to establish self-organisation within his branch and reported that his union activity had given him 'a better understanding and knowledge' of the different equality strands recognised under the Equality Act 2010 and of employment and equality issues in general. For Dave, a traffic control officer, also working in a mixed workforce in a city council:

> I just thought it would be a good thing to get in on and find out a little bit more and hopefully help to get a bit of equality across the board, because people always see equality as being a race thing or a gender thing but there are many different types of inequality – and not everybody, including myself, you don't know a lot about it to be honest, and that's what I was hoping – one to maybe gain a little bit more knowledge and two to maybe make a difference.

Dave's comment suggests that some ER's conception of equality may be wider than UNISON's historical focus upon gender, race, sexuality and disability as social categories requiring specific organisation. The narratives of ERs may also reflect more recent policy discourses, including those in public sector organisations, which emphasise diversity, as distinct from equality. The Equality Act 2010 also includes discrimination on the grounds of religion and there were mixed views amongst activists on this. Kevin was considering taking up the issue of statutory religious holidays arguing that Muslims were forced to take the statutory holidays over Christmas and Easter, but had to take annual leave at Eid or during Ramadan. Olivia, a Christian, felt that there was too much focus on non-Christian religions and that Christianity was being undermined through this, but she made it clear that this was a personal view which she would not take into UNISON. Peter was in favour of informal arrangements to allow Muslim workers time-off to celebrate Eid recognising that they were forced to take time-off at Christmas, but did not support accommodating prayer during working time:

> No, because it creates a big divide and it's like segregating a group of workers – either we're all here together, or we're not.

Early evaluation of the ER role in UNISON suggests that it is compatible with self-organisation despite being distinctive in political terms and having a different organisational basis. ERs were seen as an addition rather than as substituting for or undermining self-organisation.

ERs who were not involved in SOGs appeared to be committed to self-organisation, as for Anna, a support officer in local government:

> I think it's good that you have self organised groups to cater for people with different needs. I think the only thing you need to be careful with is that the groups don't become too exclusive and isolated from mainstream society.

Pat was a Branch Equality Officer, coordinating ERs in a health branch, and her comments reflect both support for self-organisation and a broader commitment to fairness and the possible tension between the two:

> Obviously with being chair of the women's network, but also here with the other self-organised groups, I strongly believe that they should be included and that we should be working closer together instead of in little silos, say the black members, the disabled, the women's and the LGBT, basically because sometimes we're working on the same things together and because women overarch it as well. So keeping our own identity but working towards doing some of the special campaigns and supporting each other – if need be to take motions to our individual conferences. And also, I think equality is at the heart of everything because if we haven't got it right and equal, then how do we move forward? Especially the union itself, it has to have its house in order, so we need to look at that and then go out to the employer... I've watched and seen things that aren't fair, how jobs are offered or how people are put into posts. So it's just something that I really do believe, not just something within my own personal and private life, I believe equality is an issue for us all.

There was also a view that the development of ERs could potentially stimulate or reinvigorate self-organisation in the branches – something borne out by Elizabeth:

> I think it's [self-organisation] really essential and I think there should be more of it really. In our branch there are two groups, we don't have a disabled members group and I just think that's really essential to the branch. It's one of the things I'd like to be involved with as an Equality Rep... because I think that it's a way of everybody

then being able to feed into policies – just having an opportunity to feed back.

Virdee and Grints' qualified support for self-organisation is based upon evidence that 'anti-racism in practice is critically dependent upon the existence and actions of a caucus of black and minority activists, often operating in relative autonomy from – but with the support of – the main union' (1994, p. 205). The question remains as to whether ERs will be able to mobilise resources to challenge specific forms of discrimination as effectively as self-organised groups may do, or, as Healy and Kirton put it, to address the structural constraints of union bureaucracy and democracy to achieve 'the more contested transformational change' (2000, p. 358). In the context of race Virdee and Grint proposed that 'a flexible combination of self-organised black and minority groups and conventional union organisation is most likely to succeed' (1994, p. 214). It may be that whilst self-organised networks are better placed to challenge union bureaucracies and hierarchies, the effectiveness of ERs lies in their focus upon discrimination and injustice in the workplace, suggesting the fruitful co-existence of self-organisation and equality representatives.

Conclusions

ERs have emerged in the context of the introduction of the Equality Act, 2010 and establishment of the Equality and Human Rights Commission, which recognise the complexity of disadvantage and a wider range of discriminations – in line with this ERs may provide more inclusive representation and activism. These legal changes reflect a wider shift in public discourse from equality to diversity; this approach may dilute organisation that challenges racism, sexism and other specific forms of oppression on the basis of structural divisions, focusing more upon individual relationships. The increase in individual grievances in the workplace may reinforce this.

Against the backdrop of the decline of the joint regulatory role of unions the evidence presented here suggests that ERs challenge the reassertion of managerial prerogative in the workplace, but that they also collectively frame issues arising from discrimination. Once again this suggests a more dynamic relationship between the individual and collective (Healy et al., 2004) with the focus on the workplace providing the potential to reconnect representation with mobilisation

(Fairbrother, 1996). As with union learning the exclusion of equality from collective bargaining remains a danger, but ERs were informally negotiating with local management and some actively sought a collective bargaining role in their organisations. Similarly, the refusal of government to provide statutory support for ERs may constrain their potential in the long term and has been identified as a barrier (Moore, 2010). As we have seen a number of ERs were experienced activists with existing roles in the union or new activists who acquired additional roles. As with ULRs this then raises questions as to how far the learning or equality role becomes diluted when it is not dedicated, but one of a number of roles that activists take on.

The testimonies of the activists in this chapter and throughout the book powerfully convey that race, ethnicity, gender, disability and sexuality are all integral dimensions of a fundamentally unequal employment relationship located in the workplace. Experiences of discrimination arising from this generated activism. Crucially these activists located their individual experiences of discrimination in a collective context and their concern that other workers did not share their experience led them into union activity. At the same time the presence of the union, its validation of discrimination and its responsiveness to their experience (so that they were 'giving something back') is important. The presence of self-organised structures signalled to workers that their specific experiences would be legitimated and again could encourage activism. Yet the narratives suggest that whilst experiences of discrimination in the workplace generate collectivism and the union can reflect workers' identities and help them to understand and express them, activists do not automatically construct active, fixed or politicised social identities on this basis, just as they did not actively assert class consciousness. Their testimonies support Virdee and Grints' (1994) conclusions that despite their direct experiences activism does not necessarily spring from social identity, which cannot be read off from biological characteristics, but is more contingent – social identity can be subordinated to trade union or (implicit) class interests. For most of these activists trade unionism provides the context in which their identities can be located and this is primarily because work is a key site of identity. As a consequence of the social movements of the 1970s and 1980s unions have come to reflect and reinforce a range of social identities arising from divisions in the workplace and labour market, but more importantly also workers' multiple and contingent identities. In Chapter 6 we see how unions have started to embrace migrant workers following decades of reluctance and how migrant worker activism allows for the transformation of identity.

For Virdee (2000) inter-racial class solidarity is associated with periods of strong class identification and this was the context in which self-organisation emerged and which shaped the activism of some of the older trade unionists quoted above. Newer Equality Representatives expressed their activism in terms of their practical experiences mediated by current trade union discourses and the language of equality and diversity prevalent in the public sector. Unions vary in the extent to which they reflect, mediate and shape social identity through self-organisation, whilst there are signs that self-organisation has become divorced from its political roots. The rather abstract concept of equality and/or fairness underpinning the introduction of Equality Reps is distinct not only from the collective mobilisation of politically conscious identities which characterised self-organisation in unions and wider social movements, but also from the language and vocabulary of class consciousness – it reflects a retreat from both.

6
Legacies of Self-Organisation? Migrant Worker Activists

> One company... they start messing around with the cleaners. They didn't get paid for two, three months. It was close to Christmas time and the people didn't get paid. And the cleaners they knew I was the chair for UNISON so they approached me and say this is what [is] happening. I said 'Let me go and speak to my colleagues [to see] what we can do' – so we start pushing.... You see what happen – we [were] doing well – one day immigration come, six people [were deported]. So all of this is political, it's everywhere, whatever you do nobody like it when you start [to] stand [up] for your rights. Nobody will ever, whatever you call for, nobody like it. So that's the reason sometimes we have to do it.

Jose, a Latin American migrant worker and union activist, here describes the raid in 2009 by the immigration service on largely Latin American cleaners working for a private contractor at the School of Oriental and African Studies (SOAS) and the subsequent deportation of six of them following their organisation in UNISON. This chapter explores the interplay of structure and agency in the collective representation and organisation of migrant workers in UK unions, emphasising the role played by union strategies and migrant worker activists themselves. It is based upon in-depth interviews with five migrant workers who have become active in UNISON, exploring how their specific political legacies and/or experiences in UK workplaces inform trade union activism and identity in the UK. The chapter draws upon wider research undertaken as part of UNISON's Migrant Workers Participation Project.[1] This project sought to encourage the participation of migrant workers in trade union activity recognising that according to government statistics 'foreign born' employment in Education, Health and Public Services stood at 11 per cent in 2007.[2] The chapter considers the concept of 'community unionism' as a method of engaging with migrant and other so-called 'vulnerable workers'.[3] It contemplates the implications for trade unions of moving away from the centrality of the workplace and, in terms of class consciousness, how far interest in community unionism is part of a wider shift from their class basis and identity. Such a move may substitute an uncritical and ill-defined notion of community based upon diverse social identities that is unable to challenge the fundamental divisions of labour that define migrant employment.

The context

Historically and internationally (Milkman, 2006), migrant workers have played an active role in mobilisation against injustice in the workplace, despite the frequent reluctance of trade unions to support their organisation.[4] In the UK such disputes have been about terms and conditions, but also the preferential treatment of white workers. They have also raised issues about union recognition and representation – in the case of Imperial Typewriters in Leicester in 1974 the union's refusal to allow Asian women workers to elect their own shop stewards. The Grunwick dispute 1976–1978 marked a key moment in British labour history, when a strike led by Asian women over union recognition, but also working conditions, mobilised the support not only of the workers' union, but the wider labour movement. At the same time, the inertia of trade unions has meant migrant workers have relied upon their communities for support and as a source of mobilisation and this tradition has continued in more recent disputes by (second generation) British-born Asian workers at Hillingdon Hospital in 1995 and Gate Gourmet in 2005.

This chapter is set in the context of a more recent wave of migration, including, since May 2004, the movement of around one million workers to the UK from the Eastern European Union States.[5] It also reflects the influx of Filipino workers into the UK health and care sectors as a result of a policy of state-managed migration in the Philippines – the largest exporter of registered nurses (Bach, 2007). This second wave of migration has taken place in an entirely different political and economic context from that characterising the first wave in the 1950s and 1960s and a changed situation for trade unionism. The intervening period has seen the collapse of collective bargaining in the private sector and its attenuation in the public sector through privatisation.

Virdee (2000) shows how in the 1950s and 1960s trade union strength in a period of tight labour market conditions rested upon restrictive practices to control the labour supply and collective bargaining based upon narrow and exclusive sectional interests. In the mid-1970s there was a reconfiguration of the relationship between organised labour and 'the racialised worker' as a result of the independent struggle of black workers and a shift in union strategy, which facilitated inter-racial working class solidarity. This reconfiguration reflected the recognition by trade union activists that 'their material interests could no longer be maintained solely through the operation of collective bargaining and the use of exclusionary practices' (2000, p. 557) marking an explosion of industrial action that was more inclusive and moved beyond sectionalist trade union consciousness. The political defeat of such mobilisations and the subsequent continued decline of collective bargaining has coincided with the adoption of an organising strategy by both UK and US unions characterised by attempts to 'organise the unorganised' – often migrant workers – and to build coalitions linking unions with civil society (Frege and Kelly, 2004).

For David Harvey (2005) the reassertion of the global power of capital through neoliberal restructuring has involved the elimination of barriers to the mobility of both capital and labour and this analysis provides the broader context for this chapter. Wills et al. (2010) fully document the migrant division of labour that has emerged in London, whereby migrant workers do the city's 'bottom-end' jobs largely in cleaning, care and construction. They identify the reinforcement of existing ethnic divisions of labour through the preferential access to low paid jobs that EU workers increasingly have at the expense of non-EU workers, with the points-based system restricting the entry of those considered to be 'low-skilled' from outside Europe.

Structure and agency

A range of literature on migration has attempted to synthesise macro and micro perspectives (Larsen et al., 2005) and to reflect the dynamic between structure and agency. Jon Goss and Bruce Lindquist (1995) have argued that international labour migration is not only a result of individual motivations conditioned by contextual factors. They critically reflect upon the role accorded in the literature to migrant networks as a means of articulating agency and structure, going beyond this to propose the concept of the 'migrant institution'; 'a complex articulation of individuals, associations and organisations that extends the social action of, and interaction between, these agents and agencies across time and space' (1995, p. 319). Stephen Bach has developed an industrial relations perspective on migration in order to incorporate 'the role of individuals, households and structural features of the global economy with an understanding of how institutions, especially the state and labour market institutions, regulate migration' (2007, p. 388). This approach recognises that trade unions can intervene in the labour market to influence the conditions of migrant worker employment although, since migrant workers are generally not covered by collective bargaining, this may involve unions in wider political activity beyond the workplace (for example, UNISON's involvement in campaigning against changed requirements for extending work permits for senior care workers, largely Filipino workers, introduced by the Home Office in 2007). The UNISON Migrant Worker Participation project shows that unions may also provide a means for the democratic engagement of migrant workers. The fact that UNISON's project was funded by the Union Modernisation Fund once again raises the issue of the Labour Government shaping the role of unions, in this case towards promoting the integration of migrant workers into UK society as part of its agenda on 'community cohesion'. At the same time Labour Government policy and political discourse controlled and policed migration, with a direct impact on the conditions of migrant worker employment. The potential contradiction between UK government policies based upon integration and democratic participation on the one hand and public and aggressive displays of policing on the other was starkly exposed by the raid by the immigration service on cleaners at SOAS.

Restrictions upon citizenship, access to employment and state benefits have made migrant workers particularly attractive to employers (Wills et al., 2010). In the context of the experience of migrant workers in Ireland, Tony Dundon, María-Alejandra González-Pérez and Terrence McDonough (2007) argue that the exploitation of non-Irish workers reflects the abuse of employer power reinforced by state policy, in particular the work permit system. They point to the considerable barriers to migrant workers joining trade unions arising from the work permit system and fear of deportation, but also language and lack of information about employment rights. The research undertaken as part of UNISON's migrant participation project (Moore and Watson, 2009) confirmed the importance of the legal framework in shaping activism, with citizenship status a factor. Migrant workers feared that by belonging to or by being active in a trade union they might lose their right to work in the UK, as Cassandra, a Filipino migrant activist suggested:

> For migrant workers who are mostly work permit holders, the main issue probably is fear of losing their job. They would rather bear the suffering, rather than complain. What is lacking is awareness and people are not quite educated about what are their rights and responsibilities.

Jose also described the climate of fear promoted by employers:

> They think migrant workers are illegal, this was the thing and that's my own experience, they think I was illegal...the employers, the contractors [say], 'we want to see your papers'; I say 'But you [have] already seen my papers before' 'Oh we want to see [them] again' I'd say 'What for?' 'ok so [if] you don't bring [them] tomorrow, you know...'...all of this is like bullying.

Such fears extended to EU nationals who did not need work permits, but who felt that the insecurity of their employment made them vulnerable to employer reprisals for trade union activity – as a participant from a focus group in a Health Trust described:

> At the moment we have a two tier workforce within the system, we have those who used to work for the Trust and were TUPE'd [6] over to the private contractors and then all the employees that have been taken on [since], so these people are on separate wages. If you behave, then they will put you on the same terms as the people who were TUPE'd over and if you don't behave then you'll get fired, because they normally have very, very bad employment terms and conditions. So that is the fear factor that has been created, stopping people from coming to meetings, stopping them from identifying with the union and all the other things that should really empower them.

The UNISON research identified privatisation and the contracting out of public services – and their removal from the remit of national collective bargaining – as key structural barriers to migrant worker activism. Ironically, the concentration of the delivery of privatised services in the hands of a small group of multinational companies has involved the employment of workers on a multiplicity of small contracts, characterised by divergent working conditions and fragmented representation and bargaining. This has had a direct impact on the organisation of migrant workers since they are disproportionately employed in privatised services and because of UNISON's lack of organisational strength in these areas. For example Filipino care workers working in privatised care homes were not initially aware that there was a union they could join, or that UNISON organised in privatised services or that they might be covered by a local union branch. This reflects UNISON's traditional organisation around directly employed workers in local government, health or higher education, with branches organised on the basis of the employer. Privatisation and contracting out has represented a major challenge to this model removing workers from the union's immediate influence, with directly employed branch officers denied facility time to represent or organise workers employed by contractors or to negotiate over their employment. In line with this a survey of UNISON branches[7] revealed that whilst over half (53 per cent) of branch secretaries identified migrant workers as potential UNISON recruits, approaching a third (29 per cent) did not and just under half (44 per cent) of branch secretaries reported difficulties in recruiting migrant workers. Overall just over a third (36 per cent) of branch secretaries reported that their branch did not recruit amongst private contractors – under two thirds (58 per cent) said that they did so. Strikingly, UNISON branches that reported having migrant workers in membership were more likely to report that they recruited amongst private contractors – 72 per cent did so compared to 22 per cent who did not. Whilst over a third (35 per cent) of branch secretaries stated that the branch had specifically targeted migrant workers for recruitment and organisation, the majority (62 per cent) said it had not, although in many cases this was because the branch had not specifically targeted *any* group of workers and reflected the wider organisational issues that UNISON faced – issues not just limited to migrant workers. If the responses on recruitment and organisation suggested that nearly half (46 per cent) of branch secretaries did not identify specific barriers to recruiting migrant workers, a larger proportion did report issues with transforming membership into activism. The survey suggested that the number of branches with migrant workers who were active was very low – under one in five (12 per cent) of all branches in the survey – and over three quarters, 84 per cent, of branch secretaries said there were none. The privatisation of services, often based upon an ethnic division of labour underpinned by state immigration policies, limits the development of structures of engagement for migrant workers.

Structures of engagement – the union

In exploring why migrant workers may be less active in political and civil society, Vogel and Triandafyllidou (2005) suggest that the social and political opportunity structure is important, including institutional configurations, the existence of structures of engagement, the political climate and perceptions of activism. In the UNISON survey respondents from just over a third (36 per cent) of branches that had migrant workers in membership reported that they had attempted to encourage them to become actively involved in UNISON. Nearly two thirds said the branch had not tried and approaching two thirds (61 per cent) identified particular barriers to migrant worker members becoming active. This was a much higher proportion, than the 44 per cent of branch secretaries that identified particular difficulties with recruiting migrant workers to the union.

The focus groups undertaken as part of UNISON's Migrant Worker Participation project found that in some cases migrant worker members were not integrated into their workplace branches, had not been invited to UNISON meetings and found it difficult to access UNISON branch or regional representatives. Their engagement with the union was often via community networks or UNISON's Overseas Nurses Network[8] or through individual contacts with national or regional UNISON officials. In part this reflects a wider absence of union branch activity in certain parts of UNISON, which affects not just migrant workers, but all UNISON members and particularly those based in privatised services. Yet these migrant worker members were actively recruiting other workers, but also creating a culture of trade unionism in workplaces and communities. Olivia, originally from Zimbabwe, was one of UNISON's first Equality Reps, but had also single-handedly established a union presence in a small workplace within a private health facility with no union recognition where she organised British-born workers as well as migrant workers:

> I'm moving slowly but surely and for myself, since I've joined UNISON, ten people having joined – it's amazing. And actually for people to know that if they've got any issues, they can come to me and UNISON can try and help in many ways and for them to know that if they've got any issues, could it be bullying, harassment, equalities issues, where they feel they're not being treated equally, they can go to somebody and it can be heard. And just by me being an Equality Rep has changed a lot of things...I can now tell that before

management does something they now are stopping to think – and that makes a difference.

Migrant workers emphasised the importance of existing UNSION representatives being visible and accessible in the workplace and available to talk face-to-face with workers about the union. It is not just the agency of migrant worker activists that is important – there also needs to be structures of engagement within unions. Lukasz was a Polish youth worker for a local council and was not aware of his local branch until a year after he joined the union; he then attended the branch Annual General Meetings, but these had been inquorate for three years running:

> I found them dry so I thought they are not for me. I found the environment of sitting around the table unappealing at the time. I wanted to do things, change the world and they were all just sitting there. I am a youth worker I am used to activity, something going on all the time, long boring meetings are out of my depth and I would not be effective in my role if I felt negative about what I was doing.

He did not want to become a shop steward (but was a contact point for the union), but had enjoyed UNISON's national LGBT Conference and attended regional LGBT meetings. As with the integration of new ULRs into branches, the UNISON migrant worker project suggested that this was often dependent upon the efforts of existing activists in supporting and involving migrant workers and ensuring access to union training.

Benjamin Hopkins' case study of working life in a UK chocolate factory illustrates how the influx of migrant labour, along with the precarious contractual status of workers, can fracture UK workplaces along national and ethnic lines (2009). Olivia was supporting two Eastern European workers whom she felt were being treated unfairly at her workplace, partly because of language:

> That's a problem they face…they cannot express themselves very well and other workers just whinge and whine and complain about them and sometimes you look and you think 'what are they actually complaining about, there isn't anything?'

Union organisation can overcome such divisions, but the role of activists in the workplace is important. Charles, a ULR for Unite, worked with a regional Union Learning Project officer to provide ESOL training and to organise open days in a local pub to inform largely Eastern European migrant workers about their rights and about the union. He also engaged with the agency supplying the workers about their responsibilities towards them. However, this met with opposition from other workers including union members and reps, who felt that by talking to the agencies the union was legitimising agency work, something which then manifested itself in hostility to the migrant workers in the workplace. Charles felt that the campaign he initiated around respect in the workplace had some limited impact:

> I said 'all I want to do is that when these people come on site they have proper health and safety inductions and it's a dignity at work thing, there's clearly no bullying or harassment' and I wanted to go the extra mile to give them information about the union. At the time ESOL was free, we wanted to offer them ESOL and to back that up we wanted to do some open days off site to endorse a campaign. ... I don't think we changed them [British-born workers hostile to the migrant workers] – one union rep resigned over it.

As we have seen in Chapter 4 there are a number of examples where union learning has been used to provide ESOL training for migrant workers which has also allowed them to engage with the union.

Jose joined the union when he transferred from working for a private contractor to become directly employed by the university, but following an incident when the private contractor had tried to change his terms and conditions:

> Before I worked for the contractors and then I had a little trouble with the company. I was working Monday to Friday, one day they say 'You must come to work Saturday and Sunday'. I said 'Why – [I] never did for two years now?' – 'You must or you lose your job'. So I don't know what to do, so I said 'Oh I want to speak to somebody' They say 'who's somebody?' I say 'somebody in the union'. So he [the union branch officer] help me to say 'I don't want to do it. I have a family', so he helped me with that one. And then when I passed from the contractor to the university, they say, 'Do you want to join the union?' 'Why not' [I said] 'I like to take on the union'. And then my first year in the union I was selected as Chair – I continued for four years or five years.

The union branch also defended Jose when a British-born worker, seemingly prompted by management and hostile to migrant workers, took a grievance against him, which was subsequently dropped. As we see in the opening quote to this chapter the branch responded when Jose, who by then was Chair of the branch and described by a colleague (in Gramsci's terms) as an 'organic intellectual', organised the university's largely Latin American cleaners. Union action led to the cleaning contract being brought back in-house and a campaign within the University to counter the 'invisibility' of the cleaners. In this case collective organisation was based not only upon migrant worker agency, but also the responsiveness and political leadership of the branch. Following the union organisation of the cleaners Jose was dismissed by management. He had subsequently got a cleaning job elsewhere, but in the knowledge that if he openly challenged working conditions he would jeopardise his job and/or the hours and conditions upon which he was employed.

These examples highlight the role of agency in addressing the structural conditions defining migrant labour. They reflect union strategies at national, regional or workplace level – UNISON's Participation Project identified and trained a cohort of around 90 migrant workers and a follow-up survey showed that subsequently over one third (39 per cent) held positions in their branches. The accounts of Charles and Jose demonstrate the importance of the interaction of migrant workers with unions and activists at the workplace and here the subjective and ideological dimensions of activism play a role.

Structures of engagement – community unionism

In terms of activation processes Vogel and Triandafyllidou (2005) have suggested that 'indigenous activists' may be drawn into activity by existing networks and that the role of 'recruiters' who approach individuals is important – migrant workers may be less likely to be part of such networks or to be approached by 'recruiters'. However, as Goss and Lindquist (1995) propose, networks are also important for the activation of migrants and Vogel and Triandafyllidou ask whether involvement in migrant associations leads to wider civic participation and integration or to separate activity and even to isolation and exclusion. Community unionism has emerged as a term to describe coalitions between unions and community organisations (Tattersall, 2009, p. 161), particularly, but not exclusively, in relation to migrant institutions and networks. For Amanda Tattersall interest in community unionism is a response to union crisis across the industrialised world (2009, p. 161). Research, initially drawing upon the work of US unions, has shown that the union activity of migrant workers may take the form of collective organisation based upon existing community networks which may strengthen and extend union organisation and suggest new models (Delgado, 2003). Milkman's (2006) work has shown how the organising campaigns of US unions exploded the myth of migrant 'unorganisibility'. Such campaigns involved an approach that went beyond the individual workplace and organised migrants across industries, linking up with local communities and migrant networks in order to mobilise. Similarly in the UK, Wills (2001) has suggested the capacity of community/labour coalitions to unionise 'hard to organise' workers, adopting an approach which is sensitive to racial and cultural issues.

Waddington and Kerr found that few UNISON branches had links with community organisations (2009). However, the UNISON Migrant Worker Participation project suggested that migrant community organisations and more informal migrant worker networks could encourage and reinforce unionisation. Within the broader term 'community unionism', Tattersall identifies three distinct strategies: first, coalition unionism based upon organisational relationships; second the organisation of workers on the basis of identity or interests and third, organising defined by geography or locality (2006, pl. 163). Within this framework the UNISON Migrant Worker Participation project – an essentially 'top-down' project operating from UNISON's Head Office – would fit most closely into the first, reflecting some aspects of the second, but not the third category. This definition would also apply to Unite's Justice for Cleaners' campaign.[9] The importance of community organisations to unionisation is suggested in the testimonies of migrant worker activists. Jose described how the Latin American Workers' Network encouraged members to belong to UNISON or Unite, depending upon where they worked:

> I will always say to my people 'You must join any union – that's where we fight' ... [if] something happen and you're not in the union [there's] nothing you can do. You have to join the union and you do not have to tell nobody. You don't have to tell your boss or your manager 'Oh I am in the union' – no. We say 'you work in the public sector, like a school, university or hospital, join UNISON or otherwise you have to join Unite'.

Daisy and Cassandra were both involved in the Filipino community organisation Kanlungen (meaning Shelter) and this had been a basis for engagement in UNISON. They found it easier to recruit and organise through this network than through their workplaces or branches. Daisy worked in a managerial role in a Primary Care Trust and found it difficult to get access to migrant workers based in the hospitals:

> The difficulty that I found in organising migrants is that not many work within the Primary Care Trust so we have different locations where we work. Most migrant workers are based in the hospitals and the branches within the Primary Care Trust and the Hospitals are different. When I found out that there are lots of Filipinos in acute hospitals in London, what I did was, I went through the Filipino network and tried to recruit through that network.

She described using email, but also personal networks through the church or through parties and other social gatherings:

> We like food and we like getting together that is why we look for opportunities to combine the two to find out about each other's lives and hear each other's stories. For example, we find out how we got here to the UK, where people live, work and even how much one earns. So we create or look for occasions for getting together, like if somebody has a birthday, then we cook food, invite friends – who in turn invite their friends to come and celebrate – but most importantly to get the chance to meet other people from our community. It is within these personal networks that I take the opportunity to introduce UNISON and recruit. I would say 'I'm a member of UNISON' and then I would get their details to send them the application form. Or in church groups, I try to find out who goes to a church and then contact them to send out information and applications. Sometimes I also go to a church group to meet with some people and encourage them to become members.

She had sent out around 50 application forms and had personally recruited more than ten people in two or three nursing homes. Her reference to the church reflects Ian Fitzgerald's findings on the role of faith organisations in his study of unions using a community approach to engage with Polish migrant workers in the north of England (2009). Olivia had been recruited through the church by another migrant worker seconded to UNISON to work with migrant workers in private nursing homes, which in this instance were covered by the local branch. These accounts of recruitment suggest the capacity of migrant workers to take union membership outside the workplace in a tradition that may have been lost amongst British-born workers, particularly following the break up of occupational communities. It chimes with Janice Fine's (2007) proposal that community unionism can inject trade unionism back into organisational spaces and Daisy stressed the importance of unions reaching out beyond the workplace:

> I think that it [the union] should organise outside of the workplace, because communities and community groups are important aspects in people's lives, especially migrants, outside of the workplace. From my experience of recruiting migrant workers outside of the workplace, I think that organising within community groups outside of the workplace [should] be given serious consideration because this is where you can personalise discussions and issues and then discuss about trade unions. Sometimes it is in community groups where you can have effective discussion about issues because sometimes it's impractical – there are workers who do not actually have workplaces. It can also be difficult to have discussions in the workplace because either there is conflict in time or group discussions are not allowed or recognised within the workplace.

In Scotland the engagement of many migrant workers with UNISON had come through the Overseas Nurses Network, a professional and social network providing information and support to overseas nurses and other care workers. It encouraged members to become active in their UNISON branches and met in UNISON regional premises. Its meetings were more open, informal and inclusive than traditional union meetings (recalling Lukasz's comments) implying the effectiveness of alternative models of participation. A focus group based upon the Network raised some questions about the readiness of UNISON branches in the region to engage with migrant worker activists and a feeling from branches that migrant workers demanded greater resources in terms of membership services. This suggests that community engagement may be or has been a response to the absence of structures of engagement within the union and, more generally, to weaknesses in union organisation.

Mobilising divergent social identities

Paul Stewart, Jo McBride, Ian Greenwood, John Stirling, Jane Holgate, Amanda Tattersall, Carol Stephenson and Dave Wray suggest that the prevailing interest in community unionism, as well as being an outcome of structural change in the global economy, may also reflect a related perception of a disintegration of older class identities and need for unions to transform themselves to represent 'new workers' in the service sector who may have divergent social identities (2009, p. 6). For Jane Holgate identity and culture are contingent in union mobilisation and work is only one dimension of identity. In her study of the organisation of Black and minority ethnic migrant workers in a London sandwich factory 'the opportunity to organise around identities that were important to different groups of workers was lost' (2005, p. 476). Wills describes London Citizens as a broad-based community alliance including labour, community, faith and educational groups, which engages people, including migrant workers, 'on the basis of mutual differentiation (fostering "unity across difference") whilst allowing them to enlarge their affiliations (2009, p. 158). It has undoubtedly been effective in addressing the issue of the living wage in London and it adopts a self-consciously open door policy focusing upon action rather than a commitment to a shared ideology or belief and this may involve dismissing rather than articulating potential political differences over issues such as gender and sexuality. At the same time Wills concedes that London Citizens practices a form of identity politics, although through shared experiences of collectivity it nurtures an enlarged and 'meaningful super-ordinate identity at the urban-wide scale' (2009, p. 173).

If identities do not solely rest upon work then the narratives of migrant workers also confirm that neither are they shaped solely in terms of race or ethnicity. Further, identity is not static but transformed in new geographical locations, whilst persistently defined by global and national divisions of labour. Roger Waldinger, Chris Erickson, Ruth Milkman, Daniel Mitchell, Abel Valenzuela, Kent Wong and Maurice Zeitlins' (1998) history of the Justice for Janitor's campaign suggested that both high levels of class consciousness amongst largely Latin American migrant workers and the involvement of a number of activists with left-wing or union backgrounds were key elements in the success of the movement, alongside the tactics, leadership and strategy of the Service Employees International Union (SEIU).[10] The narratives of the migrant workers interviewed here also suggest that in some cases unionisation in the UK was informed by a legacy of social or political activism. Daisy's involvement with the progressive people's movement in the Philippines had helped shape her 'understanding of the social, political and cultural structures that impact on social development and poverty'; whilst Jose had belonged to a revolutionary party in Latin America. Olivia and Cassandra had no personal experience of activism in their home countries (and were younger than Daisy and Jose), but both had relatives who had opposed the prevailing regimes there.

Whilst for Daisy and Jose involvement in UK unions appeared to be a logical outcome of their previous activism and political identities, for Lukasz, Olivia and Cassandra it was shaped more by their experiences of the UK workplace and union responses to this. Lukasz, had joined the union because in his previous job in a nursing home he had seen the role the union had played in representing a Filipino colleague who was treated unfairly by a manager, although as we saw in Chapter 5 also because it reflected his identity as a gay man. He had been on UNISON's Migrant Workers' training course. The same chapter described how Olivia was motivated to become an activist after the union helped her to challenge her dismissal for gross misconduct in a second job two weeks after drawing attention to a manager's racism. Evidence from focus groups and interviews with migrant workers revealed that they were attracted into membership because they believed that UNISON could provide support and representation in the workplace, as well as advice on employment rights. Daisy and Cassandra suggested that the experience of trade unionism in the Philippines could represent a barrier to union membership amongst Filipino workers in the UK, for Cassandra:

> Trade union activity back in the Philippines was different from here. Here it's much more formalised, much more structured, people follow, they just don't go out on the streets and demonstrate – it's more political, it's different in the Philippines when you say you are a trade union activist and it's more linked with the political agenda. I don't know but personally, there's a political history about being a trade unionist back in the Philippines and there are issues about political killings and stuff. Because people probably might feel scared that if they go back home and they've been known to be a union activist [here] ... I do a steward's job, but I don't really want to join in issues about politics and everything back home. I do want to look after the welfare and help migrant workers by giving them information, directing them to where they go and all those things or representing them with their issues. But I don't think I will be comfortable demonstrating out on the streets and everything.

Cassandra emphasises the distinctive historical and cultural contexts which define trade unionism, whilst in Box 5 Daisy describes how she highlighted conditions in UK workplaces rather than appealing to political experiences in the Philippines to recruit Filipino workers in a different context. For some workers the legacy of trade unions can be a

---

Box 5

'It depends on what your background is and your political involvement in the Philippines, the union is looked at as something that is anti-establishment. Many Filipino migrant workers equate trade unions to radicalism or being anti government. Many Filipinos are afraid of joining the unions because there is also the association with communism; Filipino migrants have the attitude of 'don't join and don't rock the boat' because if you rock the boat as in the Philippines there is a lot at stake – you can be arrested as being a communist or anti government. A lot of this fear has been experienced during the martial law years of the Marcos regime, that anything people do in protest against the Government, even if what you are doing is to exercise your right, is considered subversive, so people tend to stay away from these sorts of activities. So if you are not an activist already, then I think that the culture and the notion of aktibista [activist] being anti establishment has to be challenged'.

  So there is a lot of education I think that is needed in terms of challenging the cultural experience that non-activist migrants already have from their home country and education in terms of their rights as workers...so to stand up for their rights and also for rights in this country, it's your right to become a member of a network. If you point out actually the benefits, like I wouldn't speak about my experience, I would speak about other people's experience. I usually use practical examples recruiting in hospitals. In Oxford there were lots of Filipino nurses who were recruited as nurses, doing the jobs of trained nurses but [who] received wages equivalent to [the] wages of non-trained nurses. There were lots of issues in terms of the contracts being modified or they were working very long hours to make up for the low wages and [to] be able to afford the accommodation provided by the nursing home who charged rent; or they were given a job description which was very general and did not spell out their terms and conditions. I tried to find out what it is that they experienced in their own jobs. I found out that Filipino nurses working in nursing homes had been given contracts in the Philippines when they were recruited, but the moment that they came to the UK their contracts were changed. So I pointed out that becoming a member of the union can help them understand their rights and get support if they experience problems with their employment'.

(Daisy, International Officer)

---

resource, whilst for others it may inhibit activism and as with British-born UK activists there can be a generational effect.

  Dundon et al.'s work on migrant workers in Ireland found scepticism about unions sometimes based on the experiences of those in former Communist states (2007, p. 513). Lukasz described his parents' fears of trade union membership in Poland and attributed this to their experience of the former Communist regime (which he terms 'socialistic') where trade union membership could bring victimisation. He had been surprised when his line manager in local government had supported him joining the union:

> When I came here I kind of expected that my manager might not like it and may want to get rid of me when she finds out that I joined the union, but because she's a member herself she said to me 'everyone should be a member of a trade union', so she gave me the courage to join. Fear of trade unions was kind of planted by my parents you see...because my mum once worked at a university, she was in administration and she never joined a trade union herself as she used to say, 'they will victimise me if I am a member of a trade union, they will sack me' – a very socialistic approach, 'they are all watching us' sort of thing...I was never exposed to trade unions, I never spoke to any trade unionists, I never had opportunity to learn about them – I didn't know how trade unions work and why the public hates trade unionists and why companies want to get rid of them. So this was something which I was exposed to and I never had [the] opportunity to reflect upon this fear which was absolutely ridiculous. We learn in schools about [the] importance of 'Solidarity', but real everyday life sends a clear message that those days are gone – trade union days that is.

Whilst ideological reasons have been cited as a barrier to Eastern Europeans joining trade unions, Bridget Anderson, Nick Clark and Violetta Parutis's (2007) survey of Polish and Lithuanian workers concluded that low membership rates did not represent hostility to trade unions, since a majority of their respondents said they would be interested in joining – less than ten per cent gave ideological reasons or negative experiences of unions as a reason for not joining. Government statistics confirm that although non UK nationals have a lower union density than employees of UK nationality (21 per cent compared to 28 per cent) it is not hugely lower and this gap narrows, and reverses, when non UK nationals have been in employment for longer periods of time. Ian Fitzgerald and Jane Hardy (2010) have also outlined successful recruitment and organising strategies around Polish workers in the UK and Chapter 3 has illustrated collective organisation in a successful union recognition case. Jose suggested the different economic and political contexts in which unions operate:

> I always think how can we change when in UNISON they have good jobs and they not trouble you in [the] morning? You know when we used to have revolutionaries [it was] because the people, the poor

people, or the people we are talking about, they struggle, so they [were] suffering. So, you know, you cannot, it depends in which society you live...you can't change it...you had to struggle, you had to suffer to change it.

These testimonies suggest the dangers of assuming that migrant communities are coherent and fixed entities. For Rachel Silvey, feminist migration studies have emphasised 'the constructedness' of migrant identities (2004, p. 498). Gender is crucial to this ongoing process and these studies have illustrated how in different contexts female migrants are defined in terms of cheap, docile and disposable labour. Similarly, Sarah Dyer, Linda McDowell and Adina Batnitzky (2008) have shown how caring work is constructed at the intersection of gender with race and class in the context of the neoliberalisation of healthcare and a global division of labour where a care deficit caused by more women and men working in industrialised societies means the recruitment of caring workers from poorer and developing economies. Wills et al. (2010) show how some low paid jobs in the cleaning and care sectors have been re-gendered through migration – personified by Jose who was a qualified lawyer, but working as a cleaner. For Silvey, migrants 'participate in producing their own identities in the context of power relations and "community" politics that shape the possibilities of migrants as subjects' (2004, p. 498). She stresses the 'agentic roles' of migrant workers and the interlinkages between political-economic and subjectivity formation processes. This provides for the possibility of trade unions mediating these interlinkages, something brought to mind by a comment made by Daisy in one of UNISON's 'Pathways' courses designed to encourage migrant worker activism; in a discussion about participants' expectations of the course she suggested that it was giving something back to migrant workers in a context in which, at work, 'we are always giving'. The activism of these migrant workers challenges both the way that their gender and racial identity is constructed and by implication simplistic polarisations between structure and agency in the study of migration. The union may enable female migrants to contest stereotypical roles defined in terms of passivity and caring. Cassandra, above all, illustrates not only the way that migration can allow workers to escape national identities founded upon notions of citizenship that are both materially and symbolically exclusive in terms of gender as well as sexuality (Silvey, p. 493), but also the role that the union can play in this:

The good thing about it is they [the union] don't really judge you or it's not really an issue in terms of your sexual orientation. But in the Philippines I think I have been denied jobs because of my sexual orientation. I've been told that. It has changed me, I don't see the world as I used to right now. I've become more open minded and get to understand people where they come from and what their beliefs are. Here people believe in different ways, especially with sexual orientation and stuff; and being brought up in a Catholic family, a very, very conservative Catholic family I felt like my sexuality was not expressed, but now, I accept more who I am and what I can do and that helps me empower more of my beliefs and helps me do my union work.

When this book was been written, Cassandra underwent gender reassignment and this transformation was unveiled at a union event promoting migrant worker activism, where she was introduced as a male speaker, but took the microphone (triumphantly) as a woman; the irony was underlined by the fact that the chair of the meeting had just apologised for the fact that both speakers at the meeting (of a union with predominantly female members) were male! As we saw in Chapter 5 Lukasz stated that his work, trade unionism and activity outside of work were all defined and driven by his identity as a gay man. He had become active on lesbian and gay issues in Poland and his union activity in the UK was through UNISON's self-organised LGBT structures, although he was interested in becoming a ULR and an Equality Rep because he felt that these both related to his work as a youth worker. His identity as a Polish migrant worker was secondary to his sexuality, although he also ironically discussed potentially racist discourses which characterised Polish workers in positive terms in comparison with other groups of migrant workers. Jose suggested the instability of his identity, highlighting the way that it was also defined by his experience of attitudes towards migrants in the UK:

I'm a migrant worker. Sometime we say in Spanish 'Ni de aqui, ni de allaso' that means 'I am not from here, I am not from there' because we are not British, I am not white, I live in this country, I'm [a] British citizen. I like to be in this country...before I come to this country back home I said 'Everyone is polite, they English gentleman' *[laughing]*, but it was different when you come because they are mixed. Sometimes some people they don't like us to be here, but they don't say it, they don't say it to us, but inside they want to tell us 'Why you come to this country?'. I always say 'We come to this country for a reason, but for me I come to do my best for this country. Now I'm living here and a quarter of my life is in this country. So I'm proud to be in this country and to put my effort to this country ... about the culture I take the good things from the culture, the bad things I push away. ... Immigration will always happen ... I don't know. I don't feel British really, but I am proud to be in this country.

Insisting that the mobilisation of migrant workers is on the basis of their racial and cultural identities may deny their class and political identities, but also the way that experiences of migration, work and unionisation challenge and transform constructed and essentialised identities and allow for the expression of alternative interests based upon gender or sexuality.

Conclusions

Wills et al. locate a new migrant or ethnic division of labour within the context of 'the British class war' (2010, p. 3) – the defeat of organised labour and wholescale privatisation of public services and extensive subcontracting by multinationals through global commodity chains or production networks. The exploitation of cheap labour by multinationals in the global south has in turn fuelled migration from south to north and into these privatised, low paid jobs. The UNISON Migrant Worker Participation project found that privatisation represented a barrier to migrant worker organisation, since migrant workers were concentrated in privatised services – an area of organisational weakness for the union. This meant that branches could be unaware of the existence and potential of migrant worker activists and that there was limited engagement at local level, although this could be as much a reflection of the absence of branch activity as exclusion.

Stewart et al. (2009) imply that interest in community unionism reflects the fragmentation of work resulting from the decline in manufacturing and increase in service sectors characterised by low-wage and unregulated employment, alongside the collapse of national collective bargaining, particularly in the UK and US. The barriers that these developments pose for unionisation have prompted unions to look beyond the workplace in order to engage with so-called 'hard to organise' workers, including migrants. The narratives of activists presented here suggest a dynamic interaction between migrant worker institutions and trade unions, with the legacies and experiences of migrant workers often bringing a refreshing infusion of self-organisation to UK trade unionism. They highlight the potential for unions in reaching beyond the workplace to make alliances with community organisations and how community organisations defined in terms of ethnicity can provide sources of collective strength upon which unions can draw. Within this individual activists often play a key role in promoting trade union activity in the community (McBride and Greenwood, 2009).

Yet there is also a danger that the migrant division of labour is reproduced in the collective representation and organisation of workers. This may involve essentialising migrant communities and an assumption that migrant workers (and other 'vulnerable workers') are typically difficult to organise and need to be organised through community unionism, in contrast to British-born workers who can be organised at the level of the workplace. Fitzgerald and Hardy similarly conclude that characterising A8 migrants in terms of contingent workers can set up a binary divide between contingent and non-contingent workers, which suggests 'that they constitute a segmented and hermetically sealed part of the labour market.' (2010, p. 135), which is not the case. They suggest the importance of not only recruiting migrant workers, but also building bridges between them and British-born workers. UNISON's Migrant Worker Participation project revealed the weakness of collective representation in privatised services and the need for the union to address this as an issue which was not confined to migrant workers, but which is fundamental to the future organisation of the union itself.

Alliances beyond the workplace address the separation between economic and political struggle that historically has been seen to characterise and constrain trade union consciousness (Clements, 1977). The wider societal engagement of the activists cited here raises the possibility of a more expansive and more politicised unionism in the UK. For Wrench and Virdee (1996) there is a need for unions to extend beyond the workplace and into issues regarding the social purposes of work as part of a wider quest for a society founded on equality and they argue that when unions embark on such campaigns they are more likely to find themselves addressing political questions broader than economism and outside the remit of conventional trade union action. This implies a conscious and universal political project and Wills has suggested the importance of a political voice in connecting the experiences of work with the impact of class relations in wider society, yet the resurgence of interest in community unionism may conversely reflect union weakness and the absence of such a voice.

Whilst the political legacies of some migrant workers can inject renewed *class* consciousness into British unions, others are motivated, not by their political or cultural inheritances, but by their experiences of exploitation and discrimination in UK workplaces and the responsiveness of UK unions in terms of representation and organisation. The engagement of migrant workers at the level of the workplace in providing a trade union identity can allow them to transform constructed and essentialised identities and become a basis for integration and collective struggle. The examples of SOAS and Charle's activity in supporting migrant worker rights provide examples of engagement within the workplace – albeit problematic – and point to the important role that existing activists play in promoting integration and collectivity and ensuring that trade union identity is inclusive. This is not to say that organisation on the basis of class should elide issues of race, ethnicity, gender, sexuality, age or disability – these categories are integral to the organisation of work and should be articulated as part of workplace organisation. However, community is not a substitute for the class basis of union organisation and cannot of itself generate class politics or consciousness, although it can inform and strengthen this through a dynamic relationship which may transform both.

7
The Ideological Dimensions of Activism – Excavating Class?

> I'm much more conscious of political things now than I would
> have been. I didn't previously see that politics was any sort of
> part of my interest, but actually it is part of my job and my
> role within the union. I'm much more politically aware... it's
> through courses, but also because I'm just thinking more about
> how do you actually effect change, so if this is unfair how can
> you actually make a difference? And it seems to me that there
> are some people who have more power to change things than
> others. And that automatically leads to a political view or a
> need to have political input of some sort.
>
> Elizabeth, Equality Rep

This chapter returns to the ideological dimension of trade union activism
introduced in Chapter 2. Subsequent chapters explored the motivations
of a range of activists, rooting them within workplace and thus class
relationships defined in terms of gender, race, ethnicity and sexuality.
We now turn to the nature of consciousness produced by these relationships drawing upon an older literature on trade union consciousness
to conceptualise the values of contemporary activists, many taking on
new union roles, in a changed context. This chapter investigates how far
their trade unionism goes beyond instrumentality and a commitment
to collectivism to embrace class identity and/or consciousness. In this it
asks how far activists perceive trade unions as embracing political and
social goals as well as economic objectives and how far these extend to
the reform or transformation of the current social order – of particular
interest in a time of capitalist crisis. Finally the chapter explores the
political values of the activists asking whether they retain the traditional allegiance of trade unionists to the Labour Party or how far this

has become strained leading to alignments with political alternatives. I conclude by speculating upon the role of the trades unions in mediating prevailing ideologies and constituting social identities.

The transmission of union values

Fosh (1981) and Batstone et al.s' (1977) studies of activists' motivations and values provide a useful, if not strictly comparable, framework for the analysis of trade union consciousness 30 years later. Fosh's 1981 study of Sheffield steelworkers found that activism was based upon a commitment to collectivism and an intrinsic belief in trade unionism. Older activists had experiences of adversity in terms of unemployment, poverty or being on strike and pro-union families; younger activists, whilst less likely to have experienced adversity, tended to be surrounded by 'pro-union persons' in terms of family and friends (1981, p. 79). For the activists interviewed for this book this is generally true for family, although not necessarily for friends, and this may be a generational effect reflecting the decline of union membership. Migrant workers may be exceptions to this because of their dependence upon community networks and activists did mix socially with other activists through their union work.

Healy et al.'s more recent study (2004) of black and minority ethnic women trade unionists, has confirmed the role of solidaristic collectivism reproduced in families. Of the 30 activists interviewed for this book five reported having no previous contact with the trade union or labour movement. Half (15) reported having a parent who was or had been a union member or activist; ten others recalled another family member who was or had been a member or who had held pro-labour beliefs which had influenced them. A number recollected that a parent had told them to join the union when they started work, as in the case of Peter whose parents had been members:

> When I first started work one of the things my father always said to me, 'as soon as you go there, you sign two forms, pension, union, pension, union – done'. So that's always been embedded in me, sign your pension, sign your union … I've come from a strong trade union background, family-wise, they've always been in the union.

Similarly for Anna:

> Well my dad recommended that I join the union for protection in my job. I knew somebody who was a steward in my department at the

time, but my dad was very concerned that I should be a member of a union. He was a shop steward when he was teaching and my grandfather as well on his side of the family was a shop steward in industry.

Healy et al. (2004) also emphasise the transfer of collectivist values across national boundaries and its contribution to UK trade unionism. A number of the activists' parents had been migrants, from Ireland, the Caribbean, Asia or Africa, whilst as Chapter 6 has illustrated, some migrant worker activists had strong political legacies from their home countries. Cassandra was a Filipino migrant who had become active in UNISON:

> The earliest memory I have about trade unions was with my mum when I was eight or nine years old. She was a trade union activist back home and they were talking about collective bargaining agreements – that was my first proper memory! They were discussing it over the lunchtime and in the evening I asked her, 'Mum, what is a collective bargaining agreement?' And she said 'oh, that's not a topic for kids'. ... Well, historically my dad told us that we were related to one of our national heroes and that national hero was actually a lady hero who fought against the Spaniards when we were invaded ... they were activists and they were fighting against repression and invasion. So my dad said if there is a rebellious attitude in you, he wouldn't really be surprised. Oh I forgot to tell you, my aunt is actually an active trade union – a student union activist when she was at university, she was abducted and put in jail because she was demonstrating against the Marcos regime.

In other cases a trade union or political background was more elusive, resonating with Healy et al.'s 'unspoken political socialisation' (2004, p. 456). Some respondents initially said they had no such history before recalling a connection. Elizabeth's sister was an active trade unionist, but her parents had not been members and she had found out that her grandfather had been a steward only after she became active herself. John, Steve and Kingsley spoke about the influence of their grandfathers. John's grandfather had been a political prisoner in the World War Two and was 'a staunch trade unionist' and Socialist – 'he was quite political anyway, so that did have an influence on me, not so much the trade union, but politically in his history'.

Beynon's account of activism in Ford's describes how trade unionism is rooted historically in working class collectivism, although not necessarily class consciousness, but also how mutual identity is fostered through the labour process and work relationships (1973). In our sample older workers talked about the expectation of union membership when they started working and this was particularly strong where they had grown up in occupational communities and they reflected upon generational change. The closed shop was a key factor for Charles whose parents had not been members, but who had became a printer and was mentored by a union activist. Oreleo had started work as an electrical engineer and also recalls the closed shop:

> If you got an interview and you were given a job, and you'd start on the Monday and then by lunchtime the trade union rep, he would come to ask you 'where did you work before? Are you qualified to be here, what's your experience?' And if he said you're not able to join this union, then they went back to the employer and said he's not suitable and then you were told you couldn't stay … so in those days it was closed shops and that's where I was.

Whilst many activists talked about inheriting trade union values, others had effectively reacted against their parents. Kingsley's father had been a policeman and Conservative; 'I suppose I was the rebel'; although his grandfather, a Welsh Liberal, had talked to him about a range of ideas including socialism and communism. When asked where she thought her values had come from Josephine responded:

> Certainly not from my parents! I think my ideas about society have come from what I've seen in life itself, in moving around, meeting people, talking to people. My ideas about equality are my blooming gut feelings as to what I've seen of inequalities and how I've seen people being treated. My father was racist, and from a child I could not understand for the life of me and you knew nobody who was black at that time, or anything other than white, as we were. I could not understand why somebody would dislike somebody just because of the colour of their skin, it just seemed so wrong. I mean I had huge, huge arguments with my father, we didn't get on at all, we couldn't see eye to eye on anything like that at all. I couldn't stand his attitude.

Others, like Josephine, suggested that it was their experiences rather than family values which shaped their activism and in some cases travel outside Europe was a factor. Fosh noted that whilst for some activists an intrinsic belief in trade unionism led directly to participation, for others a 'trigger' factor was needed to 'make latent commitment manifest' (1981, p. 73). We have seen in Chapter 3 how collective workplace grievances and in Chapter 5 how individual experiences at work based upon discrimination provided such triggers. For Carrie the experience of being a single parent had also informed her activism, 'I divorced 15 years ago, I've had to fight my own corner really for quite a while, I brought up two children'. Diana suggested that for women age and parenting may give them the confidence to become active, in her case through union learning:

> You reach a certain age and you start looking around. And although I say I came in for the learning, I also came in because I could see a lot of injustice that I wasn't happy with. You've had kids, and you've started fighting for their rights in a variety of ways. Maybe your confidence is a bit higher, you've got life experience and you look around and think 'no, that's not on'.

Two thirds (20) of the activists considered their activism to be an extension of their political beliefs,[1] although one qualified this to limit it to beliefs around equality rather than what was perceived as 'the bigger game of politics'. Seven stated that they were active in the union but not interested in the political aspects, but for migrant workers the term 'political' had particular connotations. One migrant worker with a strong political history interpreted 'political' in terms of party politics rather than wider political beliefs and wanted to distance himself from these. Another was convinced that unions should not become political because of his experience of Solidarnosc and the Lech Walesa government in Poland. Two activists reported that they were active on specific issues (union learning or equality), but not involved in other aspects of the union. This was the case for Elizabeth, an ER, who in the introductory quote to this chapter talks about how she was becoming more politicised through involvement in the union and her recognition of the relationship between individual workplace grievance and wider power structures.

In social psychology the alignment of individual ideological frames with the ideological frames of social movements is seen as important; pre-existing beliefs about trade unions formed before workers enter the labour market and influenced by parental membership predict the decision to join (Klandermans, 1997). Such ideological frames shaped the activism of many of our sample and this could take the form of an active or latent, collectivism. Yet this is not the whole story, as we saw in union recognition campaigns and in the case of a number of Equality Reps and migrant workers, activism could be based upon experiences rooted in the workplace. Further, beliefs and values are transformed through activity.

The role of trade unions

As we have seen, in terms of typologies of activism Fosh distinguishes between an intrinsic as opposed to an instrumental belief in trade unionism that stressed individual benefits. Batstone et al.'s (1977) earlier study of shop steward activity differentiated between 'leader' and 'populist' stewards on the basis that leaders were more likely to believe that workers should belong to a union to defend workers' rights rather than improve wages and conditions and to hold socialist views. In conceptualising the ideological positions of trade unions Hyman (2001) deploys a triangular model of market, class and social integration. The activists were asked how they perceived the role of unions and Hyman's model is useful in characterising their responses, assuming that individual orientations will to some degree refract different union ideologies and discourses. For Hyman unions incline 'towards an often contradictory admixture of two of the three ideal types' (2001, p. 4) and in characterising the activists' frames of reference a similarly confused picture emerges. A small group (of five) saw the role of unions more in terms of a labour market function and as negotiating on terms and conditions; for Peter:

> I think the role of the trade union is to get the best terms and conditions for employees that are trade union members and to ensure we still have a plant that can earn a good standard of living for their future and the future of the workforce.

The small number in this group may reflect the composition of the sample; whilst Peter was involved in workplace bargaining for his members most others worked in the public sector where terms and conditions were negotiated nationally. Three activists in manufacturing or privatised services had worked with management to secure organisational change in order to avoid job losses or to promote competitiveness with the aim of securing the long-term survival of the company and sector. Charles described how he had negotiated an agreement guaranteeing no compulsory redundancies on the basis of an overtime ban. Simon, an activist in a privatised service also talked about working with management to negotiate organisational change. Although they increasingly operated within the market – and this was particularly true of migrant workers employed by private contractors – public service activists generally did not engage with it in the same way as those in private services or industry.

A second and larger group of over a third of the activists drew upon a more abstract notion of equality and/or fairness when discussing the role of unions and these were more likely to be (but were not necessarily) Equality Reps. Some saw the trade union as playing a welfare role in terms of supporting or helping members in the workplace as well as safeguarding equality, summed up by Simon as, 'winning fairness, looking after people'. Although the focus on promoting equality is not necessarily directly reflected in earlier typologies of union values, it appears to fit with Hyman's typology of social integration – a commitment to advancing social justice and improving social welfare and cohesion (2001). It should be noted that in the 1970s over half of Batstone et al.s' shop-floor stewards espoused trade union principles in terms of social justice (along with improving terms and conditions and the unity of workers/ collective consciousness). This was defined as ensuring members were not subject to managerial whim, opposing discrimination against the less fortunate and encompassed a notion of fairness meaning that union members should look after each other (1977, p. 28). Although this was not necessarily a concept of equality based upon race, gender, disability or sexuality, it would appear to broadly fit with the values of this group of contemporary activists and of many Equality Reps. Batstone et al. contrasted these collective values to those of staff stewards which were more individual and concerned with representing members, although this could involve ensuring fair treatment. As we concluded in Chapter 5, ERs generally located equality and/or fairness within a collective rather than an individual framework.

In terms of Hyman's typology of class, approaching half of the activists largely defined the role of unions in terms of defending workers' rights. For Daisy, 'the role of the trade union I think is to uphold the workers' rights' and she specifically mentioned the need for UK unions to support migrant workers' rights and to educate workers of their rights as part of this. For Carrie the union's role was, 'to fight for people's rights and to pull the downtrodden up a bit from the bottom'. Kingsley, another ER, also emphasised the collective role: 'It's a group backing as opposed to an individual; as a group you're stronger, as an individual you can be broken down'.

Whilst the activist values broadly reflect Hyman's triangular model, as he suggests for unions themselves activists move between typologies and between notions of collectivism and individualism and invocations of equality and class. John simultaneously articulates a class, collective and individual perspective reflecting his own purpose as a ULR, but also his belief in the union's wider social role framed in terms of a prevailing discourse of 'inclusion':

> Well for me there's a few primary functions which they have in relation to organising the working classes and offering support, representation, educational opportunities and social inclusion.

Josephine situates individual rights in the context of wider conflictual relationships:

> Still I think the role of trade unions is to act as a backup for the ordinary person when they're in conflict with management and to fight for the rights of the individual – old fashioned but still true.

Hyman talks about the reorientation of unions within the triangular model, particularly in times of change for the union movement. Rizwan perceived that unions were no longer necessarily vehicles for political conviction, possibly reflecting new representative roles:

> It certainly isn't what it was when I joined. Well you never had any of these holiday clubs or cheaper car insurance or dental care or whatever when I joined. You joined because you had conviction and you joined because you had certain politics or principles or whatever. You never joined because you thought joining UNISON meant you could get cheaper this or ... we never had that. We never had the services that the unions offer now. I just think that you have to adapt, you have to adapt, you have to have worth for members, you have to show people that you're relevant to them in their lives, that being a member of the union is relevant for them in their lives. It's an important part of their life.

As we saw in Chapter 2, activists' roles have to be situated in the context of changing workplace organisation reflecting wider political and ideological forces. These have placed constraints upon collective organisation and activists' capacity to bargain and to promote collectivism and this has probably led to the emergence of new representative roles. Yet contemporary activists' conceptions of the role of trade unions resonate with earlier models and typologies. Like Fosh's stewards they have a collectivist orientation; like Batstone et al.s' shopfloor stewards they are concerned with improvements in conditions, social justice and preventing exploitation. What is less evident are references to Socialism or workers' control and here a generational change in values and language is implied.

Industrial action

Fosh found that in her sample active union members were more likely than inactives to be willing to use collective action in the form of striking (1981, p. 72). The marked decline in industrial action over the past 30 years may suggest that current activists would be less likely to defend the use of strike action. Yet the majority had been on strike at some point in their working lives. Anand had taken part in the 2009 national strikes in the Royal Mail over changes to working practices, but recalled his first experience of strike action when after leaving school he worked in a garment factory in Mauritius. Despite the fact there was no union workers walked out because the owners brought in workers from Hong Kong on exploitative terms and conditions. Five activists were ambivalent about the use of strike action; for example, Neil was an ER and new UNISON activist in higher education who had never been on strike:

> I'm a bit sort of foot in both camps. I can see why they do it, but as yet I've not really seen any evidence that they've been effective. I think you can get your point across without having to strike and I've not seen the unions that have struck being successful in getting what they wanted just by striking.

George and Mark worked in retail and had no experience of strike action and were dubious about whether it was an option in their sector, they were committed to resolving issues without the threat of industrial action. Anna was concerned about low paid workers losing pay through strike action and others also expressed such concerns. Lukasz felt that the media response to the 2010 national strike by British Airways staff and its impact on the public questioned the value of strikes. However, the most prevalent view amongst activists was that industrial action was essential as a last resort when negotiation broke down, summed up by Elizabeth; 'I think sometimes it's necessary to do that, it's never the preferred option, but sometimes that's what it takes to actually be heard'. Kingsley expressed support in more political (if gendered) terms: 'I do believe that for the working man, his only means to fight the employers is by withdrawing his labour'. Jose talked about the weakness of industrial action in the UK in comparison with Latin America because of the illegality of secondary picketing and Charles also spoke of the need to restore the right of unions to take secondary action. UNISON activists referred to a series of one or two day national strikes on pay or pensions including or following on from the 2002 strike of one million local government workers over pay. This has been documented by Carole Thornley and Christer Thörnqvist (2009) as the largest strike by women in UK history based upon a 'complex interlinkage of class and gender issues' momentarily overcoming a historical legacy of sectionalism (2009, p. 18). As Nicola, a rep for UNISON's police civilian service group, noted with regard to the strike over pensions, these actions were not taken against workers' immediate employers and (pre-empting the title of Thornley and Thörnqvist's paper 'Where's the Enemy' on the 2002 strike), she questioned their effectiveness:

> It wasn't really against the police, we weren't striking because of the police, we were striking about local government and the government because of our pension rights. So it didn't have any effect really. I think if we were doing it for an employer, I think it would have a lot more of an impact. And I think a lot of people were afraid, they just didn't want to lose a day's pay. I didn't, but it was the principle.

As the involvement of ULRs in strike action described in Chapter 4 suggests, the experience appears to develop the confidence of activists and reinforce union identity (and Cassandra, amongst others, found it 'great fun'). However, a number of older activists compared national strikes, organised under restrictive anti-union legislation, to the more organic industrial action they had experienced as younger workers. After leaving school, Carrie had worked in a cigar factory in a strong occupational community in South Wales:

> It was blow a whistle and 'right, all out!' There it was more of a thing of 'right we're downing tools' and 'you're going to have to switch your machines off' and they get their own way.

Whilst these activists recalled a time when unions could more readily mobilise industrial action at local level, discussions of strike action were also clouded by the defeat of the 1984–1985 Miners' Strike and, in particular, the hardship experienced by the strikers and their families.

Conflicting workplace and class interests

Whilst, even amongst younger and newer activists, recognition of the necessity of collective action had not been abandoned, questions alluding to a fundamental divergence of interests between management and workers received a more varied response. These were adapted from Fosh's survey[2] and, as with her sample, activists overwhelmingly believed that teamwork was to everybody's advantage in the workplace. At the same time three activists said that this was not possible because management and workers were on opposite sides and whilst approaching two thirds of the activists said it was possible, a quarter neither agreed nor disagreed with the assertion that it was not possible. Over a third of activists agreed that good relationships between *senior* managers (as opposed to local managers at workplace level) and workers were not possible because they are on opposite sides, with a similar proportion disagreeing and a quarter neither agreeing nor disagreeing, generally on the basis that it depended upon prevailing circumstances. When asked about *actual* relationships, well over a half of activists felt that the relationship between senior managers and *unions* in their organisation was good, with four disagreeing and five saying they neither agreed nor disagreed. Interestingly a lower proportion said that relationships between *workers* and senior managers were good, over one third disagreed, with a similar proportion not committing one way or the other.

Fosh's (1981) original questions take on a different resonance in the context of a largely public sector 'sample', although she reports that in her earlier study based in the manufacturing sector both activists and non-activists felt that 'men' and management could operate as a team. She notes, however, that in Beynon and Batstone et al.s' studies activists were more likely to perceive the relationship between the workers and managers as conflictual, reflecting an ideology of working class factory consciousness (Fosh, 1981, p. 76). Batstone et al. emphasise that the specific organisation of work in domestic organisations – and here they differentiate between the shop-floor and clerical staff – fosters collective attitudes and behaviour. In our sample the managerial role of some white collar workers in the public sector (and the occasionally blurred line between their job and union roles) means the exercise of managerial power may be less stark than in a factory setting – those activists based in factory settings did appear to have a more conflictual perception of relationships.

Whilst activists differed in how far they saw a fundamental conflict of interests within their workplaces or organisations, they generally perceived divisions in wider society. Fosh found that activists were more likely to 'have a dichotomous image of society based on ideological criteria' whilst the inactives 'tended to have multi-class images based on material considerations', although both saw a divergence of interests between 'class groupings' (1981, p. 75). Drawing upon Fosh's questions the interviews with our sample of activists explored their concepts of class society 30 years later.[3] The majority of activists believed that the UK was a class society, but only half also identified themselves as working class. Lloyd expressed both; 'I think there are different social classes, yes, I would definitely put myself in the working class bracket', whilst for Elizabeth:

> I think there probably are different classes in society; I was just reading in *The Guardian* actually the gap between rich and poor has just widened again and I think it's probably too wide anyway. But there are definite classes, and definite disadvantages. I see myself as working class, I think the thing that comes to mind most is working class and I'm sort of proud of that really. And I'm proud of the fact that probably against the odds to some degree, I've got an education and I'm in a job that I love and sometimes makes a difference – yeah.

As with Fosh's sample there were differences in how respondents defined class, for some it was in terms of income, for others in terms of behaviour and lifestyle or a combination of both – for George:

> People in a bank, they give themselves a bonus – that's a different class. You can see when you go into the plane, some people are in the first class, some people are in second class so it tells you. ...

In line with this monetary definition there was some confusion as to whether activists should categorise themselves as working or middle class or lower middle class. Charles was hesitant about defining himself as working class because as a printer he felt he earned a good salary and might be seen as middle class (Box 6). This implies Fosh's distinction between multi-class and dichotomous images of society with the latter suggesting a more ideological identification that was expressed by a number of activists. Dave drew upon his experience of being a traffic warden to describe class attitudes in Bristol:

> We deal with those all the time! Well obviously there are different areas of the city we go and patrol. You might be in Burminster or in Easton one day, and then you'll be up at Clifton the next day. And there is a great, the divide is enormous, when you go into Clifton they do think that they are a cut above everybody else, even the way they talk to you: 'oh, people like you' [*said with snooty voice*] and yes, it's a massive, massive class distinction.

Rizwan defined himself as working class, but added 'I don't think it's just the economic factors. I think it's the social, cultural, I think it's identity, I think it's self identification as well'. A subjective and political definition was also implied by Diana:

> If I was going to go with any, it would be working class, it's funny because I've had this discussion with somebody quite recently ... and because of my, if you like views and aspirations, they said 'you're not working class'. I said 'but I am, because I work and I want better rights for workers'. So I don't see how you can view it any differently and I think they were coming at it from a completely different angle to me.

In contrast five of the activists resisted defining either society or themselves in terms of class. Nicola felt that this implied that some people were better than others; 'we all are human, no matter how much money you've got, you're still just the same as me'. Piotrek expressed the same view, for him the issue was of groups having too much political power in society, whether these were communists or groups from the right. Josephine similarly wanted to deny class:

> I think some people would like to think there are still classes in society. Some people want classes in society. You can view it or not as the case may be – I don't, because I refuse to. Apart from anything else I won't entertain the thought that somebody's of a different class. What is it? Traditionally there was an upper class that had money and had the land and all those sort of things, there are still people with money and land that they haven't inherited as the old upper classes did, but there are injustices!

Neil believed that changes in material circumstances had undermined class differences when asked if he thought there were different social classes he responded:

I don't think there are so much nowadays. I think the class barriers have broken down a little bit in terms of people having more money and what you would have termed upper class in the past.

Although half of activists said that they were working class when they were asked, few volunteered this as an active identity (although neither was it totally 'passive') and in these cases class was not counterposed to other social identities, such as race or gender or sexuality. A small number identified themselves in terms of their union activism or religious convictions or as parents, but as we saw in Chapter 1 some felt uncomfortable in defining themselves at all. As we have seen, Skeggs' (1997) study of young working class women found a disassociation with class, despite the fact that class was central to the way they lived their lives. She argues that whilst working class men can use class as a positive source of identity, for women class is experienced as exclusion and they may refuse to be fixed or measured by it. It is then unlikely that their actions lead to class politics, to class organisation or to class consciousness of a directly articulated form. This disassociation with class is echoed by a number of activists, but whilst historically class struggle may have legitimated men rather than women, recent working class history suggests that class as a positive identity for men has been weakened and this is to some extent reflected in the testimonies of the male activists in our sample. Even though, unlike the young working class women described by Skeggs, they are active in what remain working class organisations (Hyman, 2001) proactive class identity was tentative and there appeared to be a lack of confidence in the vocabulary of class. Yet this was not just the case for class; overall social identities, including class, whilst not entirely passive, were not generally articulated. The most active identity was gay sexuality – that is the few activists who talked without prompting about their identity were gay activists. Lukasz privileged his gay identity over his identity as a migrant worker, whilst Rizwan openly discussed his identity as a black, gay, working class man and the issues this raised for him. However, for most of the activists class was not silenced at the expense of other social identities, because there was a reticence about any subjective identification beyond trade unionism.

Whilst a number of activists, like Simon, did not necessarily have a class perspective and did not feel comfortable defining themselves in class terms, they were critical of increased inequality in society:

> I don't know if class would be – years ago I would say there were different classes but these days, I would say there's different wealth in society, but with wealth doesn't necessarily come class. And I think this is where a lot of people get confused, like years ago it would be defined by class that you were of a different class, but I think these days it's not that at all, there's a lot of wealth but that doesn't mean class. And I do think there is a huge wealth divide, and that's quite easy to see, but I don't look at it as class.

Others, like Pat had a critique of what was seen as an increased materialism in society:

> I just think that sometimes in life people have forgotten the basic things and become in time materialistic and people don't think so much about other people as they used to do. When I was a child, in the street, everybody helped everybody out. Crime and different things – sometimes I wonder if it's because some people can't have, I'm not saying they should take, but we've evolved into something where each person wants what somebody else has got and it's all on what you have, your possessions, what you own. I think it's immoral to have footballers earning what they do, I really do, I think that you've got things like that and then you've got parts of the world where people are starving – and it just doesn't balance out right.

Her unease with society resonates with the testimonies of other union activists in its perception of the absence of social and collectivist values amongst young people. A few activists went beyond a rather abstract critique of inequality and materialism to locate class within a wider economic and political system. For Elizabeth 'historically it was capitalism', whilst Daisy used the terms feudalism, imperialism and capitalism to analyse society in the Philippines, where she had been active in community politics:

> While I was going towards my last year in nursing, that was already the height of the Marcos dictatorship and I heard of people being arrested and information going around about martial law, which

was all over the news, over the radio and people talking about the military arresting people who are protesting. There were doctors coming over to the countryside to help organise medical missions and there were those who came to organise in the medical and nursing school where I was studying. That was when I heard about community based programmes and the analysis of why there is not enough healthcare services in the community and that this lack of services is related to the basic problems in the Philippines: there was unequal distribution of wealth and resources and the control of multinational companies over the health care and education system. So I started questioning – what does this mean? And then, I also reflected back at my own reality and the poverty of people in the village where I came from ... .

Her exposure to the situation there, but importantly to political ideas, had provided her with a coherent analysis – Jose had a similar analysis from his political activity in Latin America. In the context of the prevailing UK political situation these values were persistent, but residual and expressed in some way through trade union activity. Michael Mann's (1973) model of varying levels of class consciousness ranges from identifying oneself as a class member; perceiving opposition with other classes; understanding class as defining the totality of one's society; and having a vision of an alternative, classless society. Yet although it is possible to locate some of our activists on this continuum, for others class appeared to an implicit rather than an explicit or constant collective identification. Most did, however, see society as structured on the basis of class – we now move on to explore the possibilities of an alternative vision.

Unions and activism beyond the workplace

Fosh (1981) found that a further distinguishing feature of activism, beyond a commitment to collectivism, is the belief that trade unionism embraces political and social as well as economic goals and that unions have a role to play in changing society or even in transforming it. Drawing upon Fosh's questions nearly all of the activists interviewed felt that unions had a role to play in social change. One third (ten) agreed that the union should work to transform current society, nearly a third (nine) that it should work to improve society and three that it should work to redistribute income and wealth in society. Five activists said that the union should work to defend workers' share in current society. Two felt that it had no role to play in society; for Piotrek who was wary of the political role of unions from his experience of Poland, 'the trade union is trying to sort out the problems in the workplace – they should stay in the workplace'. Although the basis of the samples is so different that it is not possible to compare them, it is worth reporting that the proportion of active members supporting a role for the union in social change in Fosh's survey was 59 per cent. The responses of contemporary activists to Fosh's questions suggest some change in their resonance and in language over time. Whilst four said that unions should work to redistribute income and wealth in current society, the redistribution of wealth is both a more radical and less familiar demand than 30 years ago, whilst defending workers' share in society may have been a more radical demand in the 1980s in the context of the subsequent shift of resources from labour to capital. A further nine thought unions should work to transform (or 'reconstruct' in Fosh's language) current society, but in discussion this was not necessarily interpreted in terms of a socialist or revolutionary agenda as may have been suggested by the use of this category in Fosh's study and as we explore further below.

In terms of the role unions should play in society a number of activists mentioned campaigns around equality, for example domestic violence, the age of consent, child poverty and the role of women in political life. The union role outside of the workplace was often seen in terms of lobbying government; for Peter facing job losses in the car industry in the Midlands this involved putting pressure on the Labour Government to support manufacturing. Oreleo had put a motion to UNISON Black Members' Conference on stop and search – the disproportionate treatment of black youth by police. For Diana unions had an international role in promoting ethical trading and the rights of workers internationally. She also described how through PCS she had been leafleting with union members against the British National Party during the 2009 European Union election campaign, something she would not have had the confidence or awareness to do previously – for her this was part of her political education as an activist: 'I've been educated, this has been a process for me…it has been a huge journey'.

Many of those interviewed reported that their union activism meant that they had little time and energy for other voluntary activity, although a number attended churches and saw their religious affiliation as entirely compatible with their trade unionism. Mark, George and Neil were all active in working voluntarily for charities. As we have seen a number of migrant workers depended upon and were active in community networks and organisations. Oreleo had been involved in community campaigns on knife and gun crime. John was also active in his community; as a member of the management committee of a housing cooperative he consciously drew upon his skills as a trade unionist to set up surgeries providing advice and guidance to the long-term unemployed who comprised most of the tenants:

> When you get the opportunity to extol the virtues of the benefits of being part of an 80,000 strong collective of like minded working people who offer support to each other, then that kind of raises their interest … Going back to the comment I made about social inclusion, it's more than just something that's part of your job it's a way of life, how you live your life how you interact within the community having to carry yourself socially, do we put on one front when we're in the workplace and the trade union and leave that and close that door and be completely different and you could be sitting in the pub and be completely different from what you are in the workplace?

Like a number of the migrant worker activists John took his trade unionism beyond the workplace.

Activists embrace wider social and political goals for trade unions than the purely economic and the focus of unions like UNISON on equality encourages this, reflecting the role played by unions at different moments in constructing collective identities and interests. In defining the scope of such goals 30 years ago Fosh concluded that these are concerned with the improvement of current society rather than its transformation and tied to support for the Labour Party – how far does such support persist amongst today's activists?

The dead hand of Labour?

Fosh found that union activists were more politically aware than non-activists and more likely to support the Labour Party and believe that it was the party of working people and the trade union movement. Thirty years later Martin Upchurch, Graham Taylor and Andrew Mathers (2009) suggest a crisis in the social democratic model of trade unionism at European level and in the UK a distancing between New Labour in power and the trade union leaderships. In response to neoliberalism they argue that European unions are faced with three principal avenues of strategic and ideological orientation, embracing social partnership or the 'associational politics of the third way'; lobbying the party of labour for a return to traditional social democracy or liberating themselves from the institutional and ideological fetters of the Keynesian welfare state to re-establish themselves as autonomous movements in civil society. In the 1990s, the FBU broke formal links with the Labour Party, the RMT was disaffiliated and others have questioned the relationship. The strained but residual loyalty of activists to the Labour Party is reflected in the narratives. A small number were Labour Party members and in all but one case they predicted that they would vote for the Labour Party in the forthcoming 2010 General Election, although two had voted for the Green Party and one for an independent candidate in the most recent European Union elections (a number of migrant workers, including EU citizens did not have rights to vote in national elections). Yet around half of the activists were critical of the Labour Party, a number mentioning the Labour Government's support for military action in Iraq. Elizabeth was disillusioned with the party and like a number of others highlighted the absence of alternatives:

> I'm a bit fed up of the Labour Party and don't think there's actually any-body else who I would want to vote for, if there was a different party to vote for yes, probably, but I'm completely disillusioned with the Labour Party and I just think that they've completely betrayed working class people. I honestly don't feel that there would be anybody for me to vote for. I say that with feeling, that actually I should vote, but I really honestly do not feel that there is anybody who I agree with.

Others feared that not to vote for the Labour Party would allow other parties to get elected in marginal seats and enable the Conservatives Party to gain power, Carrie suggested this might be generational:

> Labour, I'd never vote for anybody else, I've got to be honest, not necessarily because I think they're doing things right at the moment, but I think we'd be on a loser if we voted somebody else in, because I don't think people ... and I think it's an age thing with us as well – I was around when everybody was being kicked out of work and the Maggie Thatcher years, and the steelworkers and the miners were on strike.

Lloyd and Oreleo similarly suggested they would vote Labour reluc-tantly because of their memories of unemployment under previous Conservative governments and despite the perception that 'they've turned their back on the workers of the UK'.

Whilst none of the activists argued that the union should break their existing links with the Labour Party, because of the need for a political voice in parliament, some felt that unions should have links with a wider range of political parties. Jo, a Unite, member and Labour Party member, questioned the link:

> I think that they should but only if they get something worthwhile in return and I don't think they get that at the moment. I think they're paying a lot of money to an organisation that has done very little to give them back what Margaret Thatcher took away from them. And I'm quite disappointed in how the union seem to have rolled over, personally. I would still always be in a union but I am disappointed in the unions. And I don't understand why they have done so, personally. But I do think it's important – if they don't have that link they're not going to have any influence.

Four of the activists had been in parties or movements to the left of Labour: Daisy had been in the progressive people's movement in the Philippines; Ken had been in the Communist Party when a student in the UK; Rizwan had been in the Socialist Workers Party (SWP) when younger and Jose had been in a Marxist Leninist party in Latin America. When asked (as none identified themselves voluntarily) a small number of activists said that they were socialists, Mark was a Labour Party activist who also described himself as a socialist:

> Yes, I would and I am a Labour man, I always have been and fight for the best work conditions, whatever industry you're in. That's what you go out there to earn a living [for] and you're fighting for the working people. ...

However, in general and as seen in Charles' quote in Box 6, there was a real absence of certainty and confidence in defining themselves as socialists, as Oreleo put it, 'I mean I don't know what grounds makes you a socialist'. For Peter socialism was identified with support for the SWP; 'A socialist? You mean SWP no, I'm not SWP. I'm a Labour man, I always believed in Labour'. He was critical of Asian workers in his workplace who voted for the Respect party, because of their anger over the Labour Government's war with Iraq. Pat and Diana when asked said that they were socialists, but it was not legitimated by membership of any political organisation and there remained a lack of confidence, for Pat; 'a lad I work with, he went "you're a right socialist, you" and I went

---

Box 6

I wouldn't use the word class, working class, whether that's relevant or not...I don't know. If I was a working class person who went down a mine or did the lower jobs it's an easy thing to say, I'd class myself as middle class because I do earn a good salary doing a technical job, but I see myself as a normal working guy the same as any other worker'.

'I've probably become a socialist through my union work, I went to grammar school I think I'm a bright enough lad, but politics have never been something that I was interested in, I've never thought about it...it's only when I joined the union and I suppose was facing all those things – I thought that can't be right surely...So, no I was never right wing, left wing or anything really. I can't say I am a socialist now...I don't know, I need to learn more about it and I've read lots, and I think I am a socialist, I see my role as a union representative first which puts me firmly in the socialist camp, but I'm not educated politically. As trade unionists our time is coming again, it sounds like a conflict in terms but the working landscape is changing all the time, and people will come to us the unions again for protection and help!

(Charles, ULR and workplace rep)

"no I'm not" and he went "you are. You are so a socialist!"'. Whilst for Diana:

> I probably wouldn't have done until more recently, because again it's like putting people into categories isn't it? I suppose we have to but it's something I'm never comfortable with because I always think that there are so many grey areas. But yes, I'd probably call myself a socialist now, but if you had asked me that seven or eight years ago, I probably would have said 'oh, I don't know, maybe not', but yes, I voted for Labour – I can't say that I feel particularly comfortable with that at the moment, but it was a case of the alternative. I think they've forgotten where their roots are.

Beynon (1973) concluded that the shop stewards at Ford were class conscious trade unionists, although their class consciousness was essentially a factory consciousness defined in terms of their relationship with their members. He suggests that they had a more confident commitment to socialism than the activists here, but a similar aspiration for a better society and uncertainty about how to obtain it.

Conclusions

The study of 21st-century trade unionists shows substantial continuity with those submitted to similar scrutiny in the 1970s and 1980s. Most had an intrinsic belief in trade unionism passed down through parents or other family members. However, as we have found in previous chapters such values are not a prerequisite for activism – experience of workplace relations also generated participation where the presence of a trade union provided a collective frame of reference. Whilst the majority saw their activism as an extension of their political beliefs a number said that their union activity had changed their values and given them a political perspective. Despite the decline in industrial action virtually all the activists believed that strike action was sometimes necessary to back up collective organisation. Unions were seen as having a role in improving or transforming society and there was unease with current levels of inequality and materialism. Most ascribed to a class view of society and a number of activists had a firmly antagonistic conception of management-worker relations, yet, ideological identifications with class were tentative and probably weaker than in earlier decades. At the same time there was no indication that class identity was being counterposed to other social identities.

The activist testimonies reflect conclusions for the mid-1980s that class continued to structure people's lives, but the prevailing social system was seen as 'largely unassailable' (Marshall et al., 1988, p. 157). Similarly for Batstone et al. trade union ideology in the 1970s fostered collective action and consciousness at an organisational level, but it only rarely provided a conception of an alternative social structure. If this was true for these decades it is even more evident over 30 years later following a spate of subsequent defeats for class, gender and black and anti-racist politics and this is reflected in the testimonies of contemporary activists, despite their unease with the current social system and aspirations for societal change.

Hyman's triangular model of trade unionism (2001) had a resonance with the individual orientations of activists; in particular the adherence of a number to notions of equality and fairness suggested the social integration perspective characterising their union. However, as Hyman suggests for unions, the testimonies of activists moved between his three typologies. He concludes that unions exist and function within a social framework that they may aspire to change, but which constrains their strategies and that workplace activists, even political radicals, also experience the pressures to combine order and militancy. Changing social, economic and political conditions are reflected in the nature of trade union consciousness.

Marshall et al. emphasise the importance of defining class consciousness in organisational rather than individual terms (1988, p. 193). As Wright has argued working class consciousness reflects the extent to which political parties and trade unions crystallise workers' experiences in class terms (1985, p. 264). There was little sense that this was happening to the activists here, with the possible exception of PCS[4] and the RMT – John said that he felt that his union, the RMT, 'had the voice of fighting for the rights of the working class'. This is supported by Darlington's work on the RMT (2009) where he identifies a form of political trade unionism which has become embedded within the union's activities, involving an explicit opposition to the neoliberal agenda and relationships with a range of social movements and in contrast to unions which remain wedded to Labour. In our sample allegiance to the Labour Party was strained, but persistent.

For Batstone et al. ambivalence and dual consciousness are common and attitudes are subject to manipulation and influence (1977). Sheila Cohen's study of workplace-based rank and file organisation in the UK and US over the past 30 years (2006) similarly returns to Gramsci, arguing that acceptance of the prevailing reformist nature of class consciousness is not complete; 'reformism constitutes an absence – a lack of any coherent, cohesive analysis of everyday experience, and thus an absence of an alternative to what appear as the inevitable structures of capitalist existence' (2006, p. 176), reflecting 'a profound sense of powerlessness' (2006, p. 185). Whilst this is born out in many of the activist testimonies it is important to stress first, the gap that can exist between the activity of workers at the level of the workplace and their consciousness. As Chapter 3 shows, a number of those activists who took risks in challenging employers in the face of aggressive counter-mobilisation to secure the right to collective representation and organisation, were those with weak ideological frames of reference and no active class consciousness. Second, a small number of activists had strong ideological frames of reference. These were often the residual counter-hegemonic ideologies of older activists or migrant workers, reflecting involvement in organised left politics or social movements or experiences of key class events as Kingsley had with respect to the 1984–1985 Miners' Strike. In both cases identification with contemporary movements which could transform the class basis of society was weak, reflecting a lack of confidence following political defeat and a union movement where class has gone underground (Bradley, 2008).

Conclusions

> It is quite a thing being in this environment I find myself
> watching things like Question Time and stuff like that on telly
> late at night. My wife sort of questions us on doing that, she says
> 'why have you started this?' 'I don't know', I says, 'it's just that
> I get sort of drawn into the debates and the conversations that
> people are having' which is something that I never, ever used
> to do. I don't know whether that's right or wrong or geeky or
> what [*laughing*]. It's just I never used to watch that programme,
> you know. And I'm more opinionated. I mean my wife, she's
> opinionated as well, but even things on the news and things
> like, you know, we'll sort of have conversations about that,
> quite interesting stuff we never ever used to watch or things
> we never ever used to do. The union, it's the union that's sort
> of brought my interests, broadened my interests I would say –
> that's a better word. It's broadened my interests.
>
> Steve, activist in statutory recognition campaign

This book began with Nicola and her evocation of a 'closed world'
and disavowal of consciousness and identity in spite of her activism;
it ends with Steve, who suggests the discovery of a more open world
and an awakened consciousness. They illuminate to varying degrees
the gap between activism and consciousness. All the activists featured in this book are in practice sustaining collective organisation
against the stream. This is in spite of the contraction of collective
bargaining and increased focus upon individual rights as the basis of
employment regulation, often crushing activism beneath the weight
of individual casework and the emotional injuries of class (Sennett
and Cobb, 1972) that workplace representatives deal with on a daily

basis, limiting their time and energy for organising. These activists operated as a restraint on the reassertion of managerial power in the workplace and ULRs even asserted some new space for worker interest in the face of this.

Historically, the recognition by unions that they could no longer depend upon collective bargaining to maintain their material interests allowed for the possibility of a more inclusive trade unionism which moved beyond sectional consciousness. The further decline of collective bargaining through privatisation, involving in some locations a migrant division of labour, has coincided with the adoption of organising strategies forcing unions to engage with wider and diverse constituencies – including beyond the workplace. Whilst alliances with community organisations based upon ethnicity provide a source of strength upon which trade unionism can draw and may generate a more expansive trade unionism extending beyond economism, there is also a danger that existing divisions of labour are reproduced in the collective representation and organisation of workers. However, the testimonies of the activists presented here show that where the union was seen to respond to and challenge divisions of labour in the workplace and to offer a collective identity that transcended these divisions, whilst legitimating the social identities that were defined by them, it encouraged and fostered activism.

The emergence of new trade union representative roles, shaped by government support and concerned with individual employability or equal opportunity, have been seen as further circumscribing the activity of workplace representatives and by implication also their collectivism and consciousness. Yet these new roles in their focus upon equality and workplace learning have a resonance for union members, have attracted new activists and can provide the basis for a more inclusive union activism. This book has argued that whilst they are located firmly within the structures and ideology of neoliberalism, activists are not necessarily imprisoned by them. Their narratives suggest the lived experience of the dialectic between structure and agency and the subjective and ideological dimensions of workplace activism, which also reflect union strategies. Despite the undoubted changes in the organisation and regulation of work, work remains a collective and not an individual process. The case studies of statutory recognition illustrate the way that grievances, often arising from the unfettered exercise of managerial authority in the workplace, continue to generate collective organisation, where activists are present to frame and mobilise them. The stories of Equality Reps show how individual experiences of injustice and discrimination prompted activism because workers recognised that their experience was in fact a collective one and because the union was not only present, but effective in responding, they wanted to 'give something back'.

Above all work continues to define identity and activism was rooted in workplace relations shaped by gender, race, ethnicity, sexuality, disability and class. As a result trade unions offered a collective identity which could reflect these and could confront racist, homophobic and sexist attitudes in the workplace. Yet despite real and often harrowing experiences of discrimination, union representatives did not generally articulate their activism in terms of these wider social identities. Activists did not automatically construct active, fixed or politicised social identities on the basis of gender, race or ethnicity, just as they rarely asserted class consciousness. There were exceptions, particularly for gay men, and unexpectedly gay male sexuality is a theme which reoccurs throughout the book from Kingsley's testament in Chapter 1 onwards. Discrimination on the basis of sexuality was evident in the workplace and challenged through the union, yet sexuality unlike race, gender or ethnicity, is not a category upon which the labour market is structured. Its emergence as an active identity may, as with migrant workers, reflect a stronger cultural or political presence outside of the workplace, although it was also legitimated by and expressed through the union – this needs more thought. In general, the activists here mobilised different aspects of their identity at different moments; consciousness was fleeting and could not be a pure expression of one interest, whilst agency is important. Clearly trade unions provided the context for activism and for a more constant identification, underpinned by activity and organisation, because work is a key site of identity. If these activists had an implicit class identity by virtue of their union involvement then other social identities were often subordinated to their class or union interests. Indeed, in the case of migrant workers trade union identity could allow workers to escape essentialist ethnic identities and this supports the case for the centrality of the workplace as opposed to the community as the basis of mobilisation. Materially, the relationships between work and class, race, gender and ethnicity are explicit and defined by the wider relations of a capitalist system. The articulation of these material relationships is dependent upon political organisation and language, which may crystallise or privilege one particular identity at the expense of others. In this context the assertion of politicised social identities beyond trade unionism, including class, was weak.

Kelly suggests that debates about the absence of class consciousness are cyclical (1998, p. 120). Marshall et al. (1988) describe how in the 1980s it was commonly argued that shifts in values and lifestyles supposedly encouraged individualism and privatism leading to a decline in class-based politics. Some 30 years later Reay proposed that 'the contemporary orthodoxy is that class consciousness and class awareness no longer exist' (2005, p. 912). Crompton concurs that whilst class-based inequalities are seen to persist class identity or consciousness does not (2010). Exploration of the motivations and values of activists suggests some continuity with those studies of trade union consciousness undertaken in the 1970s and 1980s, which were also concerned with the perceived obsolescence of class consciousness. Our sample of activists expressed a clear commitment to collectivism, shored up by a belief in collective action when necessary and in many cases informed by the experience of national industrial action in the public sector constrained as it was by restrictive trade union legislation. Activity was seen as an extension of political beliefs and there was a general commitment to the wider social and political role of trade unions and a strong view that unions should play a role in improving or even transforming society. Whilst there was no real evocation of feminism or a coherent black politics, there was commitment to campaigns around women's issues and to black and anti-racist struggles in the form of opposition to 'stop and search' and to the British National Party. Whilst there was broadly a class conception of society, class was often defined by money or lifestyle rather than politically or ideologically and arising from this there was some confusion about working class identity, although half of the activists described themselves as working class when asked. As in earlier studies the stranglehold of Labourism was evident, although there was a strong critique of and disillusionment with the Labour Government. There was little sense of any alternative, mirroring the 'informed fatalism' of previous generations, but reflecting an increased lack of confidence in socialist politics.

Cohen locates workplace activism within the prevailing reformist ideology of the labour movement and warns of the dangers of judging activists in terms of 'extraneous political agendas' which open up 'the familiar gap between where rank and file trade unionists are and where radical commentators would like them to be' (2006, p. 170/171). She emphasises the importance of workers' capacity 'to collectively resist the demands of capital at the point of production' in a period of union decline and recognises that reformism is contested and not completely endorsed by workers and 'riven with contradictions'. The focus upon the narratives of activists here has exposed the gap between activity and consciousness. The case studies of statutory recognition show that those activists who were prepared to take risks and stand up to and challenge aggressive employer counter-mobilisation were not necessarily those with strong ideological frames of reference. The case study of Sportsco is one where an activist and workforce with a history of suspicion and hostility to trade unionism from Eastern Europe achieved collective organisation in the most inauspicious circumstances.

The narratives suggest how union representatives mediated the neo-liberal forces and ideologies in which their activism has to be located. Whilst they clearly use prevailing language to define their activity they also draw upon a range of other discourses, producing testimonies that are often confused and contradictory. Union Learning Reps legitimated their activity in terms of the language of individual employability, but this was in terms of a real commitment to addressing the historical exclusion of unskilled workers from training and their often negative experiences of the education system – their narratives are simultaneously infused with a universalist discourse of education as providing the possibility for personal development and empowerment. Since particular social, economic and political conditions shape consciousness it is also important to acknowledge that the activism of previous generations of trade unionists was also constrained by the conservatism and sectionalism of the prevailing ideologies and languages of labourism, in particular an exclusionary language that reflected divisions of labour based upon gender and race and subordinated these to class. It is possible that the language of neoliberalism has reversed this subordination in its attempt to ideologically dissipate collective categories through the assertion of individualised identity based upon the market. Whilst Equality Reps often expressed their activism in terms of a prevailing public discourse on equality and/or fairness refracted by some unions, this was not necessarily in opposition to an earlier politics of self-organisation based upon more active and conscious social identities which explicitly recognised wider structural divisions rather than individual relationships. An exploration of the wider motivations, ideas and values of activists found that their reproduction of prevailing language was not necessarily counterposed to the articulation of a class identity and values. Further, engagement in the union strengthened and transformed collectivist values and, as we saw in a number of cases, offered the possibility of politicisation.

The availability of political ideas and language remains important to the articulation of identity and the emergence of consciousness. New union representative roles have emerged from the Labour Government's neoliberal offensive and in a period of weak class identification following the defeat of class movements. As Virdee has suggested (2000) inter-racial class solidarity is associated with periods of strong class identification and the same can be said of social movements based upon gender. Struggles, described by Gilroy (2002) as rendering the connections between class, race and gender, have been in retreat. This challenges those who argue that decisive shifts in the structuring of social inequalities have generated forms of sectionalism replacing long-standing solidarities associated with social class. Race and gender have always been integral to class relations and must be integral to class movements striving for social change. The expression of social identity is unleashed or constrained by the hegemonic forms and impulses sustaining material relations in a particular conjuncture. The testimonies of the activists here reflect a conjuncture in which hegemonic versions of gender, race, ethnicity and class are powerful – counter-hegemonic identifications based upon gender, race, ethnicity as well as class are alive, but, in the language of Williams, residual or emergent.

Despite this, for a number of older union representatives their renewed or sustained union activity was informed by the residual ideologies of older social movements. For some older migrant workers these were strong political legacies. There was a residual counter-hegemonic impulse drawing upon memories of political struggle based upon class, gender and race. Political defeat had buried these impulses and reframed them in prevailing discourses – but they survived, however tentatively. The relationship between beliefs and action is indeterminate and the actions of workers are not necessarily 'unambiguously indicative of consciously held values or beliefs' (Marshall, 1988, p. 120). For most of the activists an intrinsic belief in trade unionism had been inherited, but this was not always the case. For younger activists experience grounded in workplace relations also generated a practical consciousness at odds with prevailing ideologies – their values were changed by their activism, but also constrained by prevailing trade union ideologies and language, yet they offer prospects for union renewal.

The testimonies of the activists powerfully illustrate that trade unions remain one of the few channels through which collectivist impulses can be expressed. Where they are present and responsive they are able to translate grievance into a collective challenge to the fundamental inequality of the workplace relationship. They not only remain vehicles for class identity and interest, but can also articulate and critique the experience of inequalities based upon the gender, racial and ethnic divisions of labour which are integral to the way workplace relations are structured under capitalism. These experiences, grounded in the workplace, provide a basis for activism and support Cohen's argument for the forging of a conscious link between socialist politics and everyday workplace organisation (2006, p. 181). Yet activism is shaped and constrained by a changed political and ideological context for trade unionism reflecting changes in the balance of resources and power between capital and labour and an intensification of work undermining collective organisation. The life histories of activists suggest that an emergent consciousness of changing class relations has not necessarily been superseded by identities based upon other social categories, yet they are inextricably bound and refracted through these categories. In this Marxist theories of consciousness have not been eclipsed by post-modernist notions of identity (Bradley, 1996) and remain relevant to any understanding of activism and essential as a basis for change, providing they can reflect dialectical relationships between class, race, ethnicity and gender.

Notes

Introduction

1. A question raised by Ellen Meiksins Wood (1986).
2. Black is used to describe activists of Afro-Caribbean or Asian heritage.
3. None of the women interviewed identified themselves as lesbian and this clearly has a bearing on findings, it may be that gender is as important as sexuality to lesbian activists, but it is not possible to draw conclusions from this sample.
4. For the purposes of the book the term working class is used to include workers divorced from the ownership of the means of production and dependent upon selling their labour power (Lockwood, 1958, p. 14).
5. A number of the Union Learning Representatives were taking a Certificate in Professional Development in Union Learning taught by the Working Lives Research Institute and Centre for Trade Union Studies at London Metropolitan University.

1   Identity and Consciousness – An Unstable Relationship?

1. Industrialisation involved a renegotiation of gender relations, with variation between industrial processes within sectors and regions, which had political expression in both informal and formal working class activity. Working class male trade unionism and its political expression, Chartism, often represented the reassertion of male power in response to a perceived threat to existing gender relations and increase in female wage labour (Moore, 2010). As Barbara Taylor has shown Owenite Socialism reasserted gender interests in response to this (1983).
2. This is ethnicity rather than race, but at the same a hierarchical immigration regime creates a hierarchy of migrant labour supply reinforcing racial divisions and racism (Wills, 2010, p. 104).
3. A question about identity was asked at the end of the interview after respondents had been given ample opportunity to locate themselves, the question was; 'when you think about your own identity in society how would you define it?'

2   Structure and Agency – The Dynamics of Workplace Activism

1. Trade union membership in the UK declined from 13.2 million in 1979 to 7.6 million in 2008, with membership levels stabilising since 1995, but density

falling because of increased employment levels. Trade union density fell by 3.9 per cent for those in employment between 1995 and 2008, from 28.8 per cent to 24.9 per cent. A higher proportion of women than men are trade union members because higher proportions of women work in the public sector. However, union density in the public sector was falling faster than at any time since 1995. Union density was highest amongst black or black British employees at 30.3 per cent in 2008 (Barratt, 2009).

2. The Review appeared to recognise a changed context for workplace representation, it asked:
   * Whether new methods of working at the modern workplace seriously affect the ability of workplace representatives to function well; and
   * Whether the effectiveness and efficiency of workplace representatives can be enhanced in order to optimise the net benefits they bring to employees, employers and society more generally.

3. This impression may be supported by WERS 2004 data showing that 44 per cent of senior representatives reported that they spent five or more hours a week on their duties in 2004 whereas only 24 per cent did in 1998. At the other end of the distribution, 52 per cent of union representatives in 1998 said they spent less than two hours a week on their duties compared to 24 per cent in 2004 (Kersley et al., 2006).

3 The Role of Activists in Collective Mobilisation – Statutory Recognition Ballots

1. The names of the companies where recognition was achieved have been anonymised to protect the activists.
2. Since the company names are anonymised the CAC documentation is not referenced.
3. To trigger the procedure a union must formally approach the employer for recognition, if the employer rejects the request or fails to respond the union may refer the case to the CAC and for the application to be valid it must be in writing, the union must be independent and the employer must employ at least 21 workers. The application can be accepted if at least 10 per cent of the proposed bargaining unit are union members, if there is not already a collective bargaining agreement covering some or all workers in the proposed bargaining unit and if the CAC is satisfied that a majority of workers in the bargaining are likely to be in favour of recognition (Wood et al., 2003).
4. The CAC reported in its 2008–2009 Annual Report that the historical average was 37 per cent.
5. Classic organising campaigns have a participative or mobilising dimension through a representative organising committee comprised of workplace activists which plans tactics, identifies organising issues, maps the workplace and becomes involved in one-to-one recruitment. Generally there is reliance on paid lead organisers to oversee campaigns and foster activism. (Heery et al., 2000)
6. These required employers with over 50 workers to establish consultative forums.

4 Agents of Neoliberalism? The Contested Role of the ULR

1. Skills for Life courses were part of the Labour Government's Skills for Life strategy covering basic literacy, language, numeracy and computer skills.
2. These are first, case studies of the relationship between learning and organising carried out for unionlearn (Moore, 2009a), but second, case studies produced by three of the ULRs interviewed as part of their participation in a Continuing Professional Development (CPD) in Union Learning which encouraged reflection on practice (Working Lives Research Institute, 2009).
3. Reasonable time-off is granted to ULRs for training, the analysis of members' learning or training needs; the provision of information and advice about learning or training matters, arranging or promoting learning or training and discussing activities as a ULR with the employer.
4. The publication of *A Fresh Start – Improving Literacy and Numeracy* (DfEE 1999, ref: CMBS 1), what became known as the Moser Report, claimed that up to 7 million adults in England have difficulties with literacy and numeracy, with one in five adults functionally illiterate.
5. The Skills Pledge is a commitment by employers to train and support their employees to develop basic literacy and numeracy skills and work towards a level 2 qualification equivalent to five GCSEs A* to C.
6. At the same time a survey conducted by Bacon and Hoque for the Trade Union Congress (2009) found that three quarters of ULRs reported an increase in training in their workplaces.

5 The Mobilisation of Social Identity? The Emergence of Equality Reps

1. One of the six priority themes which applications had to meet was 'improving the ability of unions to respond to the increasing diversity of the labour market, and to supply services geared to the needs of a diverse membership'.
2. The TUC (2010) reported that in addition to their own project for the training and development of ERs, there were seven Equality Rep projects running in UNISON, Unite, the NUT, Prospect, PCS, GFTU/Connect and the TSSA.
3. In Bacon and Hoque's survey for the TUC 46 per cent of respondents were female and 81 per cent white (TUC, 2010).
4. An Equality Impact Assessment (EqIA) is a tool for identifying the potential impact of a public sector organisation's policies, services and functions on its users and staff, ensuring they reflect the needs of the community.

6 Legacies of Self-Organisation? Migrant Worker Activists

1. The research is based, first, upon a telephone survey of UNISON branch secretaries and, second, upon five focus groups of migrant worker members and activists designed to identify factors that inhibit or encourage activism.

2. For the purposes of UNISON's Migrant Worker Participation project migrant workers were defined as workers who have come to the UK specifically to find or take up work whether or not they intend to remain in the UK. According to government statistics for the three months to June 2008 foreign-born workers made up 13 per cent of the UK workforce with 50 per cent first arriving after 1999, but 81 percent of people employed who were born in the EUA8 countries arriving after 2004. The Office for National Statistics uses country of birth to define a foreign worker, however, it also points out that the Labour Force Survey for April to June 2008 (on which its statistics are based) shows that of the 5.2 million non-UK-born working age individuals resident in the UK, 38.1 per cent (2 million) defined themselves as UK nationals. Previous statistics showed that 'foreign born' employment in Education, Health and Public Services increased from 7.6 per cent in 1997 to 11.3 per cent in 2007 or 859,000 workers – the figure for 2008 was 973,000.
3. Defined by the TUC as those in precarious work that places them at risk of continuing poverty and injustice resulting from an imbalance of power in the employer–worker relationship (Hard Work, Hidden Lives, TUC, 2007).
4. In the UK, these include a number of industrial disputes led by Asian workers; for example, at Woolf's rubber factory in Southall in 1965 and at Mansfield Hosiery in Loughborough in 1972.
5. This coincided with these countries' accession to the EU, which granted their nationals the right to work freely in some member states including the UK.
6. Referring to staff transferred from one employer to another under TUPE legislation.
7. The survey conducted in 2008 was based upon a random sample of 100 UNISON branches stratified by region and service group. This represented 10 per cent of UNISON's branches spread over the 12 UNISON regions and 3 service groups, local government, health and higher education. The number of branches selected was proportionate to the total number of UNISON branches in each region and service group, but on the basis that it was desirable to survey at least one branch in each service group in each region numbers were slightly adjusted in order to do so. The survey aimed to map migrant worker members and activists and to identify attempts or initiatives by branches to recruit and encourage activism.
8. This professional and social network was launched by UNISON in 2003 in Glasgow and provided information and support to overseas nurses and other care workers and an opportunity for them to meet and get to know each other. It gave information on employment rights and access to training, including union representative training, as well as UNISON welfare support.
9. Unite's Justice for Cleaners campaign organised migrant and other vulnerable workers within the cleaning sector at Canary Wharf, on the Tube and in the City of London.
10. This campaign reorganised the building services industry in Los Angeles, bringing over 8000 largely migrant workers under a union contract (Waldinger et al., 1998).

7   The Ideological Dimensions of Activism – Excavating Class?

1. Respondents were asked which of the following statements they most strongly identified with: I am not currently active in union; I am active as a Equality Rep/workplace rep/ULR but don't get involved in other aspects of the union; I am active but not interested in the political aspects of the union; I am active and see the union as an extension of my political beliefs.
2. Fosh asked her respondents to agree or disagree with two statements:
   (1) A firm is like a football team because good teamwork on a side means success and is to everyone's advantage and;
   (2) Team work in industry is impossible, because employers and men are really on opposite sides.
      In my version I differentiated between workplace and senior management to reflect public sector structures. The statements were:
      • In my workplace teamwork is to everybody's advantage;
      • In my workplace teamwork is not possible because managers and workers are on opposite sides;
      • In the organisation in which I work good relationships between senior managers and workers are not possible because they are on opposite sides;
      • In the organisation in which I work relationships between senior managers and unions are good;
      • In the organisation in which I work relationships between senior managers and workers are good.
3. The question was 'some people think there are different social classes, what do you think about that?'
4. The General Secretary of the PCS, Mark Serwotka was an exception in providing a strong voice for workers.

Bibliography

Acker, J. (2006) *Class Questions: Feminist Answers* (Lanham: Rowman & Littlefield Publishers).

Anderson, B., Clark, N. and Parutis, V. (2007) *New EU Members? Migrant Workers' Challenges and Opportunities to UK Trade Unions: a Polish and Lithuanian Case Study* (London: TUC).

Anderson, P. (1977) 'The Limits and possibilities of trade union action', in Clarke, T. and Clements, L. (eds) *Trade Unions under Capitalism* (Glasgow: Fontana).

Atzeni, M. (2009) 'Searching for injustice and finding solidarity? A contribution to the mobilization theory debate', *Industrial Relations Journal*, 40, 1, 5–16.

Bach, S. (2007) 'Going global? The regulations of nurse migration in the UK', *British Journal of Industrial Relations*, 45, 2, 383–403.

Barratt, C. (2009) *Trade Union Membership 2008* (London: BERR).

Batstone, E., Boraston, I. and Frenkel, S. (1977) *Shop Stewards in Action: The Organisation of Workplace Conflict and Accommodation* (Oxford: Basil Blackwell).

BERR (2007) *Workplace Representatives – A Review of Their Facilities and Facility Time* (London: BERR).

Beynon, H. (1973) *Working for Ford* (Harmondsworth: Penguin).

Bourdieu, P. (1999) *The Weight of the World* (CA: Stanford University Press).

Bradley, H. (1996) *Fractured Identities: The Changing Patterns of Inequality* (Cambridge: Polity Press).

Bradley, H. (2008) 'No more heroes? Reflections on the 20th anniversary of the miners' strike and the culture of opposition', *Work, Employment, Society*, 22, 2, 339–349.

Brah, A. (1996) *Categories of Diaspora* (London: Routledge).

Bronfenbrenner, K. and Juravich, T. (1998) 'It takes more than house calls: organising to win with a comprehensive union-building strategy', in Bronfenbrenner, K., Friedman, S., Hurd, R.W., Oswald R. and Seeber R. (eds) *Organising to Win: New Research on Union Strategies* (Ithaca, NY: ILR Press).

Brown, W., Deakin, S., Nash, D. and Oxenbridge, S. (2000) 'The employment contract: from collective procedures to individual rights', *British Journal of Industrial Relations*, 38, 4, 611–629.

Brown, W. and Oxenbridge, S. (2005) 'Trade unions and collective bargaining: law and the future of collectivism', in Deakin, S. and Wilkinson, F. (eds) *The Law of the Labour Market: Industrialization, Employment, and Legal Evolution* (Oxford: Oxford Monographs on Labour Law).

Bryson, A. (2001)'*Union Effects On Managerial and Employee Perceptions of Employee Relations in Britain*', Centre for Economic Performance Discussion Paper 494 (London: London School of Economics).

Bryson, A. (2006) 'Working with Dinosaurs? Union Effectiveness in Britain', in Gall, G. (ed.) *Union Recognition: Organising and Bargaining Outcomes*, (London: Routledge).

Bryson, A. and Gomez, R. (2005) 'Why have workers stopped joining unions? Accounting for the rise in never-membership in britain', *British Journal of Industrial Relations*, 43, 1, 67–92.

Buitelaar, M. (2006) '"I am the ultimate challenge": accounts of intersectionality in the life-story of a well-known daughter of Moroccan migrant workers in the Netherlands', *European Journal of Women's Studies*, 13, 3, 259–279.

Cassell, C. and Lee, B. (2009) 'Trade union learning representatives: progressing partnership?' *Work, Employment and Society*, 23, 2, 213–230.

Charlesworth, S. (2000) *A Phenomenology of Working Class Experience* (Cambridge: Cambridge University Press).

Charlwood, A. (2003) 'Willingness to unionise amongst non-union workers', in Gospel, H. and Wood, S. (eds) *Representing Workers: Trade Union Recognition and membership in Britain* (London: Routledge).

Charlwood, A. and Terry, M. (2007) '21st century models of employee representation: structures, processes and outcomes', *Industrial Relations Journal*, 38, 4, 320–337.

Clarke, T. (1977) 'The Raison D'Etre of Trade Unionism', in Clarke, T. and Clements, L. (eds) *Trade Unions under Capitalism* (Glasgow: Fontana).

Clements, L. (1977) 'Reference groups and trade union consciousness', in Clarke, T. and Clements, L. (eds) *Trade Unions under Capitalism* (Glasgow: Fontana).

Clough, B. (2004) 'From spear holders to stakeholders: the emerging role of unions in the UK learning and skills system', in Cooney, R. and Stuart, M. (eds) *Trade Unions and Training: Issues and International Perspectives* (Monash University).

Coffield, F. (1999) 'Breaking the consensus: lifelong learning as social control, *British Educational Research Journal*, 25, 4, 479–499.

Cohen, S. (2006) *Ramparts of Resistance: Why Workers Lost Their Power and How to Get It Back* (London: Pluto).

Colling, T. and L. Dickens (1989), *Equality Bargaining—Why Not?* (Manchester, EOC).

Crompton, R. (2010) 'Class and employment', *Work, Employment and Society*, 24, 1, 9–26.

Cully, M., Woodland, S., O'Reilly, A. and Dix, G. (1999) *Britain at Work* (London: Routledge).

Danieli, A. (2006) 'Gender: the missing link in industrial relations research', *Industrial Relations Journal*, 37, 4, 329–343.

Daniels, G. and McIlroy, J. (2009) *Trade Unions in a Neoliberal World: British Trade Unions under New Labour* (Oxford: Routledge).

Darlington, R. (1994a) *The Dynamics of Work Place Unionism: Shop Stewards' Organisation in Three Merseyside Plants* (London: Mansell).

Darlington, R. (1994b) 'Shop stewards' organisation in Ford Halewood: from Beynon to today', *Industrial Relations Journal*, 25, 2, 136–149.

Darlington, R. (2009) 'Leadership and union militancy: the case of the RMT', *Capital & Class*, 99, 3–32.

Delgado, H. (1993) *New Immigrants, Old Unions* (Philadelphia: Templeton University Press).

De Turberville, S. (2007) 'Reorganising UNISON within the NHS', *Employee Relations*, 29, 3, 247–261.

DfES (2005) *Skills: Getting on in Business, Getting on at Work* (London: DfES).

Donnelly, E. and Kiely, J. (2007) 'Learning representation in the United Kingdom: helping unions organise or not?', *International Journal of Employment Studies*, 15, 1, 69–88.

Drinkwater, S. and Ingram, P. (2005) 'Have industrial relations in the UK really improved?' *Review of Labour Economics and Industrial Relations*, 19, 3, 373–398.

Dundon, T., Gonzalez-Perez, M. and McDonagh, T. (2007) 'Bitten by the Celtic Tiger: immigrant workers and industrial relations in the new "glocolized" Ireland', *Economic and Industrial Democracy*, 28, 4, 501–522.

Dyer, S., McDowell, L. and Batnitzky, A. (2008) 'Emotional labour/body work: the caring labour of migrants in the UK's NHS', *Geoforum*, 39, 2030–2038.

Eagleton, T. (1989) 'Base and Superstructure in Raymond Williams', in Eagleton, T. (ed.) *Raymond Williams Critical Perspectives* (Cambridge: Polity Press).

Eagleton, T. (1991) *Ideology: An Introduction* (London: Verso).

Earle R. and Phillips, C. (2009) ' "Con-viviality" and beyond: identity dynamics in a young men's prison', in Wetherell, M. (ed.) *Identity in the 21st Century: New Trends in Changing Times* (Basingstoke: Palgrave Macmillan).

Ewing, K., Moore, S. and Wood, S. (2003) *Unfair Labour Practices: Trade Union Recognition and Employer Resistance* (London: Institute for Employment Rights).

Ewing, K. (2005) 'The function of trade unions', *Industrial Law Journal*, 34, 1, 1–22.

Fairbrother, P. (1989) 'Workplace unionism in the 1980s: a process of renewal?', *Studies for Trade Unionists (WEA)*, 15, 57.

Fairbrother, P. (1996) 'Workplace trade unionism in the state sector', in Ackers, P., Smith, C. and Smith, P. (eds) *The New Workplace and Trade Unionism* (London: Routledge).

Fairbrother, P. (2005) book review of G. Gall (ed.) 'Union organising: campaigning for trade union recognition', *Capital & Class*, 37, 257–263.

Fantasia, R. (1995) 'From class consciousness to culture, action, and social organisation', *Annual Review of Sociology*, 21, 269–287.

Fentress, J. and Wickham, C. (1992) *Social Memory* (Oxford: Blackwell).

Fine, J. (2007) 'A marriage made in heaven? Mismatches and misunderstandings between worker centres and unions', *British Journal of Industrial Relations*, 45, 2, 335–360.

Fitzgerald, I. (2009) 'Polish migrant workers in the north – new communities, new opportunities?' in McBride, J. and Greenwood, I. (eds) *Community Unionism: A Comparative analysis of Concepts and Contexts* (Basingstoke: Palgrave Macmillan).

Fitzgerald, I. and Hardy, J. (2010) 'Thinking outside the box? Trade union organising strategies and polish migrant workers in the United Kingdom', *British Journal of Industrial Relations*, 48, 1, 131–150.

Flanders, A. (1970) *Management and Unions: The Theory and Reform of Industrial Relations* (London: Faber).

Forrester, K. (2004) 'The quiet revolution? Trade union learning and renewal strategies. Research Notes', *Work, Employment and Society*, 18, 2, 413–420.

Forrester, K. (2005) 'Learning for revival: British trade unions and workplace learning', *Studies in Continuing Education*, 27, 3, 259–272.

Fosh, P. (1981) *The Active Trade Unionist: A Study of Motivation and Participation at Branch Level* (Cambridge: Cambridge University Press).

Fosh, P. (1993) 'Membership participation and workplace trade unionism: the possibility of renewal', *British Journal of Industrial Relations*, 31, 4, 577–592.

Fraser, N. (1997) *Justice Interruptus: Critical Reflections on the "Postsocialist" Age* (London: Routledge).

Freeman, R. and Diamond, W. (2003) 'Young workers and trade unions', in Gospel, H. and S. Wood, S. (eds), *Representing Workers: Union recognition and membership in Britain* (London: Routledge).

Frege, C. and Kelly, J. (2004) *Varieties of Unionism: Strategies for Union Revitalisation in a Globalising Economy* (Oxford: Oxford University Press).

Fryer, R. (1997) *Learning for the twenty-first century: first report of the national advisory group for continuing education and lifelong learning* (London: National Advisory Group for Continuing Education and Lifelong Learning).

Gilroy, P. (2002) *There Ain't No Black in the Union Jack* (London: Routledge).

Gilroy, P. (2006) 'Multiculture in times of war: an inaugural lecture given at the London School of Economics', *Critical Quarterly*, 48, 4, 27–45.

Glucksmann, M. (2009) *Women on the Line* (London: Routledge).

Goodman, J. and Whittingham, T. (1973) *Shop Stewards* (London: Pan Books).

Goss, J. and Lindquist, B. (1995) 'Conceptualizing international labour migration: a structuration perspective', *International Migration Review*, 29, 317–351.

Government Equalities Office (2008) *Equality Bill White Paper 'Framework for a Fairer Future'* (London: GEO).

Gramsci, A. (1971) *Selections from the Prison Notebooks of Antonio Gramsci*, Hoare, Q. and Nowell Smith, G. (eds) (London: Lawrence and Wishart International).

Green, F. (2006) *Demanding Work: the Paradox of Job Quality in the Affluent Society* (Princeton: Princeton University Press).

Greene, A.-M., Black, J. and Ackers, P. (2000) 'The union makes us strong? A study of the dynamics of workplace union leadership at two UK manufacturing plants', *British Journal of Industrial Relations*, 38, 1, 75–93.

Harvey, D. (2005) *A Brief History of Neoliberalism* (Oxford: Oxford University Press).

Healy, G., Bradley, H. and Mukherjee, N. (2004) 'Individualism and collectivism revisited: a study of black and minority ethnic women', *Industrial Relations Journal*, 35, 5, 451–466.

Healy, G. and Kirton, G. (2000) 'Women, power and trade union government', *British Journal of Industrial Relations*, 35, 3, 343–360.

Heery, E., Simms, M., Simpson, D., Delbridge, R. and Salmon, J. (2000) 'Organising unionism comes to Britian', *Employee Relations*, 22, 1, 38–53.

Heery, E., Healy, G. and Taylor, P. (2004) 'Representation at work: themes and issues' in Healy, G., Heery, E., Taylor, P. and Brown, W. (eds) *The Future of Worker Representation* (Basingstoke: Palgrave Macmillan).

Heyes, J. (2009) 'Recruiting and organising migrant workers through education and training: a comparison of Community and the GMB', *Industrial Relations Journal*, 40, 3, 182–197.

Holgate, J. (2005) Organising migrant workers: a case study of working conditions and unionisation in a London sandwich factory, *Work, Employment and Society*, 19, 3, 463–480.

Hollingrake, A., Antcliff, V. and Saundry, R. (2008) 'Explaining activity and exploring experience – findings from a survey of union learning representatives', *Industrial Relations Journal*, 39, 5, 392–410.

Hopkins, B. (2009) 'Inequality Street? Working Life in a British Chocolate Factory', in Bolton, S.C. and Houlihan, M. (eds) *Work Matters: Critical Reflections on Contemporary Work* (Basingstoke: Palgrave Macmillan).

Hoque, K. and Bacon, N. (2008) 'Trade unions, union learning representatives and employer-provided training in Britain', *British Journal of Industrial Relations*, 46, 4, 702–731.

Howard, J.A. (2000) 'Social psychology of identities', *Annual Review of Sociology*, 26, 367–393.

Humphrey, J. (2000) 'Self-organisation and trade union democracy', *Sociological Review*, 48, 2, 262–282.

Hyman, R. (1971) *Marxism and the Sociology of Trade Unionism* (London: Pluto).

Hyman, R. (2001) *Understanding European Trade Unionism: Between Market, Class & Society* (London: Sage).

Keep, E. (2002) 'The English vocational education and training policy debate – fragile 'technologies' or opening the 'black box': two competing visions of where we go next', *Journal of Education and Work*, 15, 4, 457–459.

Kelly, J. (1998) *Rethinking Industrial Relations: Mobilization, Collectivism and Long Waves* (London: Routledge).

Kelly, J. (2005) 'Social movement theory and union revitalization in Britain', in Fernie, S. and Metcalf, D. (eds) *Trade Unions Resurgence of demise?* (London: Routledge).

Kerr, A., Perks, L. and Waddington, J. (2002) *The Characteristics, Role and Activities of UNISON Stewards*, (London: UNISON).

Kersley, B., Alpin, C., Forth, J., Bryson, A., Bewley, H., Dix, G. and Oxenbridge, S. (2006) *Inside the Workplace: Findings from the 2004 Workplace Employment Relations Survey* (London: DTI).

Kessler, I. and Heron, P. (2001) 'Steward organisation in a professional union: The case of the Royal College of Nursing', *British Journal of Industrial Relations*, 39, 3, 367–391.

Kilkauer, T. (2004) 'Trade union shopfloor representation in Germany', *Industrial Relations Journal*, 35, 1, 2–18.

Kirk, J. (2007) *Class, Culture and Social Change: on the Trail of the Working Class* (Basingstoke: Palgrave Macmillan).

Kirton, G and Healy, G. (1999) 'Transforming union women: the role of women trade union officials in union renewal', *Industrial Relations Journal*, 30, 1, 31–45.

Kirton, G. and Greene, A.-M (2002) 'The dynamics of positive action in UK trade unions: the case of women and black members', *Industrial Relations Journal*, 33, 2, 157–172.

Kirton, G. (2006) *The Making of Women Trade Unionists* (Aldgate: Ashgate).

Klandermans, B. (1997) *The Social Psychology of Protest* (Oxford: Blackwell).

Larsen, J.H., Allan, H., Bryan, K. and Smith, P. (2005) 'Overseas nurses' motivation for working in the UK: globalization and life politics', *Work, Employment and Society*, 19, 2, 349–368.

Lloyd, C. and Payne, J. (2002) 'Developing a political economy of skill', *Journal of Education and Work*, 15, 4, 365–390.

Lockwood, D. (1958) *The Black-Coated Worker* (London: Allen and Unwin).

Logan, J. (2006) 'The union avoidance industry in the United States', *British Journal of Industrial Relations*, 44, 4, 651–675.

Ludvig, A. (2006) 'Differences between women? Intersecting voices in a female narrative', *European Journal of Women's Studies*, 13, 3, 245–258.

Lukacs, G. (1974) *History and Class Consciousness* (London: Merlin).

Machin, S. (2000) 'Union decline in Britain', *British Journal of Industrial Relations*, 38, 4, 631–645.

Mann, M. (1973) *Consciousness and Action Among the Western Working Class* (London: Macmillan).

Marshall, G., Rose, D., Newby, H. and Vogler, C. (1988) *Social Class in Modern Britain* (London: Hutchinson).

Marshall, G. (1988) 'Some remarks on the study of working-class consciousness', in Rose, D. (ed.) *Social Stratification and Economic Change* (London: Hutchinson).

Martinez Lucio, M. and Stewart P. (1997) 'The paradox of contemporary labour process theory: the rediscovery of labour and the disappearance of collectivism', *Capital and Class*, 62, 49–77.

McAdam, D. (1988) 'Micromobilization contexts and recruitment to activism', *International Social Movement Research*, 1, 125–154.

McBride, J. and Greenwood, I. (2009) *Community Unionism: A Comparative Analysis of Concepts and Contexts* (Basingstoke: Palgrave Macmillan).

McDowell, L. (1997) *Capital Culture: Gender at Work in the City* (Oxford: Blackwell).

McIlroy, J. (2008) 'Ten years of new labour: workplace learning, social partnership and union revitalisation in Britain', *British Journal of Industrial Relations*, 46, 2, 283–313.

McIlroy, J. and Croucher, R. (2009) 'Skills and training: a strategic role for trade unions or the limits of neoliberalism?', in Daniels, G. and McIlroy, J. (eds) *Trade unions in a neoliberal world*, (Oxford: Routledge).

McKay, S. and Moore, S. (2009) 'The impact of economic and political change upon workplace trade union representation in the UK', *Bulletin of Comparative Labour Relations*, 70, 97–112.

Meiksins Wood, E. (1986) *The Retreat from Class: A New 'True' Socialism* (London:Verso).

Metocchi, M. (2002) 'The influence of leadership and member attitudes in understanding the nature of union participation', *British Journal of Industrial Relations*, 40, 1, 87–111.

Milkman, R. (2006) *L.A. Story: Immigrant Workers and the Future of the U.S. Labor Movement* (New York: Russell Sage Foundation).

Moore, S. (2004) 'Union mobilization and employer counter-mobilization in the statutory recognition process', in Kelly, J. and Willman, P. (eds) *Union Organisation and Activity*, (London: Routledge).

Moore, S. (2009a) *Integrating Union Learning and Organising Strategies: Case Studies of Good Practice* Unionlearn Research Paper 8 (London: TUC).

Moore, S. (2009b) ' "No matter what I did I would still end up in the same position": age as a factor defining older women's experience of labour market participation', *Work, Employment and Society*, 23, 4, 655–671.

Moore, S. (2010) *Establishing Equality Reps in UNISON: An Evaluation* (London: UNISON).

Moore, S. (2011) 'Gender and class consciousness in industrialisation – the Bradford worsted industry', in Davis, M. (ed.) *Class and Gender in British Labour History: Renewing the debate (or starting it)?* (London: Merlin).

Moore, S. and Wood, H. (2007) *Union Learning, Union Recruitment and Organising*, Unionlearn Research Paper 1 (London: TUC).

Moore, S. and Ross, C. (2008) 'The evolving role of union learning representatives', *Journal of In-service Education*, 34, 4, 423–444.

Moore, S. and Watson, M. (2009) *UNISON Migrant Workers Participation Project: Evaluation Report* (London: UNISON).

Moser C. (1999) *A Fresh Start: Improving Literacy and Numeracy*, Department for Employment and Education (London: DfEE).

Munro, A. (2001) 'A feminist trade union agenda? The continued significance of class, gender and race', *Gender, Work and Organisation*, 8, 4, 454–471.

Nash, J. (2008) 'Re-thinking intersectionality', *Feminist Review*, 89, 1–15.

Oxenbridge, S. and Brown W. (2002) 'The two faces of partnership? An assessment of partnership and co-operative employer/trade union relationships', *Employee Relations*, 24, 3, 262–276.

Peetz, D. and Pocock, B. (2009) 'An analysis of workplace representatives, union power and democracy in Australia', *British Journal of Industrial Relations*, 47, 4, 623–652.

Pilemalm S., Hallberg, N. and Timpka, T. (2001) 'How do shop stewards perceive their situation and tasks? Preconditions for support of union work', *Economic and Industrial Democracy*, 22, 4, 569–599.

Pollert, A. (1981) *Girls, Wives, Factory Lives* (Basingstoke: Palgrave Macmillan).

Pollert, A. (1996) 'Gender and class revisited; or, the poverty of patriarchy', *Sociology*, 30, 4, 639–659.

Pollert, A. (2007) 'Individual employment rights: "Paper tigers, fierce in appearance but missing in tooth and claw"', *Economic and Industrial Democracy*, 28, 110–139.

Pollert, A. and Charlwood, A (2009) 'The vulnerable worker in Britain and problems at work', *Work, Employment and Society*, 23, 2, 343–361.

Pollert, A. and Smith, P. (2009) 'The limits of individual employment rights: the reality of neoliberalism' *Bulletin of Comparative Labour Relations*, 70, 113–132.

Reay, D. (2005) 'Beyond consciousness? The psychic landscape of social class', *Sociology*, 39, 5, 911–928.

Rees, J. (1998) *The Alegebra of Revolution: The Dialectic and the Classic Marxist Tradition* (London: Routledge).

Robinson, C. (1982) *Black Marxism: The Making of the Black Radical Tradition* (London: Zed Press).

Rundle, J. (1998) 'Winning hearts and minds in the era of employee-involvement programs', in Bronfenbrenner, K., Friedman, S., Hurd, R.W., Oswald, R. and R. Seeber, R. (eds) *Organising to Win: new Research on Union Strategies*, (Ithaca, NY: ILR Press).

Savage, M. (2000) *Class Analysis and Social Transformation* (Buckingham: Open University Press).

Sennett, R. and Cobb, J. (1972) *The Hidden Injuries of Class* (New York: Knopf; London: Fontana).

Silvey, R. (2004) 'Power, difference and mobility: feminist advances in migration studies', *Progress in Human Geography*, 28, 4, 490–506.

Skeggs, B. (1997) *Formations of Class and Gender* (London: Sage).

Stedman-Jones, G. (1983) *Languages of Class: Studies in English Working Class History, 1832–1982* (Cambridge: Cambridge University Press).

Stevenson, H. (2010) 'Challenging the orthodoxy: union learning representatives as organic intellectuals', in Alexandrou, A. (ed.) *Union Learning Representatives: Challenges and Opportunities* (Oxford: Routledge).

Stewart, P., McBride, J., Greenwood, I., Stirling, J., Holgate, J., Tattersall, A., Stephenson, C. and Wray, D. (2009) 'Understanding Community Unionism', in McBride, J. and Greenwood, I. (eds) *Community Unionism: A Comparative analysis of Concepts and Contexts* (Basingstoke: Palgrave Macmillan).

Stoney C. (2002) 'Partnership and workplace learning in the UK: pioneering work at British Telecommunications plc', *Journal of Workplace Learning*, 14, 2, 58–67.

Stuart, M. (2007) 'The Industrial Relations of learning and training: A new consensus or a new politics?', *European Journal of Industrial Relations*, 13, 3, 269–280.

Stuart, M., Martinez Lucio, M. and Charlwood, A. (2009) *The Union Modernisation Fund – Round One : Final Evaluation Report*, Employment Relations Research Series No. 104, (London: BIS).

Tattersall, A. (2009) 'Using their sword of justice: The NSW Teachers 161 Federation and its Campaigns for Public Education Between 2001 and 2004', in McBride, J. and Greenwood, I. (eds) *Community Unionism: A Comparative analysis of Concepts and Contexts* (Basingstoke: Palgrave Macmillan).

Taylor, B. (1983) *Eve and the New Jerusalem* (London: Virago).

Terry, M. (1995) 'Employee representation: shop stewards and the new legal framework', in Edwards, P. (ed.) *Industrial Relations – Theory & Practice*, 2nd edn, (Oxford: Blackwell).

Terry, M. (2000) *Redefining Public Sector Unionism: UNISON and the Future of Trade Unions* (London: Routledge).

Thompson, D. (1984) *The Chartists* (Hounslow: Temple Smith).

Thompson, P., Warhurst, C. and Findlay, P. (2007) *Organising to Learn and Learning to Organise: Three Case Studies on the Effects of Union-Led Workplace Learning*, Unionlearn Research Paper 2. (London: Trades Union Congress).

Thornley, C. and Thörnqvist, C. (2009) Where's the enemy? A comparison of the local government workers' strike of July 2002 in the UK and the municipal workers' strike of spring 2003 in Sweden, Paper presented to BJIR Conference in honour of Richard Hyman, London 28–29 May 2009.

Tilly, C. (1978) *From Mobilzation to Revolution (New York: McGraw-Hill)*.

TUC (1998) *Union Gateways to Learning*. TUC Learning Services Report (London: TUC).

TUC (2006) *The Union Learning Representative: Challenges and Opportunities*, Organisation and Services Department (London: TUC).

TUC (2006) *Making a Real Difference, Union Learning Reps: a survey, Unionlearn Union Impact on Learning and Skills* (London: TUC).

TUC (2007) *Hard Work, Hidden Lives* (London:TUC).

TUC (2009) *Equality Reps Project Report* (London: TUC).

TUC (2010) *TUC Equality Reps Project Extension Report* (London: TUC).

TUC (2010) *Unionlearn Fact Sheet* (London: TUC).

Upchurch, M., Danford, A. and Richardson, M. (2002) 'Research Note: Profiles of union workplace representatives: evidence from three unions in South West England', *Industrial Relations Journal*, 33, 2, 127–140.

Upchurch, M., Taylor, G. and Mathers, A. (2009) 'The crisis of "Social Democratic" Unionism: The "Opening up" of Civil Society and the Prospects for Union Renewal in the United Kingdom, France, and Germany', *Labor Studies Journal*, 34, 519–542.

Virdee, S. and Grint, K. (1994) 'Black self-organisation in trade unions', *Sociological Review*, 42, 2, 202–226.

Virdee, S. (2000) 'A Marxist critique of black radical theories of trade-union racism', *Sociology*, 3, 545–565.

Vogel, D. and Triandafyllidou, A. (2005) 'Civic activation of immigrants. An introduction to conceptual and theoretical issues', in Vogel, D. (ed.), *Building Europe with New Citizens. Active civic participation of immigrants in Europe* (Luxembourg: Office for Official Publications of the European Communities).

Waddington, J. and Whitson, C. (1996) Empowerment versus intensification: union perspectives of change at the workplace', in Ackers, P., Smith, C. and Smith, P. (eds) *The New Workplace and Trade Unionism* (London: Routledge).

Waddington, J. and Whitson, C. (1997) 'Why do people join unions in a period of membership decline? *British Journal of Industrial Relations*, 35, 4, 515–546.

Waddington, J. and Kerr, A. (2009) 'Transforming a trade union? An assessment of the introduction of an organizing initiative', *British Journal of Industrial Relations*, 47, 1, 27–54.

Walby, S. (1992) 'Post-post-modernism? Theorising social complexity', in Barrett, M., and Phillips, A. (eds) *Destabilizing Theory. Contemporary Feminist Debates* (Cambridge: Polity Press).

Waldinger, R., Erickson, C., Milkman, R., Mitchell, D., Valenzuela, A., Wong, K. and Zeitlin, M. (1998) 'Helots no more: a case study of the justice for janitors campaign in Los Angeles', in Bronfenbrenner, K., Friedman, S., Hurd, R.W., Oswald, R. and Seeber, R. (eds) *Organising to Win: New Research on Union Strategies* (Ithaca, NY: ILR Press).

Wallis, E., Stuart, M. and Greenwood, I. (2005) ' "Learners of the workplace Unite!" An empirical examination of the trade union learning representative initiative', *Work, Employment and Society*, 19, 2, 283–304.

Wallis, E. and Stuart, M. (2004) 'Trade unions, partnership and the learning agenda: evidence from a seven country European study', in Cooney, R. and Stuart, M. (eds) *Trade Unions and Training: Issues and International Perspectives* (Leeds: National Key Centre in Industrial Relations Monograph).

Warhurst, C. and Nickson, D. (2007) 'Employee experience of aesthetic labour in retail and hospitality', *Work, Employment and Society,* 21, 1, 103–120.

Weller, S. (2007) 'Discrimination, labour markets and the labour market prospects of older workers: what can a legal case teach us?' *Work, Employment and Society*, 21, 3, 417–437.

White, S. (2004) 'Markets, time and citizenship', *Renewal: A Journal of Labour Politics,* 12, 3, 50–63.

Williams, R. (1977) *Marxism and Literature* (Oxford: Oxford University Press).

Willman, P. (1980) 'Leadership and trade union principles', *Industrial Relations Journal,* 11, 4, 39–49.

Willman, P. and Bryson, A. (2006) Centre for Economic Performance Discussion Paper 768 (London: London School of Economics).

Wills, J. (2001) 'Community unionism and trade union renewal in the UK: moving beyond the fragments at last,' *Transactions of the Institute of British Geography,* 26, 4, 465–483.

Wills, J. (2009) 'Identity making for action: the example of London Citizens', in Wetherell, M. (ed.) *Theorising Social Identities and Action* (Basingstoke: Palgrave Macmillan).

Wills, J., Datta, K., Evans, Y., Herbert, J., May, J. and McIlwaine, C. (2010) *Global Cities at Work: New Migrant Divisions of Labour,* (London: Pluto).

Women and Work Commission (2006) *Shaping a Fairer Future.*

Wood, S., Moore, S. and Ewing, K. (2003) 'The impact of the trade union recognition procedure under the Employment Relations Act, 2000–2', in Gospel, H. and Wood, S. (eds) *Representing Workers: Trade Union Recognition and Membership in Britain* (London: Routledge).

Wood, H. and Moore, S. (2005) *An Evaluation of the UK Union Learning Fund – Its Impact on Unions and Employers,* (London: Working Lives Research Institute, London Metropolitan University).

Working Lives Research Institute (2009) *The Goose That Lays the Golden Egg? ULR Case Studies of the Wider Impact of Union Learning from the WLRI CPD in Union Learning* (London: Working Lives Research Institute, London Metropolitan University).

Wrench J. and Virdee S. (1996) ' "Race", poor work and trade unions', in Ackers, P., Smith, C. and Smith, P. (eds) *The New Workplace and Trade Unions* (London: Routledge).

Wright, E.O. (1985) *Classes* (London: Verso).

Yuval-Davis, N. (2006) 'Intersectionality and feminist politics', *European Journal of Women's Studies,* 13, 3, 193–209.

Žižek, S. (2000) 'Class Struggle or Postmodernism? Yes, please!' in Butler, J., Lauclau, E. and Zizek, S. (eds) *Contingency, Hegemony and Universality: Contemporary Dialogues on the Left* (London: Verso).

Index

Acker, Joan, 15–16
activists, 3–5
  class identity, 153–157
  involvement in campaigns,
    158–159
  family background, 143–145
  mobilisation theory, 53, 68–69
  new, 75–77, 92–94, 104–105
  relationships with managers, 152
  statutory recognition ballots, 52,
    65–69
  values, 146–150
  see also workplace representatives
AEEU (Amalgamated Engineering and
  Electrical Union), 32, 69
agency workers, 61, 89, 128
Anand, 3, 75, 78, 89, 93, 150
Anna, 4, 113, 116, 143, 150
anti-racism, 7, 24, 29, 109, 117, 163,
  168
Atzeni, Maurizio, 56, 68

Ballots, see statutory recognition
  ballots
Batstone, Eric, Boraston, Ian and
  Frankel, Stephen, 42–47,
    101, 143, 147, 148, 150, 152, 163,
    164
Beynon, Huw, 46, 47, 65, 68, 69, 144,
    152, 162
black self-organisation (UNISON), 90,
    108, 109, 112, 117, 122, 158
Bourdieu, Pierre, 7, 8, 21
Bradley, Harriet, 17–18, 19, 28, 164,
    171

CAC (Central Arbitration
  Committee), 50–1, 59, 60, 62
capitalism
  injustice, 56, 171
  race and gender, 16
  restructuring of, 15–17
  unions and, 44

care workers, 123, 125, 132, 137
caring responsibilities, 35, 76, 104,
  137, 146
Carrie, 4, 19, 26, 38, 105, 113, 146,
  148, 151, 160
Cassandra, 5, 19, 37, 38, 106, 124, 130,
  133, 134, 137, 138, 144, 151
Cassell, Catherine and Lee, Bill, 82–83
Charles, 3, 53, 75, 78, 83–84, 86–88,
  89, 90, 127–128, 129, 145, 147,
  151, 153, 161, 162
class, 13–14, 15, 27–28, 29, 121, 141,
  153–155, 163–164, 167, 168,
  169, 170
  gender and class, 15–16, 20, 29, 57,
    151
  race, and class, 15–16, 18, 20, 170
  unions and, 147, 148–149
class consciousness, 2, 6–9, 18–20, 25,
  27–29, 56, 133, 145, 155–157, 162,
  163–164, 167, 168, 171
class identity, 20, 153–157
closed shop, 12, 39, 145
Cohen, Sheila, 164, 168, 171
collective action, see industrial action
collective bargaining, 40–41, 44–45,
  165–166
  community unionism and, 139
  equality reps and, 98–99, 102, 103
  migrant workers and, 121–124
  statutory recognition and, 50, 51
  union learning and, 85–86
collectivism, 46–47, 56–58, 68–69,
  102–108, 142–146, 149–150, 167
communism, 55, 57, 70, 135, 145, 154
Communist Party (British), 69, 161
community unionism, 129–133, 139
consultative bodies, 57–58, 65–66,
  103, 114
counter-mobilisation, 7, 10, 52–53,
  58–63, 69, 70, 164, 169
CWU (Communication Workers
  Union), 3, 89

Daniels, Gary and McIlroy, John, 2,
    42, 44, 48, 77, 96–97, 98
Daisy, 5, 21, 25, 108, 111, 130–132,
    133–135, 137, 148, 156, 161
Darlington, Ralph, 36, 43–45, 47, 53,
    101, 164
Dave, 3, 115, 154
Diana, 4, 43, 46, 75, 76, 77, 80–81, 84,
    86, 88, 90–93, 112, 146, 154, 158,
    161, 162
disability, 19, 102, 103, 105,
    108, 114
  self-organisation of disabled
    workers, 113, 116–117
Disability Discrimination Act (1995),
    102
discrimination, 25, 26, 78, 96, 99,
    101, 105–108, 110, 113, 115, 117,
    118, 148, 167
divisions of labour
  ethnicity, 16, 121–122, 125, 137,
    139, 140, 166, 167
  gender, 17, 70, 169
  global, 137
  race, 99, 169
domestic division of labour
  activism and, 34–35
Donnelly, Eddie and Kiely, Julia, 73,
    75, 87, 90, 92, 94
dual systems theories, 15

Eagleton, Terry, 20, 27
elections
  European Union, 158, 160
  General Election 2010, 160
  workplace representatives, 36–37
Elizabeth, 4, 32, 102–103, 106, 116,
    142, 144, 146, 151, 153, 156, 160
employability, 29, 72–74, 77–82, 94,
    166, 169
employers
  attitudes to unions, 38–39
  counter-mobilisation, 58–63
  facility time, 34
  relations with, 152
  statutory recognition ballots,
    53–56
  union learning, 82–85
Employment Act 2003, 73

Employment Relations Act 1999
    (ERA), 50
Employment Relations Act 2004
    (ERA), 51
equality, 11, 24, 28, 57, 96, 97,
    113–119, 145, 148, 156, 158,
    159, 166, 169
Equality Act, 97, 102, 115, 117
Equality Bill, 97–98
Equality Impact Assessments,
    102–103
Equality Reps
  numbers, 98
  role, 98–104
  statutory rights, 97–98
ERA, *see* Employment Relations Act
ESOL (English for Speakers of Other
    Languages), 89, 128
ethnicity, 16, 20, 24, 57, 107, 133,
    137–139, 140, 166
European Employment Strategy, 74

facility time, 31–40, 125
  equality reps, 97
  UK Government Review of Facilities
    and Facility Time (2006), 31
  ULRs, 77
Fairbrother, Peter, 45, 48, 53, 118
fairness, 1, 11, 24, 96, 97, 113–119,
    148, 163, 169
Fantasia, Rick, 6–7, 23
FBU (Fire Brigades Union), 160
feminism, 1, 7, 24, 25, 29, 110, 111,
    168
Filipino workers, 5, 21, 107, 110, 121,
    123, 124, 125, 130–131, 134, 135,
    144
Fosh, Patricia, 36, 43–44, 46, 143, 145,
    147, 150, 152–153, 157–159

gender, 17, 24
  activism and, 34, 75–76
  class and gender, 15–16, 20, 29, 57,
    151
  collective bargaining, 99
  migration, 137
George, 3, 35, 54, 67–68, 150, 153,
    158
Gilroy, Paul, 13, 17, 24, 28, 170

globalisation, 74, 122, 139
Glucksman, Miriam, 8
GMB (General, Municipal and
    Boilermakers' union), 32, 64, 69
Gramsci, Antonio, 9, 10, 18, 20–21,
    29, 73, 164
Green Party, 160
grievances, 53–57, 100–104, 166

Healy, Geraldine, Bradley, Harriet and
    Mukherjee, Nupur, 69, 96, 104,
    109, 118, 143–144
Healy, Geraldine and Kirton, Gill, 25,
    34, 109, 117
hegemony, 9–10, 20–21, 29, 170
homophobia, 26, 100–101, 137–138
Hyman, Richard, 10, 13–14, 44, 71,
    147–149, 156, 163

identity, *see* social identity
immigration *see* migration
individual rights, 10, 40–42, 45, 46,
    47–48, 57, 64, 88, 96, 99–101,
    104, 117, 146, 148
industrial action, 12, 22, 41, 82, 93,
    121, 143, 150–2, 163, 168,
Information and Consultation
    regulations, 57, 66
instrumentality, 54, 64, 73, 75, 142,
    147
intersectionality, 6, 7, 9, 14, 15, 26,
    28, 107
Iraq, 69, 160, 161

Jo, 3, 21, 41–42, 56–57, 66, 67, 68–69,
    161
John, 4, 72, 75, 77, 78–79, 83, 84, 88,
    93, 144, 149, 159, 164
Jose, 5, 120, 124, 128, 129, 130, 133,
    134, 136–137, 138, 151, 157, 161
Josephine, 4, 24, 25, 27, 102, 103, 110,
    111, 145, 149, 154
Justice for Janitors (SEIU), 64, 133
Justice for Cleaners (Unite), 89, 130

Kelly, John, 2, 6, 53–54, 56–57, 68,
    70, 168
Ken, 3, 23, 50, 58, 60–61, 67, 69, 161
Kevin, 4, 105, 106, 115

Kingsley, 4, 12–13, 14, 16, 21, 22–23,
    24, 25, 114, 144, 145, 148, 151,
    164, 167
Kirk, John, 8, 21–22
Klandermans, Bert, 53, 56, 102, 146

Labour Government, 2, 9, 10, 41–42,
    48, 50, 72, 74, 77, 95, 97–98, 123,
    158–159, 168, 170
Labour Party, 11, 68–69, 142,
    159–162
language, 14, 23, 24, 27–28, 29,
    81, 85, 95, 97, 119, 150, 158,
    169, 170
Latin American workers, 5, 120, 129,
    130, 133, 151, 157, 161
LGBT (Lesbian, Gay, Bisexual and
    trangender) self-organisation,
    107, 110, 127, 138
lifelong learning, 74, 78, 80, 94
Lloyd, 4, 23, 37, 74, 75, 77, 78, 79, 89,
    90, 92, 107, 153, 160
Lockwood, David, 1–2
London Citizens, 133
Lukacs, Geog, 7, 9
Lukasz, 5, 110, 127, 132, 134, 135,
    138, 150, 155

Mark, 3, 67, 68, 150, 158, 161
Martinez Lucio, Miguel and Stewart,
    Paul, 47–48
Marshall, Gordon, 3, 6, 170
    and Rose, David, Newby, Howard
    and Vogler, Carolyn, 18, 163, 168
Marxism, 14, 16, 17, 20, 27, 44, 56,
    171
McIlroy, John, 64, 77, 86, 87, 94
    and Croucher, Richard, 10, 72
McKay, Sonia and Moore, Sian, 32,
    33, 34, 35, 38, 39, 40, 41
Meiksins Wood Ellen, 14, 27–28
migrant workers, 5, 6
    class consciousness, 133
    networks, 122, 126, 129–132, 135
    rights, 124, 135
    social identity, 108, 132–139, 155
    union learning, 89
    union organisation, 54–55, 57, 70,
    120, 121, 125–129, 134–137

migration
  patterns, 121–123, 139
  points-based system, 122
  state immigration controls, 120,
    123–125
Milkman, Ruth, 64, 65, 70, 92, 121,
  130
Miners' Strike 1984–5, 22–23, 152,
  164
mobilisation theory, 10, 50, 53–58,
  68–70, 73

Nash, Jennifer, 7, 26, 109
National Labor Relations Board, 63, 65
Neil, 4, 102, 114, 150, 155, 158
Neoliberalism, 42, 48, 72, 94, 122,
  137, 159, 164, 166, 169, 170
New Labour, *see* Labour Government,
  Labour Party
Nicola, 1, 4, 9, 39, 102, 113, 151, 154,
  165
NLRB, *see* National Labor Relations
  Board

offshoring, 26, 27
older workers, 16, 17, 22, 23, 24, 29,
  34, 76, 119, 145, 151, 164, 170
Olivia, 5, 35, 100, 101, 105, 112, 115,
  126, 127, 131, 133, 134
Oreleo, 4, 30, 42, 75, 78, 80, 82, 83,
  89, 90, 92, 107, 145, 158, 159, 160,
  161
organising, trade union, 36, 45, 47,
  52, 53, 55, 63–65, 68, 166
  learning and organising, 87–92
  migrant workers, 122, 130–132

partnership, 40, 48, 74, 77, 82–85, 98,
  103, 159
Pat, 4, 25, 33, 36, 99, 101, 104, 116,
  156, 161
PCS, (Public and Commercial Services
  union), 4, 77, 91, 93, 158, 164
Peter, 5, 107, 108, 109, 115, 143, 147,
  158, 161
Poland, 69, 135, 146
Polish workers, 3, 5, 55, 56–57,
  61–62, 65, 88, 110, 127, 131,
  136, 138, 158

Philippines, 25, 121, 133, 134, 135,
  138, 156–157, 161
  Marcos regime, 21, 135, 144, 156
Piotrek, 3, 55, 61, 63, 65, 69, 154, 158
Pollert, Anna, 15, 29, 41
  and Charlwood, Andy, 99, 101
postmodern theories, 14–15
private sector
  collective bargaining, 41, 101
  management support for unions, 39
  workplace representation, 31, 100
privatisation, 21, 31, 32, 33, 47, 121,
  124–125, 139, 166
public sector
  industrial action, 151
  reform, 32, 38
  unionism, 6, 32, 36, 44, 152
  workplace representation, 31

race, 20, 24, 25, 28, 106, 108–109,
  111, 117, 133
  class and, 15–16, 18, 20, 170
racism, 101, 105, 107–109, 111, 134
recruitment, union, 44, 45, 62, 87–90,
  125, 131, 136
recognition, *see* statutory recognition
  procedure
religion, 97, 115, 131, 155, 158
Respect (political party), 161
Rizwan, 5, 18, 81, 101, 107, 110, 111,
  112, 149, 154, 155, 161
RMT (Rail, Maritime and Transport
  union), 4, 93, 160, 164
Robinson, Cedric, 15
Royal Mail, 75, 89, 150

SEIU (Service Employees
  International Union), 64, 133
self-organisation, 25, 97, 104, 106,
  110–119, 158, 169
sexuality, 6, 13, 15, 16–17, 18–19,
  25–27, 96, 110, 112, 137–138,
  155, 167
sickness procedures, 64, 100
Silvey, Rachel, 137
Simon, 5, 25, 26, 27, 34, 36, 40, 96,
  100, 102, 105, 147–148, 156
Skeggs, Beverley, 8, 9, 19, 20, 25,
  29, 155

skills
    agenda, 10, 72, 74, 77–78, 80, 86, 95
    for Life, 72, 79, 83
    Pledge, 83
SOAS (School of Oriental and African
        Studies), 120, 123, 141
social identity, 14–15, 17–20, 26,
        104–119, 132–139, 153–157,
        167, 170
socialism, 69, 109, 144, 147, 158,
        161–162, 168, 171
Socialist Workers' Party, 161
staff forums, *see* consultative bodies
statutory recognition ballots, 51–52,
        59–63
statutory recognition procedure, 41,
        50–51
Steve, 3, 55, 64, 69, 144, 165
stress, 41, 101
strikes, *see* industrial action
supervisors, 38, 60, 63

Terry, Michael, 44
trade union consciousness, 11, 25,
        28, 30, 44, 95, 109, 122, 140, 142,
        143–150, 162–163
trade unions
    class and, 13–14, 147–150, 152–157
    education, 33, 78, 81, 89, 92, 93
    membership, 31, 136
    role of, 147–150, 157–159
    training, 32, 33, 39
Trades Union Congress (TUC), 73, 74,
        75, 77, 78, 97, 98, 102, 105, 109
training
    basic skills training, 74, 79, 82
    employer, 78–79, 85–86
    vocational, 74, 78–80, 84, 85

unfair labour practices (ERA, 2004),
        51, 62
union learning, 74
    learning agreements, 82, 83
    time-off for learners, 84
Union Learning Fund, 73–74, 77, 83
Union Learning Reps, 3–5, 10, 48
    activism, 75–77, 92–94
    collective bargaining, 85–87
    development of ULR role, 73

recruitment and organising, 87–92
relationship with employers, 84–85
values, 77–82
Union Modernisation Fund, 97–98,
        123
UNISON, 4–5, 6, 8, 12–13, 79, 159
    community networks, 130–132
    national industrial action 2002,
            151
    Overseas Nurses Network, 132
    representation in, 33–34, 36, 38, 39,
            40, 45
    self-organisation in, 11, 25, 97, 104,
            110, 111, 113, 115, 116, 138, 158
UNISON Equality Reps project, 96,
        98–108, 112, 113, 116
UNISON Migrant Workers'
        Participation Project, 120,
        123–127, 134, 137, 139, 140
Unite the union, 3–5, 50, 54, 55, 58,
        64, 83, 89, 108, 127, 130, 161
Upchurch, Martin, Taylor, Graham
        and Mathers, Andy, 159–160
US union organising, 52, 60, 63, 64,
        65, 70, 130, 122, 130, 133, 164

victimisation of activists, 62, 63, 65,
        66–67
Virdee, Satnam, 44, 98, 109, 119, 122,
        170
    and Grint, Keith, 109, 113, 117, 118

Waddington, Jeremy and Kerr, Allan,
        33, 34, 39, 45, 114, 130
Weight of the World, The, 8
Williams, Raymond, 10, 21–25, 27,
        29, 170
Women and Work Commission
        (2005), 97
Women's Movement, 24, 25, 110
women's self-organisation, 1, 19, 25,
        104, 109, 110, 112, 116
work
    centrality of, 13, 14, 16–17, 69
    intensification, 10, 31, 32, 37
    restructuring of, 12, 16–17, 22,
            31–34, 102–103
working class, *see* class identity
work-life balance, 33–36, 54

Workplace Employment Relations
  Survey 2004 (WERS), 31, 34, 39,
  40–41, 85
workplace representatives
  characteristics of, 31
  decline of, 31, 33, 36

facilities, 31–39
government support, 42
managerial support for, 38–40
time spent on union duties, 34, 41

Yuval-Davies, Nira, 14, 26, 109